PUT OPTIONS

PUT OPTIONS

How to Use This Powerful Financial Tool for Profit and Protection

Jeffrey M. Cohen

McGraw-Hill

New York   Chicago   San Francisco
Lisbon   London   Madrid   Mexico City
Milan   New Delhi   San Juan   Seoul
Singapore   Sydney   Toronto

5 6 7 8 9   IBT / IBT   0 9

ISBN 0-07-141665-X

This publication is designed to provide accurate and authoritative information in regard to the subject matter covered. It is sold with the understanding that neither the author nor the publisher is engaged in rendering legal, accounting, futures/securities trading, or other professional service. If legal advice or other expert assistance is required, the services of a competent professional person should be sought.

—From a Declaration of Principles jointly adopted by a Committee
of the American Bar Association and a Committee of Publishers

McGraw-Hill books are available at special quantity discounts to use as premiums and sales promotions, or for use in corporate training programs. For more information, please write to the Director of Special Sales, Professional Publishing, McGraw-Hill, Two Penn Plaza, New York, NY 10121-2298. Or contact your local bookstore.

Library of Congress Cataloging-in-Publication Data

Author:	Cohen, Jeffrey M.
Title:	Put options : how to use this powerful financial tool for profit & protection / by Jeffery M. Cohen
Published:	New York : McGraw-Hill, 2003.
Description:	p. cm.
LC Call No.:	HG6024.U6C64 2003
Dewey No.:	332.63/228 21
ISBN:	007141665X (hardcover : alk. paper)
Notes:	Includes biliographical references.
Subjects:	Options (Finance)—United States.
Control No:	12988283

For Cyndi and Adam.
May your reasoned minds help you through
the quagmire of popular thought.

CONTENTS

viii   Contents

FOREWORD

Only rarely does a book come along that has the potential to redefine the way Americans invest. This is one of those rare books.

As a writer for several prominent business and investment sites and the author of seven books and more than 200 articles, I am regularly asked to read and review a number of investment books. No matter what the claims of the author, most such books fit neatly into existing, already full categories such as value investing, diversification, momentum investing, stock picking, bottom fishing, market timing, day trading, index investing, or mutual fund investing.

Put Options is an entirely new type of book. Regardless of your investment orientation, this book will make you a much more successful investor. How?

Not by telling you what stocks to buy. Hundreds of other books claim to do that. You probably already have a favorite investment orientation or stock selection methodology. Stick with it. Not by telling you when to buy stocks. Again, many other books will offer you advice on timing. This book is different in that whatever stocks you decide to buy or whenever you decide to buy them, Jeff Cohen will show you how to take a position in them *in a way that will significantly increase the likelihood of your making money.*

Do you love Wal-Mart, Amgen, Microsoft, General Electric, or some other stocks? You will love them even more if you learn to make money on them even if they go down after you take a position in them. Think this is impossible? Think again. Jeff Cohen shows you how to accomplish this.

Jeff Cohen will show you how to make 15 to 20 percent per year, on stocks just like those, *even when the market is flat.* If you are selecting high-quality stocks, this approach to investing is both conservative and rewarding. With Jeff's system, you won't lose money if your favorite stocks drop 15 to 20 percent, and you'll make over 15 percent a year even if they stay level.

Jeff Cohen is not a stockbroker. He is not trying to sell you stocks or mutual funds. Instead, for whatever high-quality stocks you decide to buy, he is giving you a better way of taking a position in them. Moreover, you can use his system at any major stock brokerage firm or discount firm. The only requirement is that the stock must have options, as do the stocks of most midsize and large American companies. Even the stocks of many small companies have options.

As an active investor, I have used these strategies for years, primarily with indexes. These ideas are not theories to me. I know they work from my own personal experience and success. If you are risk averse, you may want to consider doing the same.

I have used these strategies not once or twice but hundreds of times using my own money. These are real trades, not hypothetical ones. I learned all of this the hard way, without Jeff's guidance or this book. Fortunately, even learning on my own, the vast majority of my trades have been profitable. If you combine the wisdom contained in this book with intelligent stock selection, I am confident that almost all of your trades will be profitable. Whatever the level of success you have had with investing in the past, you should be able to increase it with the techniques shared in this book.

In this remarkable volume, Jeff Cohen shows you how to dramatically reduce the risk of investing in the stock market. *Full disclosure*: If you want to learn how to double or triple your money in a year or less, this book is not for you. If you want to get rich overnight, this book is not for you. I, personally, have never seen a get-rich-quick scheme that worked, and I do not believe in get-rich-quick schemes. However, if you want to learn how to *consistently* outperform most mutual funds and take on much less risk, this is the book you have been waiting for.

It gives me great pleasure to wholeheartedly recommend Jeff Cohen's book because I know it will help many investors increase their returns while lowering their risk. To enjoy enhanced returns with lower risk is the Holy Grail of investing. With other systems, some investors do temporarily get market-beating returns—but at the price of high risk. Other systems offer low risk, but investors also have to settle for subpar returns. This book shows you how to achieve the best of both worlds: above-average returns with below-average risk.

Many investors, especially beginning investors, become obsessed with "beating the market." They swing for the fences, take huge risks, and eventually suffer substantial losses. They then, belatedly, focus on lowering risk and end up settling for very low returns. Here you will learn how to enjoy a relatively high rate of return with much reduced risk.

Most investors and financial planners hope for a rising stock market. Why? The vast majority of people—professionals, and average investors alike—can make money only when the stock market is going up. Their definition of a "good market" is limited to one with rising stock prices. Not Jeff Cohen. He can make money under almost all (but not all) stock market conditions: rising market, flat market, or moderately declining market. In this book, he will show you how to do the same. Moreover, he does this *without* short selling stock.

You don't have to know which stocks are going to go up or down or when they will do so to profit from Jeff's system. You don't need a crystal ball. You should do your research to select the highest-quality stocks you can find. Morningstar is one of the best resources you can use to research stocks. Buy quality stocks you think are going to go up, and, even if you are wrong, you will usually make money using this system. This is the power of Jeff Cohen's SafetyNet Trading System.

What if the stock market crashes and your stocks crash? As you know, the markets tend to rise over time. True stock market crashes are very rare. If a crash does occur, even with Jeff's system, you will probably lose money. However, you will lose much less money than everyone else who bought stocks the conventional way. While average investors might lose 25 percent of their money, you might only lose 3 or 4 percent—and you took positions in exactly the same stocks! In addition, using Jeff's system, you will be able to recover your losses and book profits much more quickly once any recovery starts taking place.

If you are like me, you probably have some very thick books on investing sitting on your bookshelf collecting dust. Most of those tomes are full of complex theories, charts, and graphs that average people either can't understand or don't want to take the time to understand. Some of these books need extra chapters to explain or justify why their risky systems are deserving of consideration. In contrast, the ideas that Jeff Cohen presents in this book will probably make intuitive sense to you. *The results* of this higher-reward, lower-risk investing system speak for themselves. The book's clear real-life examples illustrate the superiority of this investment system.

As I write this in late August 2002, American investors have collectively lost more than $7 trillion over the past two and one-half years. This is the largest stock market loss in history. Had these investors and their financial advisors used the strategies recommended by Jeff Cohen, hundreds of billions of dollars could have been saved.

The strategies recommended by Jeff Cohen are powerful and conservative. Best of all, he explains them clearly and makes them easy to understand and use. How many books can make that claim?

I have been hired to speak to, train, and motivate thousands of stockbrokers, financial planners, and accountants over the past 20 years. As a group, financial advisors are some of the hardest-working professionals I have encountered. Unfortunately, during the bull market of the past two decades, only a few of these advisors learned how to use the conservative strategies explained in this book. I think one of the best gifts any investor could bestow upon his or her financial planner or stockbroker is a copy of this book.

The techniques described in this book are not new. If they were, I could not endorse them. These are time-tested proven techniques and strategies. These investment strategies have been used by an elite group of sophisticated investors for many years to limit stock market risks. What Jeff Cohen has done, and it is indeed a remarkable achievement, is to present these strategies in such a way that almost any serious investor can understand and immediately use them.

While many investors and even financial advisors mistakenly believe that "stock options are risky," Jeff Cohen conclusively proves that the proper use of certain kinds of options significantly *lowers* investment risk. In fact, some of the techniques advocated by Jeff, such as buying protective put options, are so powerful that certain stockbrokers and financial planners are now being sued by their clients for millions of dollars because the financial advisors did not use these risk-reduction strategies. There is simply no excuse for ignoring risk-reducing strategies.

If you would like to learn how to *significantly* reduce the risks inherent in traditional stock market investing while still enjoying gains that outdistance those of most investors, I strongly recommend you read and reread this book.

Donald Moine, Ph.D.
Investment Psychologist, Financial Planning Columnist

PREFACE

Pretend for a minute that you live in the 1400s. You were brought up to believe that the world is flat. All your teachers have told you that. All the maps have indicated that the world is flat. And then one day you are miraculously transported miles above the earth, and you see that it is actually round. When you come back to earth, you start to notice a lot of things that should have been clues to you that the earth is round all along. You see a round sun. You see a curved reflection of the earth on the round moon. You notice objects slowly move over the horizon. You hit yourself in the head and think, why didn't I see that? Why did I just accept what everyone else was telling me? Why didn't I investigate this myself?

Well, this book is going to produce a similar reaction in you. It's a process I went through as I began to investigate the inner workings of the financial markets. I decided to set aside what everyone else said and what I was previously taught, and research and evaluate for myself how certain aspects of the market work. What I found was incredible. I found that a great majority of financial professionals do not understand the industry they work in. I found that many supposed experts who write books on the subject are completely wrong! I found that major brokerage firms, out of their ignorance, prohibit the average investor from employing trading techniques that would have saved them billions of dollars over the past few years. During the course of this book I'm going to show you, and prove to you beyond any doubt, that what I learned about investing is true. I'm going to prove that, like all those who thought the world was flat, most current market commentators are absolutely wrong in their assessment of option trading. I'm going to prove that what they say is conservative option trading is actually risky and what they say is risky option trading is actually much more conservative. And when I'm done, I'm confident that you'll step back and say, Why didn't I see that before?

Why is that important and why now? Very few would dispute that the stock market paradigm has changed radically.

There are several indications of this, but the most prominent characteristics of the new paradigm are (1) greater market volatility, (2) less reliance on traditional factors (that is, price-earnings ratios and book values) for stock movement, and (3) much higher individual company valuations across the board as compared to historical valuation standards. As a result, we need a new investment paradigm.

The old "buy 'em and hold 'em" strategy has not been working lately. We need a strategy that takes advantage of that increased market volatility and a strategy that increases our probability of making winning trades because investing in today's market is a lot more like gambling than ever before. It is also important to have a strategy that will protect us in the event of a major market correction without our having to sit on the sidelines and miss a possible market recovery. Most people insure their lives, their cars, their homes, and their businesses, but they never insure their portfolios. Many don't even know it's possible. Fortunately, such a strategy exists. I call it the SafetyNet Trading System.

But don't expect miracles. This strategy will not produce 100 percent annual returns. It is not a get-rich-quick scheme. It is designed to provide reasonable returns with substantially less risk than buying stocks or traditional mutual funds. It's hard to believe how many people fall for the outlandish claims made by some financial marketing firms. Look at these actual redacted advertisements I recently clipped from Internet e-mails:

You Can Turn $10,000 into $1 Million with Just Two Stocks!

To reach total financial independence, all you need is the right two

stocks. This new special report shows you exactly how three

trades—two buys and one sell—can give you a seven-figure net worth.

Click here for details.

What If You Could Have Known to Get Out of the Market in 2000?

Order The XXXXXXXX and learn how to follow a

simple strategy based on interest rate moves of our federal

reserve. Spend just a few minutes a day and make periodic

adjustments to your portfolio to outperform buy-and-hold.

These are real ads. Imagine how much money the individuals who have these unbelievable stock-picking systems have accumulated for themselves by now. Then try to imagine why they are still working. Why are they trying to sell you a system for $39 if they can truly double their money every year? If they started with just $50,000 and could double it every year, in just 5 years they would have an annual income of over $1.5 million. These same people are hawking their wares at every financial trade show. I recently went to a large symposium and noticed that the salespeople in over 80 percent of the booths were claiming they can show you how to accurately pick the direction of a particular stock. If they can really do that, why are they spending weekends away from their families and 12 hours a day on their feet, begging individuals to visit their expensive booths? The answer: They can't. Their real job is to convince you they can.

If you are looking for a system that produces those types of results, this book is not for you. On the other hand, if you are looking for a way to make double-digit gains with significantly less risk than buying stock, this book can show you how.

Jeff Cohen

ACKNOWLEDGMENTS

I would like to acknowledge the following people for their help in the final publication of this book. First, to Donald Moine for his continued encouragement to expand on my initial concepts and ideas and bring this thorough manuscript to the investing public. Next, to Jim Huguet of Great Companies, whose ideas about how to choose the right universe of stocks have been an inspiration and the primary basis for the chapter on that subject. And last, to Kelli Christiansen of McGraw-Hill for her insightful editorial comments and suggestions.

INTRODUCTION

Never buy stocks, or traditional mutual funds that buy stocks, again!

Many would find this suggestion outlandish. However, I'm confident that by the time you finish reading this book, you will agree that the suggestion is, with minor exceptions, appropriate.

In any event, it certainly raises the question, Why not? The answer has three parts. The first part can be found in the answer to the following two questions. First, why do people buy stocks instead of investing their money in bank CDs or Treasury bills that have much less risk? The obvious answer is that they want to achieve higher returns.

Second, what kind of returns do equity investors expect, over the long term, to adequately compensate them for taking the additional risk? I ask that question often as I tour the world speaking on this subject. Most people, according to my nonscientific polling, want somewhere between 10 and 15 percent returns on their stock and mutual fund portfolio. Occasionally I get a 20 or 25 percent answer, but that is unusual.

Based on those two answers, the first reason you should not buy stocks and mutual funds is that you can reach your financial goals, even if you want 20 to 25 percent returns, without assuming the high risk associated with buying stocks or mutual funds. And if you can achieve your financial goals with less risk, then why voluntarily assume the greater risk?

The second reason is that no one knows what the market or any particular stock is going to do. Just watch the talking heads on CNBC for a couple of days, and it will become evident that even the supposed market pundits have no clue. One of the best examples I can give involves Enron. Most people know that Enron was at one time one of the largest U.S. companies, and its stock was selling at $85 a share. During November 2001, the Securities and Exchange Commission (SEC) began to uncover some accounting irregularities with the company. The stock price fell rapidly as the story unfolded, eventually landing at about $4 on Tuesday, November 30. Of the 15 analysts covering

the stock on that Tuesday, 7 rated it a strong buy, and 7 rated it
a buy. Wednesday the stock dropped to 40 cents! From $85 to 40
cents with almost all the analysts rating it a buy or better!
Better yet, on Thursday most of the analysts dropped their rating, and the stock proceeded to rise 300 percent in the next 3
days. I repeat: No one knows what the market or a particular
stock is going to do.

So why does that indicate that you shouldn't buy stocks?
Because the only way you can make money when you buy stocks
is to pick ones that go up. You have to be *right* to profit. I'm
going to show you in this book how to profit even when you're
wrong—and that's the second reason you shouldn't buy stocks.
Because you can win more often by not buying them.

The third reason you shouldn't buy stocks or traditional
mutual funds is that the stock market is subject to potential
large drops if some unforeseen and disastrous economic or
world event takes place. The average investor cannot afford to
risk his or her financial well-being in hopes that natural or
human-made disasters won't occur. However, you can protect
your portfolio from such a disaster by not buying stocks and traditional mutual funds.

In this book, I will show you how to structure your portfolio in a way that substantially reduces your risk while still providing you the potential for double-digit gains. The book is
divided into three parts. The first part will summarize the overall strategy and give you a cursory look at how it works. The
second part will provide a detailed tutorial on how to implement
the trading strategy. The third part will provide you historical
examples and some sample trades (based on today's market).

New ideas are always met with resistance from those who
promote the status quo. You can't expect your current financial
advisors, who have been recommending that you buy stocks and
traditional mutual funds, to immediately recognize that times
have changed. They have a significant investment in their
beliefs, and it will take some time and persuasion to convince
them their previous recommendations may expose you to too
much risk in this market environment.

Many reading this book know all too well how much risk they
have been exposed to over the past couple of years. Unfortunately,

most didn't know it was possible to avoid it without giving up too much of the potential upside. If you haven't lost everything, there is still time to reduce that risk and participate in the market's ultimate recovery.

Unlike many writers who persuade you to their point of view by sneak attack, I'm going to present my premises right up front and then present the evidence to support them. Here are my basic opinions on the market:

1. Nobody (other than some insiders) knows what the market or a particular stock is going to do.
2. The market is influenced by people who do not have your best interests in mind.
3. Wall Street analysts are no help because they either don't know the direction of a stock or they are purposely misleading you.
4. You can't trust the numbers produced by supposedly independent accounting firms.

If my premises are accurate, then why should we ever invest in the market? The answer is that we shouldn't, at least not in the traditional sense. Buying stock or traditional mutual funds in today's market environment is much too risky. Unfortunately, a lot of investors didn't realize how risky it is until a couple of years ago. They bought into the Wall Street story that the market always goes up over time, but now they may have to wait 15 years for the "over time" to occur. When do you think the Nasdaq will reach 5000 again? It will take about 15 years if it grows at 10 percent per year.

On the other hand, does this level of overall risk mean that you should avoid the market altogether? I don't think so, as long as you strictly adhere to a strategy that (1) rewards you even when you're wrong, (2) insures you against a market crash, and (3) restricts your participation to the world's finest companies. With that approach, I am convinced that you can earn consistent, double-digit annual gains and still sleep at night. But before I explain how to do that, let me address my opinions and prove why you should employ such a conservative investment strategy.

If you needed to find a local address, the obvious person to ask would be the letter carrier walking down the street. If you needed to find a particular grocery item, the store manager would be a likely person to question. And if you wanted some stock market information, who better to ask than people who get paid lots of money to manage billions of dollars and have every conceivable resource at their fingertips to aid them in their analysis. Of course, large mutual fund managers, if anybody, should know the direction of markets and individual stocks.

Well, do they? I was recently sent a *Performance Update* by Travelers, which showed the recent performance of the stock funds within their variable universal life product. Here were the 1-year performance results for some well-known investment managers as of August 31, 2001:

AIM Capital Appreciation Portfolio	−46.54%
Alliance Growth Portfolio	−29.41%
Janus Capital Appreciation Fund	−46.59%
Fidelity VIP Growth Portfolio	−35.51%
Janus Aspen Series Aggressive Growth	−61.04%
Smith Barney Large Cap Growth Portfolio	−27.87%

Of course, this list could go on and on with any number of high-profile investment managers included. I certainly don't mean to imply that the Travelers' fund managers have a monopoly on poor performance. In fact, most high-profile manager's missed the market top and continued to buy stocks as their prices plummeted over the past 2 years. That is exactly my point.

The bad stock picks didn't stop there. As I was doing my final edit for this book, I came across some interesting stock picks by some other high-profile managers from early in 2002. In "Tyco, Target, Qwest Among Managers' Favorites," an article by Christopher Davis, published by Morningstar.com on February 12, 2002, he points out that "Hoby Buppert, the long-tenured and successful manager of Deutsche Flag Value Builder Fund," remained "a big fan of Tyco International despite its recent accounting-related troubles." Buppert believed the company would "generate a lot of free cash, which they can reinvest in its businesses, pay dividends, or save for a rainy day." He also picked Cendant, which "spins off a lot of cash from its real-estate and travel-related businesses." Buppert was also bullish on Qwest Communications International, which he says is extremely undervalued.

Well, how were those three stocks performing 6 months after Buppert picked them? Tyco had gone from $31.25 to $12.23, a drop of more than 60 percent. Cendant had gone from $16.74 to $13.59, a drop of only 18.8 percent. But Qwest, an "extremely undervalued" stock according to Buppert, had fallen over 86 percent to $1.24 from $9.36.

He's not the only manager with egg on his face. According to the same article by Christopher Davis, Dreyfus Growth & Income Fund's Doug Ramos "thought that an economic rebound [was] in the works" so he added some smaller semiconductor and software companies to his fund. He picked up shares of Altera and Adobe Systems. Six months later both stocks were down over 50 percent. To be fair, he also picked three other stocks that have remained flat.

Davis's article concludes with picks from two other funds. JDS Uniphase (down 57 percent 6 months later) and Ciena (down (61 percent 6 months later) were picked by Red Oak Technology Select's Doug MacKay and Jim Oelschlager. And Novo Nordisk (down 27 percent 6 months later), GlaxoSmithKline (down (13 percent 6 months later), and Astrazeneca (down 24 percent 6 months later) were favorites of T. Rowe Price European Stock's management team.

The point is that even experienced money managers with unlimited resources at their disposal have not been able to avoid big losses. And even during the market heydays, were fund managers really responsible for big gains? It's my opinion that they were not. Yes, with good research and superior analysis, a manager or investor can be a better guesser than others, but no one will ever **know** the direction in which the market or any particular stock will go. A subscription to the Psychic Hotline may prove as equally valuable.

The second group of people who should know a stock's direction, if anyone does, is market analysts. They spend all their time analyzing specific companies from every perspective.

But, as will be abundantly clear, they don't know either, or they purposely deceive the investing public with their self-serving proclamations. Let's take a look at their record and then examine how it became so abysmal.

Some of the worst recommendations in history were made during the recent technology bubble. Paine Webber's Walter Piecyk put a price target on QUALCOMM of $1000 a share in 1999. Although he subsequently reduced that target to $200 a share in 2000, at the time of this writing, it was trading in the 20s. Henry Blodgett, about whom we will talk more later, put a $250 price target on Amazon.com, which at the time of this writing was trading in the teens. Mary Meeker, an analyst for Morgan Stanley, had a buy rating on Priceline when it was trading at $165 in 1999 and reiterated her buy recommendation as it fell to $78. Since then it has traded under $3. In another brash call, Meeker told investors to buy WebMD when it was trading at over $100 a share. At the time of this writing, it had lost over 95 percent of its value.

Here are some other interesting picks as reported by the *Wall Street Journal* at the end of 2000. Ariane Mahler of Dresdner Kleinwort Benson put a $120 price target on Lucent on May 15, 2000. By the time of the *Journal*'s story, Lucent was trading at $17.81. At that time she lowered her price target but said, "I still think this business is going to become very important." At the time of this writing, the stock was trading under $2.

On March 14, 2000, Anthony Noto of Goldman Sachs put a price target of $150 on Priceline while it was trading at around $55 a share. As previously mentioned, at the time of this writing, it was trading under $3. Then there is Richard Juarez at Robertson Stephens who put an $86 price target on PSINet when it was trading at $42 a share on March 9, 2000. By December 2000, the stock was under $2.

At J.P. Morgan, William Epifanio placed a price target of $115 on Red Hat on February 8, 2000. Ten months later the stock had fallen from $88.94 to $8.63. According to Epifanio (December 18, 2000), "The price target on the stock was contingent on a variety of things happening that did not happen. It is irrelevant right now." It's probably not irrelevant right now to the investors who took his well-heeled advice. Even after the fall, J.P. Morgan retained a long-term buy rating on the company, which at the time of this writing, a year and a half later was trading under $5 a share. I wonder if a long-term buy rating means you have to hold it a long time to get your money back.

And then there was Arthur Newman at Schroder & Co. He put a price target of $300 on Yahoo! on January 4, 2000. By December 2001, it was trading in the 30s. The *Journal* quoted him as saying, "By setting our price target only 25 percent above the stock's current price we were indicating there was only a little more upside on the stock." That's an understatement.

It's not just a few analysts who have gone wrong on just a few high-profile technology stocks. According to a study by Investars.com, a Web site that reports on analysts' track records, since January 1997, 16 of the 19 largest U.S. brokerage firms have issued money-losing investment advice. According to the study, if you had followed the advice on 633 different stock recommendations by Robertson Stephens, you would have lost over 40 percent of your capital from January 1997 to June 6, 2001. Remember, that includes 2½ years of a torrid market. Rounding out the worst five firms from the study are USB Piper Jaffrey (down 22.7 percent), Dain Rauscher (down 21.5 percent), CIBC World Markets (down 14.7 percent) and Deutsch Banc (down 14.4 percent). Even the best firm (Credit Suisse First Boston) would have produced just a 6.9 percent gain for the entire period. During the same period the S&P 500 went from 786 to 1255. That means that while the overall market was going up almost 60 percent, the average investor taking the advice of market analysts from the largest firms actually lost money.

Not only have major analysts lost money for investors who have taken their advice but they also missed picking the winners. According to a study done by the University of California at Berkeley's Haas School of Business, performed for the Securities Industry Association (SIA), the stocks most often recommended by analysts lost, on average, 48.7 percent of their value in 2000. The stocks that analysts recommended least often made 31.2 percent. "I don't think the SIA liked what we found," says Brett Trueman, professor and a coauthor of the study. "But it's interesting to see that as concern over analysts' involvement in investment banking grew in magnitude last year, the skill of analysts diminished in magnitude."

How can so many analysts, who get paid millions of dollars by huge brokerage firms, be so wrong? They are either very bad stock analysts, or they have another agenda. There is no shortage of financial writers who suggest the latter. Peter Elkind, author of "Where Mary Meeker Went Wrong" (*Fortune* magazine, May 2001), suggests in his article that the competitiveness for investment banking business causes analysts to hype stocks regardless of the merit's of the company issuing the stock. The article reports on how Morgan Stanley's Mary Meeker issued a glowing report on eBay on the first day of trading which 7 months later led to her firm's being awarded half of a $1.1 billion secondary offering. Morgan Stanley had previously lost eBay's initial offering to Goldman Sachs. However, after Meeker's report was published, Goldman Sachs was forced to give up 50 percent of the secondary offering to Morgan Stanley.

According to Michael Sincere, coauthor of *The Long-Term Day Trader* and author of *The After Hours Trader,* this is exactly how Wall Street does business:

> Basically, the investment banking divisions of major brokerage firms raise money for companies that need cash, so they strongly encourage their analysts to be bullish on companies the firm represents. The bottom line: Most analysts are not going to say anything controversial or negative about a current or future client.

Kent Womack, a professor of business administration at the Amos Tuck School of Business at Dartmouth College, also finds a problem with apparent or real conflicts of interest. According to Professor Womack, "Some analysts are employed by firms that underwrite or invest in the companies they cover, while the salaries and bonuses of others depend on their bank's financial performance." Womack, a former Goldman Sachs vice president, cited a Morgan Stanley memo leaked to the press several years ago stating that it was company policy to "not make negative or controversial comments" about clients.

The coauthor of *Tools and Tactics for the Master Day Trader,* Oliver Velez, suggests an even more sinister set of motives. He points out that there is an eternal conflict of interest between retail and institutional divisions of large Wall Street brokerage firms. According to Velez:

> The retail brokerage arms of most Wall Street firms have historically been money-losing enterprises, but are primarily used as the other side of the transaction for their institutional clients. For instance, how does an institutional mutual fund that is a client of a major Wall Street brokerage firm get out of 4.4 million shares of an individual stock in a short period of time? To sell 4.4 million shares close to the desired price in a short period of time, you need a buyer. To help support the buy side is a brokerage upgrade, an analyst recommending the stock to retail investors. Although this action is not illegal, I think if more retail market players were aware of this activity, they might be a little more cautious about brokerage upgrades and downgrades. Historically, they have a horrible record.

The studies previously mentioned certainly support Velez's opinion.

Others suggest that analysts attempt to control the market for their own benefit. An August 2002 article in the *New York Times*, by Gretchen Morgenson, suggests that Jack Grubman, WorldCom's cheerleader at Salomon Smith Barney, helped top executives at major telecom companies get initial public offerings shares of upstart companies like Juniper Networks who would later win major equipment contracts from these same companies. She quotes David Chacon of Salomon's Los Angeles office and Phillip Spartis of their Atlanta office as claiming that their firm offered "sweetheart allocations" to the telecom executives. With the failure of WorldCom, Grubman is on the hotseat. As late as March 13, 2002, with WorldCom trading down to $7.39, Grubman still rated WorldCom a buy even as a fellow analyst at Salomon, Tobias Levkovich, dropped the stock from his recommended list. Imagine how confused Salomon's retail clients must have been with the divergent reports from the firm. In what has to be one of this year's most outlandish responses, a spokesperson for Salomon said, "It wasn't sending its clients mixed signals about WorldCom." You decide.

Several lawsuits have also recently been filed against analysts alleging that they issued positive reports for their personal benefit. According to the *Wall Street Journal*, Henry

Blodgett of Merrill Lynch has been accused, in a lawsuit filed by
a former Merrill Lynch client, of issuing "overly optimistic pro-
jections" on a company called Infospace, Inc., in order to ensure
that Infospace could successfully acquire another Merrill
investment banking client—Go2Net, Inc.—for about $4 billion.
According to the arbitration case, "Blodgett's recommendation
lacked a reasonable basis in fact, and Blodgett failed to disclose
a serious conflict of interest with the company whose stock he
was touting."

That's not the only stock Merrill was pushing publicly
while internal memos and e-mails suggested otherwise. An
investigation by the state of New York's attorney general's office
revealed some interesting comparisons between Merrill's public
and internal opinions. For instance, on July 20, 2000, a Merrill
Lynch public research report about Excite@Home said, "We do
not see much more downside to the shares." Their short-term
rating: Accumulate. But a month *earlier*, star Internet analyst
Henry Blodgett wrote an e-mail that said, "ATHM is such a
piece of crap."

On December 4, 2000, Merrill Lynch published a rating of
2 (accumulate), their second highest rating, on Lifeminders,
and it stated in a research report on December 21, 2000, "We
think LFMN presents an attractive investment." At the same
time, Henry Blodgett was writing an internal memo about
Lifeminders that said, "I can't believe what a POS [piece of shit]
that thing is."

On October 5, 2000, Merrill published an accumulate rating on the Internet Capital Group (ICGE), and the company
had placed the stock on their list of the top 10 technology stocks
("Top Ten Tech" list) as late as September 12, 2000. At the same
time internal memos said the stock was "going to 5" (it closed at
$12.38) and that there was "No helpful news to relate [regard-
ing ICGE], I'm afraid. This has been a disaster. . . . There really
is no floor to the stock."

On July 11, 2000, Merrill had this to say publicly about one
of its major investment banking clients: "InfoSpace continues to
be one of the best ways to play the wireless Internet." It rated
the stock a buy, its highest ranking. It was also on the firm's
"Favored 15 List" from at least August 2000 until December 5,

2000, even though analyst Henry Blodgett had acknowledged, as early as June 2000, that the stock was a "powder keg" and that "many institutions" had raised "bad smell comments" about it and in October had referred to it as a "piece of junk."

And finally on January 11, 2001, Merrill publicly said, "We believe GoTo.com will be a survivor." But a week earlier analyst Kirsten Campbell had written, "I don't think it deserved a 3-1 [short-term neutral, long-term buy rating]."

Other high-profile lawsuits have been filed against Morgan Stanley's Mary Meeker. The suits allege that Meeker provided biased research on AOL Time Warner, Amazon.com, and eBay, Inc. One lawsuit claims that "Meeker crossed over the 'Chinese wall' that is supposed to exist between analysts and their firms' investment banking units." Peter Elkind, author of the previously mentioned article in *Fortune* magazine, seems to concur. According to the article:

> Analysts have become far more involved in the process of landing banking business than they once were. The modern analyst helps the banking team smoke out promising companies, sits in on strategy sessions, and promises—implicitly at least—to "support" the company once it has gone public with favorable research. That this makes tough-minded, independent stock research difficult, if not impossible, is no longer even an issue at most firms. Investment banking brings in far more money than, say, brokerage commissions from grateful investors, thankful for unbiased research. Indeed, these days most analysts' pay is directly linked to the number of banking deals they're involved in.

The same article in *Fortune* states that Meeker went far beyond the usual analyst's accommodation. Instead of just supporting Morgan's Internet banking effort, she became the driving force behind it. She was the firm's key deal-maker and primary relationship person. "She'd almost bring her bankers in as a sort of execution team," said a confidential source. For her part, Ms. Meeker said: "Our bankers were great. I was part of a team."

Even though Meeker often pointed out that only 3 of 10 Internet companies would survive, none of the companies she covered were ever on the potential fail list. Because she did not downgrade her stocks, even as they dropped 70 percent, 80 percent, or more than 90 percent in some cases, she's been accused of selling out investors to keep Morgan Stanley's banking clients happy. According to the *New York Times*, in December 2000 Meeker still had an outperform rating on all of her Internet stocks—down an average of 83 percent.

One problem in relying on analysts is they almost never tell investors to sell a stock. According to Multex.com, only one-fifth of 1 percent of all stock recommendations were sells at the height of the market in spring 2002. And despite a 14-month market spiral, even fewer sell recommendations are outstanding as of this writing. Analysts just can't afford to bite the hand that feeds them. So you decide: Are analysts just inept, or are they purposely deceiving the investing public in order to accomplish their personal objectives? It really doesn't matter which answer is true. In either case you just can't count on most of their analysis and certainly not on their recommendations.

Adding to the analyst problem is the unreliability of corporate financial reporting. Analysts, mutual fund managers, and individual investors have historically relied on audited financial reports to gauge a company's fundamental value, profitability, and growth prospects. It has only come to light recently that these reports may be more fiction than fact. The problem is manifested in three areas: (1) the use of questionable accounting rules and practices, (2) the use of pro forma reporting, and (3) outright fraudulent reporting.

Certainly the most widespread problem relates to the use of questionable accounting rules. Executives, trying to constantly keep a short-term-focused Wall Street happy, have employed accounting strategies designed to enhance stock values rather than accurately report the companies' financial condition. For instance, many companies use vendor financing as a means to increase revenues. A company will sell products to a customer and accept a note for payment, but they report the sale as current revenue. In some cases, this may be an appropriate course of action, but when abused, it can lead to severely overstated earnings. For example, by the end of 2000, telecom equipment suppliers were collectively owed $15 billion by customers. These debt-funded purchases served to exaggerate the size and sustainability of their earnings. The article "The

Numbers Game" by David Henry (*BusinessWeek*, May 14, 2001) states that according to Hank Herman, chief investment officer for fund manger Waddell & Reed Financial, "It is only now, in hindsight, that it is turning out that it wasn't real revenue growth at all, just bad receivables."

A specific company example of inaccurate reporting of debt-funded earnings is Motorola's $1.5 billion sale of equipment to Telsim, a wireless carrier in Turkey. Motorola made no mention of the financing arrangement in their February 2000 press release. According to *BusinessWeek*, "The risk is not just that the customer won't pay, but that the customer won't buy more products unless Motorola lends it more."

Another ploy used by today's corporate executives is the taking of a large restructuring charge during one year, many times in a year with already high losses, to get it off the books. This gives the company a fresh start going forward with low or no cost assets on its balance sheet. If some of the assets written off can be salvaged in some later reporting period, those assets artificially enhance the company's profitability. For example, according to Howard Schilit, head of the Center for Financial Research and Analysis, Sterling Software, Inc., took a charge right before it was acquired by Computer Associates, a move that may have accelerated expenses to the benefit of Computer Associate's future earnings.

Yet another technique used to manage earnings is the questionable timing of reporting revenues and expenses. One way to increase reported earnings is to extend the depreciation schedule for certain assets, which lowers current operating expenses. Another approach is to reduce the bad debt assumption. According to Robert Olstein, manager of Olstein Financial *Alert* Fund, *Reader's Digest* decided to assume that more customers would pay their bills on time, which resulted in a gain of 16 cents per share in the December quarter. When questioned about this assumption, *Reader's Digest* responded by saying the change was not implemented to "affect earnings in any way" and explained that the modification was a result of a change in the mix of business. Earnings reports can also be enhanced by lengthening amortization schedules. The SEC took issue with Verizon Wireless over its decision to amortize wireless licenses over 40 years, in spite of the fact that new technology may make its current licenses obsolete much sooner. Another example involves AOL. For years, the company aggressively deferred the expense of mailing millions of free disks to potential customers. Finally, after an SEC inquiry, the company agreed to pay a $3.5 million fine and restate prior earnings.

A common approach to enhance earnings is to not report the cost of issuing stock options to employees. In the recent past, especially during the roaring stock market of the 1990s, it was popular to use stock options to attract and retain key employees. Making it even more popular was an accounting rule that permits companies to merely footnote the expense without reporting its actual impact on current earnings in the same way they have to report the impact of paid salaries or bonuses. (Recently, a few companies have voluntarily agreed to start expensing stock options as salaries and bonuses.) Pat McConnell, an accounting analyst with Bears Stearns, suggests that the average earnings growth rate for S&P 500 companies would have been reduced by 2 percent if stock options grants had been fully expensed during the 3 years ending in mid-2000. According to *BusinessWeek*, some noted individual examples would be Cisco, which would have reduced reported income by $1.1 billion or 42 percent and Starbucks, which would have reduced earnings by $28 million, or 30 percent.

Companies can also use their pension plans to enhance reported earnings. Many large public companies have what are called *defined-benefit pension plans*. That means the plan defines the ultimate benefit its employees will receive rather than defining the amount the company will contribute each year. If the plan's assets perform well, the company can contribute less and still have enough money to cover its retirement liabilities. Some companies change their funding assumptions after a few good investment performance years without regard to the possibility that the good years may be followed by some lean years, during which larger employer contributions would be required. Changing pension assumptions in this way can help executives manage reported earnings growth in an artificial way. For example, according to Gabrielle Napolitano of

Goldman Sachs, IBM increased earnings in 2000 by raising its assumed investment return on pension assets to 10 percent from 9.5 percent. Of course, with the latest market results, a lot of companies may have to make up pension shortfalls that will reduce future earnings at a time companies can least afford to do it.

The use of pro forma reporting probably creates the most confusion. The SEC requires companies to report their earnings based on generally accepted accounting principles (GAAP), but it allows companies to issue pro forma reports. GAAP methods are designed, although they do not always accomplish it, to present the true financial picture of a company. Pro forma reports exclude certain items that management does not feel are appropriate in evaluating the actual financial state of a company. Obviously, the intent is to present the company in its best light by omitting expenses. I have never seen a pro forma report that omitted large revenues.

BusinessWeek, in a story on this subject, reported some interesting examples of how pro forma reporting enhanced company valuations. Yahoo!, in January 1999, presented results 35 percent better than GAAP by excluding the cost of buying Internet companies. In 2001 it excluded even more items, including payroll taxes on stock options. Network Associates dropped a loss-making 80 percent–owned subsidiary (McAfee Corporation) to reduce its GAAP losses. (I wonder if it would have dropped the subsidiary results had they been positive?) And Xcare.net, Inc., reported revenues before subtracting the cost of warrants to buy Xcare shares that it gave to customers to induce them to buy software from the company. Although the value of the warrants was provided lower in the press release, "the headline numbers boosted the company's apparent sales by 69% and cut its losses by 40%" according to *BusinessWeek*.

The *New York Times* reported that by changing how it accounts for software sales, Computer Associates changed a GAAP loss of 59 cents a share to a pro forma gain of 42 cents a share. *BusinessWeek* further reported that Qwest Communications International, Inc., reported $2 billion in quarterly earnings before interest, taxes, depreciation, and amortization (EBITDA) in a January 24, 2001, press release, but eventually it reported a GAAP quarterly loss of $116 million! The scenario has gotten so bad that an SEC chief accountant now refers to pro forma results as "EBS" earnings—everything but bad stuff.

Some companies can't even decide on their own definition of pro forma earnings. Amazon.com on April 24, 2001, reported a "pro forma operating loss" of $49 million. It also reported a "pro forma net loss" of $76 million. Its actual GAAP loss was reported at $234 million.

To make matters worse, recent news shows that corporate executives are not above fraudulently cooking the books or burying particular personal expenditures in the numbers, sometimes with the help of their supposedly independent auditors. Just ask WorldCom, Enron, or Tyco shareholders how they feel about the executives that were running their companies. And ask yourself why one of the largest accounting firms in the world would shred documents used in preparing public financial statements.

The sad truth is we can't completely trust corporate executives, independent accounting firms, or Wall Street analysts. In light of that revelation, we either have to settle for low investment yields offered by government bonds or bank CDs, or we have to employ a market strategy that allows us to win when we're wrong and protects against a market crash that could occur for any number of reasons. During the course of this book I will explain how to arm yourself against this world of uncertainty and reduce your risk sufficiently to allow you the opportunity to achieve double-digit gains without risking the farm. As the market has certainly shown us, any equity-based approach involves risk. It is my charge to show you how to reduce it.

PART ONE

AN OVERVIEW OF THE SAFETYNET TRADING SYSTEM

1

Understanding Risk
You Can't Avoid What You Don't Understand

During the last couple of years many people have found out just how risky the market can be. In my travels I have met people who have lost over 90 percent of their portfolio in less than 2 years. These same people were giving their stockbrokers and financial advisors rave reviews just a year earlier for the tremendous gains they had achieved.

Unfortunately, they didn't realize how much risk their advisors were assuming on their behalf to achieve those splendid results. In fact, many did not even know that risk could be and should be estimated. I asked one gentleman that lost 97 percent of his portfolio if he had ever asked his money managers what they were doing to reduce risk in his portfolio, and he answered, "Never."

If we want to reduce risk, we first need to understand what it is. When it comes to investing, risk has two components. The first is *frequency*. How often are we going to make losing trades? If we enter 30 positions, how many of them will result in a loss? The second component of risk is *severity*. How much can we lose in any given transaction?

Too many people enter a transaction without first considering the downside. What is my breakeven point on this trade? How much could I lose in a worst-case scenario? These are the components of risk that we must evaluate before we invest our retirement nest egg. The strategy given in this book will help investors make such evaluations. Let's first look at *frequency*. How often will we make a losing trade? What are the probabilities of a trade's going south? In order to evaluate that, let's take a look at the five things that can happen after you have taken a position in a stock. Let's assume that it is a *bullish position*— that is, you expect the stock to go up in price. The stock can go up a lot, it can go up a little, it can remain relatively flat, it can go down a little, or it can go down a lot (see Figure 1.1).

As you can see in Figure 1.2, you will make a profit if it goes up; you will lose money if it goes down; and you will break even if it stays flat. However, as you can see from Figure 1.3, with the SafetyNet Trading System, you will make a profit if the stock goes up, or if it stays flat, or even if it goes down a little. The only time you will lose money is if the stock goes down a lot. And even then, it is possible that you will break even.

This approach significantly reduces the probability of placing a losing trade since you can make money even when a stock you picked to go up, actually goes down a little. In other words, you will lose less frequently when using this approach. And

FIGURE 1.1

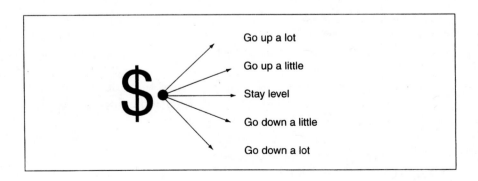

FIGURE 1.2

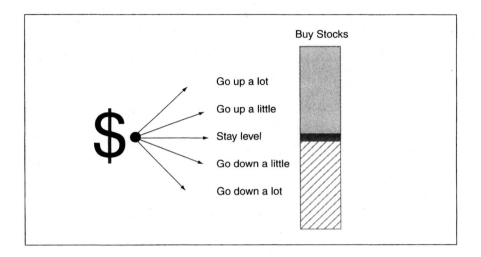

your odds of making a successful trade will increase because you can actually make money when you are wrong.

Now let's consider *severity*, or how much you can lose on any one trade. The amount you can lose when you buy stock is the amount the stock falls in price after you take a position in it. There is the potential to lose money with any bullish investment strategy when a stock you pick to go up actually falls in price.

When you *buy* stock, that loss is the full amount of the drop in price. However, with the SafetyNet Trading System, any losses generated as a result of a drop in price will be offset by up to four factors:

1. The out-of-the-money factor
2. The premium factor
3. The interest factor
4. The hedge factor

As a result, *all* losses will be lower than if you had bought the stock because they are *always* offset by a number of positive factors.

FIGURE 1.3

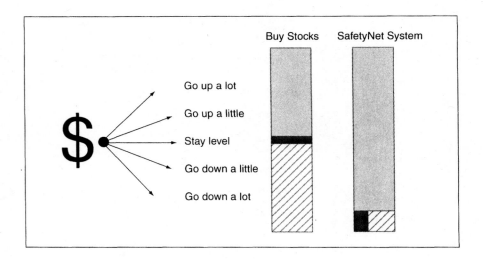

In other words, by using the SafetyNet Trading System, you will be reducing both the *frequency* and *severity* of money-losing incidents that affect your portfolio. In the next chapter, it will become clear how the risk components work in your favor instead of against you.

CHAPTER 2

Using Options to Reduce Risk

Increase Your Odds of Successful Trading

One of the components of the SafetyNet Trading System is selling puts on individual stocks, which is probably the most misunderstood financial concept on the planet.

Many people in the investment community really don't understand what puts are. If you called 100 stockbrokers right now and told them you wanted to open a brokerage account to sell puts, it's likely that at least 99 of them would tell you that you can't or shouldn't because that would be too risky. In reality, as I will prove to you, selling puts is much less risky than buying stock—something every broker will let you do all day long.

Let me give you an analogy that will make puts easy to understand. A put is like car insurance. When you buy a new car, one of the first things you do is call your insurance agent and ask him or her for collision insurance for your new car. You want to make sure that if your car gets totaled, the insurance company will give you the value of the car before it crashed.

If you want a low deductible, you will pay a high premium. If you are satisfied with a higher deductible, you can pay a lower premium. In any event, the idea behind the insurance is that you can "put" your car to the insurance company at the value of the car before it crashed. Well, cars aren't the only things that crash. Stocks do too. And for the last couple of years, a lot more often.

Stock puts work the same way as car insurance. A stock put allows you to put a particular stock to someone else at the price of the stock before it crashed. You pay a premium for the put, and the premium amount depends partly on how large a deductible you are willing to accept.

Let's say IBM is trading at $100 a share. By purchasing a put, you can get someone to guarantee to purchase IBM from you for $95 no matter how low IBM goes. You can pay a lower premium if you are willing to be guaranteed a $90 price (a $10 deductible). Or you could pay a higher premium if you want a $100 price guarantee (no deductible). The amount of the deductible impacts the put premium, in the same way deductible amounts affect car insurance. With stock puts, the deductible is referred to as how much the put option is *in* or *out of the money*.

Since I am talking about a risk-averse strategy, you might be thinking that I am suggesting you buy puts as insurance against falling stock prices. But I'm actually suggesting the reverse. I am proposing that you sell puts. Let me explain why.

First, imagine what class of companies has more money than any other in the world. The answer: insurance companies. How did they get all that money? Answer: selling premiums. And how did they get to keep those premiums? Answer: only insuring risks they didn't think would result in a claim. Well, that's exactly what I suggest you do—become like an insurance company and sell puts on stocks that you don't think are going to go down. These, of course, would be the same stocks you ordinarily would have bought. But instead of buying them, you would sell puts on them.

Let's take a look at some historical examples and see how the results differ between buying stock and selling puts. A couple of years ago during a speech at the San Francisco Money Show, I used the following examples to show how much less risky it is to sell puts than it is to buy stock. The examples compared buying certain stocks to selling puts on the same stocks with an expiration date 17 months into the future.

The first example was Wal-Mart (WMT). On Friday, August 4, 2000, the stock closed at $53. A stock buyer could have bought the stock for $53 a share. To do that, the investor, if he or she didn't want to borrow money and pay interest to a broker, would have needed to send $53 per share to the broker to pay for the stock.

The alternative would have been to sell puts on Wal-Mart at a $50 *strike price*. That means an investor would have been obligated to buy Wal-Mart for $50 a share even if Wal-Mart's stock price dropped below $50. (Remember, this approach is designed as an alternative to buying the stock, an investor shouldn't mind being obligated to buy Wal-Mart at a lower price tomorrow than he or she was willing to pay for it today.) In return for assuming that (that is, the put) obligation, the investor would have received a premium of $7.25 a share. In addition, he or she would have had to send his or her broker only $25 as collateral for that trade, rather than sending $53 to buy the stock. (In Part 2 you will find detailed explanations about options that will make this transaction clearer.)

Now let's look at which transaction is really more risky. To do that, we need to look at the downside. What would have happened if the stock had gone down? Let's assume that Wal-Mart fell from $53 to $39. If you had bought the stock, you would have lost $14 per share—the full drop in price of the stock.

On the other hand, if you had sold a put at a $50 strike price, you would have lost only $2.31 a share. That's because you would have bought the stock for $50 (the put strike price), not the $53 a stock buyer would have paid. Your loss on the stock would have been just $11 a share ($50 − 39 = $11). This $11 per share loss would have been offset by the $7.25 premium you had received for selling the put and the interest you would have earned on the $25 you sent your broker and the interest you could have earned on the $7.25 premium ($11 stock loss − $7.25 premium − $1.44 interest = $2.31 loss). Figure 2.1 illustrates this point. (By the way, many people have the misconception that if they don't sell a stock when it drops, they really don't have a loss yet. They may not have a loss for tax purposes, but I assure you your banker sees it as a loss.)

As you can easily see from Figure 2.1, the severity of loss is much lower when you sell the put than it is when you buy the stock. But what about the frequency? Will you lose more or less often when you sell a put?

Frequency is merely a function of the breakeven point of a transaction. In this example, the breakeven price for buying Wal-Mart stock is $53. But the breakeven price when selling the put is just $41.31. That's because when you sell the put, you are obligated to buy the stock for $50, but the $50 purchase price is reduced by the premium you receive ($7.25) and the interest earned during the transaction period ($1.44). The question is then, "Is it more likely or probable that Wal-Mart will end up below $53 or $41.31?" Obviously, it is much more likely that Wal-Mart will end up below $53 than below $41.31. Therefore, it is much less likely that you will lose money when you sell the put than when you buy the stock (see Figure 2.2).

You can clearly see that the risk, from both severity and frequency standpoints, is substantially less when you sell a

FIGURE 2.1

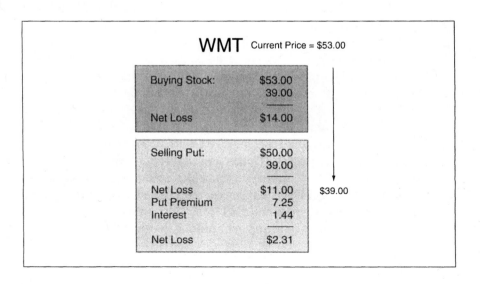

FIGURE 2.2

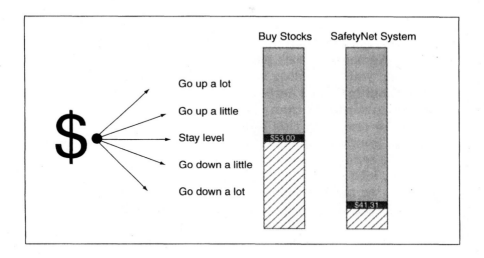

Wal-Mart put than when you buy a Wal-Mart stock. Of course, if we reduce the risk, we must also reduce the potential reward. And selling puts does reduce the potential reward.

No matter what price Wal-Mart rises to, the put seller will make only $8.69 a share ($7.25 premium and $1.44 interest). However, on a $25 investment, that is still a 35 percent profit in 17 months (25 percent annualized gain) even if Wal-Mart goes down a little but stays above the $50 strike price. A buyer of Wal-Mart stock could have made much more if the stock went up beyond $71. It's that upside potential that is given up in order to get the downside protection. But if your goal is 15 percent annual returns, why would you take the extra risk when you can make more than 15 percent with much less risk? The answer: You wouldn't if you or your current advisor knew it was possible to reach your investment goals with less risk.

Our next example was Computer Associates (CA). The company had recently announced that it would not reach its projected revenues as a result of lower sales in Europe. The stock plunged from the $50 to $60 range, and on Friday, August 4, 2000, it closed at $27. As a stock buyer, you could have bought the stock for $27 a share. To do that, if you didn't want to borrow money and pay interest to a broker, you would have sent $27 per share to the broker to pay for the stock.

The alternative would have been to sell puts on Computer Associates at a $25 strike price. That means that you would have agreed to buy Computer Associates for $25 a share even if Computer Associates' stock price dropped and stayed below $25. (Remember, you are selling the put in lieu of buying the stock, and you shouldn't mind agreeing to buy Computer Associates at a lower price tomorrow than you were willing to pay for it today.) In return for assuming that obligation, the put, you would have received a premium of $6.25 a share. In addition, you would have had to send your broker only $12.50 to make that trade.

Again, let's look at which transaction is really more risky. To do that, we need to look at the downside. What would happen if the stock were to go down? Let's assume that Computer Associates fell about another 25 percent from $27 to $21. If you had bought the stock, you would have lost $6 per share (see Figure 2.3).

If instead you had sold a put at a $25 strike price, you would have actually made $3.11 a share. That's because you

FIGURE 2.3

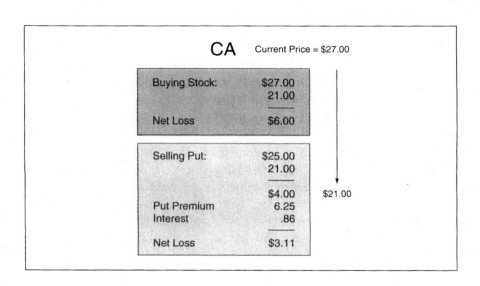

would have bought the stock for $25, not the $27 a stock buyer would have paid. Your loss on the stock would have been just $4 a share ($25 − $21 = $4). This $4 per share loss would have been more than offset by the $6.25 premium and the interest you would have earned on the $12.50 you sent your broker as collateral for the position and the $6.25 premium you received for selling the put ($4.00 stock loss + $6.25 premium + $0.86 interest = $3.11 gain!).

As you can easily see, the severity of loss is much lower when you sell the put than when you buy the stock. In fact, as in this case, sometimes the offsetting factors are so significant they actually turn a loss into a profit. Wouldn't it be nice to make a profit even when you're wrong?

But what about the frequency? Will you lose more often or less often when you sell a put on Computer Associates?

As I mentioned, frequency is a function of the breakeven point of a transaction. In this example, the breakeven price for buying Computer Associates stock was $27. But the breakeven price when selling the put was just $17.89 (see Figure 2.4). The question is then, "Is it more likely or probable that Computer Associates will end up below $27 or below $17.89?" Of course, it is much more likely that Computer Associates will end up below $27 than below $17.89 for the simple reason that if it falls below $17.89, it will already be below $27. But it doesn't have to be below $17.89 just because it falls below $27. Therefore, it is much less likely that you will lose money if you sell the put than if you buy the stock.

Once again, you can clearly see that the risk, both from a severity and frequency standpoint, is substantially less when you sell a Computer Associates put than when you buy Computer Associates stock. Of course, if we reduce the risk, we must also reduce the potential reward. As I said, selling puts does reduce the potential reward.

No matter what price Computer Associates rises to, the put seller would make only $7.11 a share ($6.25 premium and $0.86 interest). However, on a $12.50 investment, that is still a 57 percent (41 percent annualized gain) profit even if Computer Associates goes down a little. A buyer of Computer Associates stock could have made much more if the stock went up beyond

FIGURE 2.4

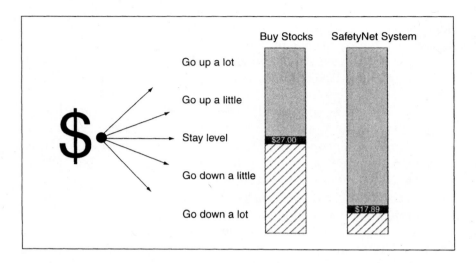

$27. It's that upside potential that is given up in order to get the downside protection.

Next let's look at QUALCOMM. The stock on August 4, 2000, had closed at about $64. As a stock buyer, you could have bought the stock for $64 a share. To do that, if you didn't want to borrow money and pay interest to a broker, you would send $64 per share to the broker to pay for the stock.

The alternative would have been to sell puts on QUALCOMM at a $60 strike price. That means that you would have agreed to buy QUALCOMM for $60 a share even if QUALCOMM's stock price dropped below $60. In return for assuming that obligation, the put, you would have received a premium of $13.50 a share. In addition, you would have had to send your broke only $30 to make that trade.

Once again, let's look at which transaction is really more risky. To do that, we need to look at the downside. What would happen if the stock were to go down? Let's assume that QUALCOMM fell from $64 to $41. If you had bought the stock, you would have lost $23 per share (see Figure 2.5).

On the other hand, if you had sold a put at a $60 strike price, you would have lost only $3.54 a share. That's because

FIGURE 2.5

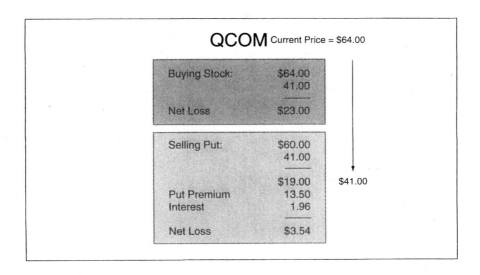

you would have bought the stock for $60, not the $64 a stock buyer would have paid. Your loss on the stock would have been $19 a share ($60 − $41 = $19). This $19 per share loss would have been offset by the $13.50 premium and the interest you would have earned on the $30 you sent your broker and the interest on the $13.50 premium you received on day 1 ($19 stock loss − $13.50 premium − $1.96 interest = $3.54 loss).

As you can easily see, the severity of loss is much less when you sell the put than when you buy the stock. But what about the frequency? Will you lose more often or less often when you sell a QUALCOMM put?

As I mentioned, frequency is a function of the breakeven point of a transaction. In this example, as can be seen in Figure 2.6, the breakeven price for buying QUALCOMM stock was $64. But the breakeven price when selling the put was just $44.54. The question is then, "Is it more likely or probable that QUAL-COMM stock will end up below $64 or $44.54?" Obviously, it is much more likely that QUALCOMM will end up below $64 than below $44.54. Therefore, it is much less likely that you will lose money if you sell the put than if you buy the stock.

FIGURE 2.6

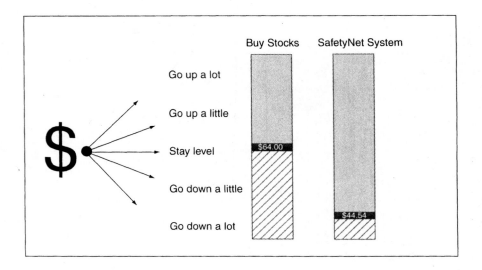

Once again, you can clearly see that the risk, both from a severity and frequency standpoint, is substantially less when you sell a QUALCOMM put than when you buy QUALCOMM stock. Of course, if we reduce the risk, we must also reduce the potential reward. And, once again, selling puts does reduce the potential reward.

No matter what price QUALCOMM rises to, the put seller would make only $15.46 a share ($13.50 premium and $1.96 interest). However, on a $30 investment, that is still a 52 percent profit (37 percent annualized gain) even if QUALCOMM goes down a little. A buyer of QUALCOMM stock could have made much more if the stock went up beyond $91. It's that upside potential that is given up in order to get the downside protection.

A thousand examples would all produce the same kind of results. The indisputable conclusion is that (1) selling puts is less risky than buying the same stock, and (2) it is possible, and even likely, to earn over 12 percent a year (24 percent with the use of minimal leverage) selling puts, even in a flat market. As a result, those with financial return goals of less than 15 percent should not assume the significant risk of buying stocks but should reduce that risk by selling puts instead on the same stocks they would have purchased. Not only will this reduce risk but it also will increase the likelihood of achieving reasonable financial goals since this approach will produce profits even when the stocks chosen stay flat or go down slightly.

Some may argue that when you buy a stock, you can sell it if it starts to fall and thereby limit your losses. However, you can limit your losses selling puts as well. It is important to understand that you can close out a losing put sale early if a stock begins to fall in price and you think it appropriate to close the transaction. The put you originally sold will increase in price as the stock falls and you will have to pay more to buy it back and close out the transaction, but just like buying stock, you can close out the transaction early to limit your losses.

Although most in the industry still don't understand options, they have begun to finally receive some positive attention. The Options Clearing Corporation (OCC) recently announced that options trading activity has increased again for the tenth straight year and that 2001's volume was almost 50 percent higher than the previous year's. Even the *Wall Street Journal* recently published some positive comments about selling options when it wrote, "Investors might sell puts as a way to pocket a premium upfront while setting a price at which they will be willing to buy stock." They also quoted Tim Biggam, chief options strategist at Man Securities, as saying, "Given the current combination of low stock prices and high volatility, this is a great time to pick up stocks you like while selling options to capture the rich premiums and help pay for the stocks."

In summary, selling puts reduces the frequency and severity of potential losses while simultaneously increasing the likelihood of making successful trades since you can actually make a profit when you sell a put and the stock goes in the opposite direction from what you thought it would. These increased odds are achieved by giving up some of the upside potential, but not to the point that you fail to reach your financial goals.

In the next chapter we will discuss how to insure your portfolio against a major market correction.

3

Using Someone Else's Money to Insure Your Assets

A Tranquilizer for Your Portfolio

The second component of the SafetyNet Trading System is designed to protect you from a major market crash. As I stated in an earlier work,* I suggested in 2000 that we might be headed for a significant market downturn. Here is a repeat of what I said then:

> What might cause a downturn in the overall economy? It's anyone's guess. The one thing that every major market crash in U.S. history has in common is that most investors never saw it coming. Looking back, we can see the warning signs that preceded each one, but at the time most investors were oblivious to those warnings. One thing we do know is that most market crashes are precipitated by a huge run-up in stock prices and the belief that the overall economy is very strong.
>
> So, are we overdue for a major market correction, and, if so, what might cause it? Are there any warning signs we should be looking for?

---

* Jeffrey M. Cohen, *Don't Trade Without a Net* (2000).

Warning Sign 1: While some people suggest that the Federal Reserve Bank has done a good job so far keeping inflation "at bay" with small, incremental rate increases, others worry that the very "medicine" the Fed is using to fight inflation could ultimately backfire and cause an economic downturn. Higher interest rates almost always cause a slowdown in consumer spending and an increase in the cost of goods sold in a large number of market sectors.

Warning Sign 2: Low unemployment figures and the tightness in the skilled-labor pool could eventually push labor costs up dramatically. Add to that the possibility of continuing increases in the price of fuel oil, and the threat of higher inflation becomes even more threatening.

Warning Sign 3: Some economists are alarmed at the amount of margin loans outstanding. The concern is that if a market correction takes place while investors are heavily leveraged, there might not be enough liquidity afterward to help bring about the quick recovery or rebound we've all come to expect. Investors facing margin calls could be forced to sell their already beleaguered shares, causing a further downward spiral. Several bearish-type analysts have quietly voiced concerns that this could lead to a disastrously deep recession, followed by a long, slow recovery.

Those are just a few concerns. There are always the old standbys: fear of war, drought, or some other widespread natural disaster. And then there's always the threat that politicians will use economic policy shenanigans to gain popularity before, during, or immediately after an election year.

The problem, of course, is that there is no way to know for certain exactly when this economy will finally begin to slow down, and nobody wants to sit on the sidelines waiting for the next big stock market crash. I considered pulling out in 1997 because I felt certain a major correction was coming. Had I not had a system that allows me to stay in the market without the risks associated with a general market correction, I would have missed out on several years of incredible profits.

Well, we did get a major market correction, and some of the factors mentioned above and some new ones never thought imaginable before September 11, 2001, may still drive the market lower.

How do we protect ourselves in such an event? The answer is hedging. Hedging is to take two opposing positions at the same time in the hopes that, if the primary position goes down and you lose money, the other position will make profits to off-set the loss on the first position.

If you sell puts on a diversified portfolio of individual stocks, you could lose a lot of money if the market crashes. You wouldn't lose as much as you might have if you had bought the stocks, but you could still lose a lot of money. In order to protect against such an occurrence, I suggest that you use some of the premium you received from selling the individual stock puts to buy puts on the overall market by purchasing *index puts*.

You can buy puts on the Dow Jones index, the S&P index, or the Nasdaq index, to name just a few. The idea is to buy puts on an index that relates to the stocks on which you sold the individual stock puts.

It is important to realize that there is no perfect hedge. There will always be what is called dispersion. That means that your individual stock choices will never react exactly the same as the index as a whole. As a result, if you sell puts on stocks that underperform the market when it falls, you will not make enough profit on your index puts to completely offset the losses on your stock puts. Conversely, if your stocks outperform a falling market, you would actually make a profit during the market correction. Now even though there is no perfect hedge, think of how much better an imperfect hedge is than no hedge at all. On the other hand, the typical stock buyer would have no cash to use to buy the index puts (they used their cash to buy the stocks), whereas the put seller can use about 20 to 25 percent of the put premium received from someone else to insure his or her portfolio with the index puts.

Let's take a look at how this investment approach compares to others. Pretend that you just walked into a financial advisor's office and told him that your portfolio was full of Amazon.com, eBay, CMGI, and Yahoo! stock. You realized after the last couple of years that, with these stocks, you can make or lose a lot of money and you can't take the rollercoaster ride anymore (see Figure 3.1).

FIGURE 3.1

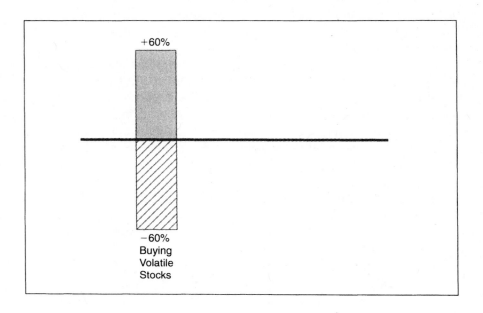

He might suggest that you liquidate these volatile stocks and buy stocks like GE, Wal-Mart, and Lehman Brothers instead. He would explain that these stocks are less volatile and would probably return less than more volatile stocks, but they would also reduce the downside. He would be correct. However, now, instead of losing or making maybe 60 percent a year, you may fluctuate between 30 percent losses or gains (see Figure 3.2). The point is: *This change doesn't increase the probabilities of successful trading; it merely constricts the possibilities.*

The same would be true of *asset allocation*. With this increasingly popular approach to managing risk (see Figure 3.3), you would hold 50 percent stocks and 50 percent bonds with the idea of reducing your risk. Once again, you wouldn't be increasing the probabilities of success; instead, you would just be constricting the possibilities. What we need is an approach that increases the probabilities of success and decreases the potential risk. The SafetyNet Trading System does just that (see Figure 3.4).

FIGURE 3.2

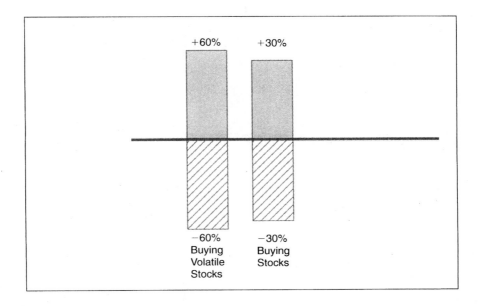

Let me show you a hypothetical example. Let's assume that you sell puts on a diversified group of stocks on January 1. The puts you sell have an average strike price 5 percent below the stocks' current prices. Let's assume that by the end of the year the market has crashed. The overall market has gone down 40 percent. Worse yet, the stocks you sold puts on did 15 percent worse than the overall market. Let's see what happened.

First, since the market went down 40 percent and your stocks did 15 percent worse than the market—your stocks went down 46 percent! (40 percent × 15 percent worse = 6 percent more). Of course, your losses will be offset by the four factors we discussed earlier.

Because you sold puts 5 percent below the stocks' current price, you lost only 41 percent on those stocks since you don't start losing money until the stock drops below the option's strike price. That's a 5 percent reduction in losses. We call that

FIGURE 3.3

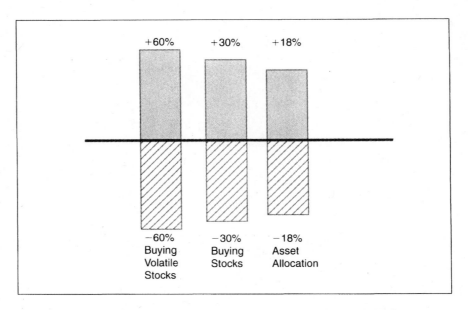

the *out-of-the-money* factor. You originally sold the put 5 percent below the stock's then-current price.

You then reduce your losses by the amount of the net premium you took in. We'll assume you took in only 12 percent in premium and spent 3 percent of the 12 percent on the index puts. That leaves you a net 9 percent premium to further reduce your loss. You then reduce your loss even further by the profits you make on the index put hedge.

We'll assume that you reduced the strike price on the index puts by 14 percent. Remember, we are trying only to insure against a loss, and, since we took in a net 9 percent premium and sold puts 5 percent out of the money, theoretically we won't lose money unless the market drops more than that. Since the market, in our scenario, went down 40 percent, your net gain on the index puts is 26 percent, because you purchased those index puts 14 percent below the index price at the time of the transaction.

You can then further reduce your losses by the interest earned on the cash collateral you deposited with your broker

FIGURE 3.4

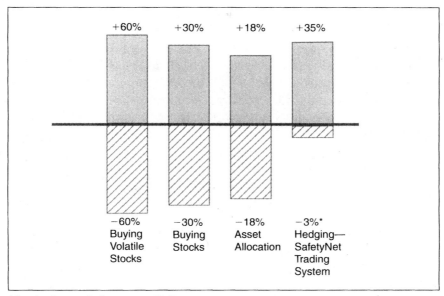

* Based on the example given on pages 39–41.

and the net premium you received. That amounts to about another 3 percent.

So here's the summary: You lose 41 percent on the stocks after considering that the puts were sold 5 percent below their then current price; you gain 9 percent from the net put premiums; you gain 26 percent on the index puts; and you gain 3 percent in interest. A total net loss of only 3 percent under a terrible scenario! A stock buyer would have lost 46 percent! That example is theoretical, but I'll show you some actual examples in Part 3.

It should now be clear that using this system is significantly less risky than buying stocks or mutual funds. And even though you give up potentially large gains if a stock or the whole market takes off, you still earn returns in excess of your long-term goals. Why would anyone take additional risk to exceed his or her goals? That would be like someone who never drives over 30 miles per hour buying a Corvette.

In this industry, it is called an *unsuitable approach*. It is illegal for a financial advisor to suggest that a client take risk that is inappropriate in relation to his or her stated goals and risk tolerance. Yet almost every financial advisor has suggested to clients that they buy traditional mutual funds and/or stocks. In most cases, they make such recommendations probably because they truly didn't know a better alternative was available. The real question is, Why haven't the leaders of these large financial firms taught their representatives about these risk-averse approaches so that the representatives could explain and implement these strategies to those clients who want 10 to 15 percent annual gains with less risk than accompanies direct stock purchases? Is it because they don't know themselves, or is there some hidden agenda?

I don't know the answer to that question, but I can recount an incredible, yet true story. Until recently, I had been using Merrill Lynch as my broker to clear option trades. One day, I received a telephone call from one of their compliance officers who told me that I had sold too many puts in my accounts. I replied that I was well within their margin limits and didn't understand what the problem was.

The compliance officer then explained that they have a rule regarding the number of contracts that can be sold, regardless of the put strike prices. This, of course, has no basis in logic since it is the value of the puts sold that fixes your liability. Selling 100 contracts at a $100 strike price establishes a lot more liability than selling 300 contracts at a $10 strike price. (Of course, the reason put sellers currently sell a large *number* of contracts is that stock prices have fallen so far.)

The compliance officer didn't care that I had over $3 million in cash in the accounts and that I was well within published margin limits—the company had a rule about the number of contracts that can be sold, and that was it. By the way, they have no similar rule about the number of shares of stock you can buy. The compliance officer had also spoken to the office manager, and between them they decided that put selling was much too risky anyway. Of course, she would have no problem with my investing all of my assets in their wonderful mutual funds. The following is a sample of the 2001 results for some of their in-house funds as quoted by Morningstar:

Merrill Lynch Large Cap Core—down 5.0 percent
Merrill Lynch Large Cap Growth—down 10.3 percent
Merrill Lynch Mid Cap Growth—down 36.6 percent
Merrill Lynch Premier Growth—down 52.6 percent
Merrill Lynch Disciplined Equity—down 8.2 percent
Merrill Lynch Focused Twenty—down 70.1 percent
Merrill Lynch Fundamental Growth—down 19.4 percent
Merrill Lynch Global Growth—down 26.3 percent
Merrill Lynch Global Technology—down 44.0 percent
Merrill Lynch Global Value—down 13.7 percent

If you had diversified your holdings over these 10 funds, you would have lost almost 30 percent of your assets in 1 year—and paid a nice management fee for the privilege! But, if you had used the examples we posted freely on our Web site during 2001, you would have earned over 15 percent. It kind of makes you wonder if the same people who came up with that Merrill Lynch rule manage those funds.

The point is that Merrill Lynch not only does not advise its clients on how to use this less-risky strategy but they actually require them to use a more risky one (buying stocks or mutual funds) if they want to be in the market since according to them "put selling" is too risky.

It continues to amaze me how few people in the investment business actually understand how to use options to reduce risk. And it is even more incredible that most actually think that the use of options increases risk. By the time you finish this book, you will probably know more about investing than the person who has been advising you.

If you doubt that, call up a few stockbrokers and ask them if they know how you can make money in the market when you're wrong. Or ask them if they know how you can insure your portfolio against a major market correction with someone else's money. The heavy odds are that they won't know.

TWO

OPTION TRADING: A DETAILED TUTORIAL

4

Understanding Options

They're Simpler Than You Think

The SafetyNet Trading System involves the conservative use of equity and index options. This chapter is devoted to a functional explanation of these financial instruments. There is a multitude of ways that options can be used—both aggressively and conservatively. Rather than trying to describe every conceivable use, in this chapter my goal is to teach you about their use with regard to the SafetyNet Trading System.

If you want to learn more about options, I have listed several good sources in the "Recommended Reading" section at the back of the book. If you are an old pro on options, you could skip this chapter altogether or consider it a refresher course.

EQUITY OPTIONS

An equity option is a financial instrument that gives the option owner the right, but not the obligation, to buy (a *call option*) or sell (a *put option*) a particular stock at a predetermined price by a certain date. That definition sounds more complicated than options really are. Let's start by discussing the first type of option: *calls*.

CALLS

A call option gives its owner the right, but not the obligation, to purchase a particular stock from the person who sold him or her the call option. Thus the option owner has the right to buy that stock at a predetermined price, but he or she must do so before the option expires.

Think of it as an agreement between you and another person. You are speculating that the price of a particular stock, we'll call it Gizmonics (GIZ), might rise substantially from its current price of $38 within the next 30 days. Instead of purchasing the stock outright, you decide to enter into an agreement that says that you have the right to buy 100 shares of Gizmonics stock for $40 per share any time between now and the third Friday of the following month. That means that if the price of Gizmonics stock goes up to $40, or $50, or even $150 before the option expires, you have to pay only $40 per share for 100 shares.

If, on the other hand, Gizmonics shares stay at $38 or if they drop in price, you are not obligated to buy the stock.

OPTION PRICING

Strike Prices

In the previous example I said you had the right to purchase Gizmonics stock at $40. That amount is called the *strike price*. We could have purchased an option to buy the stock with a strike price of $45, or $50, or $55, and so on.

In the Money and Out of the Money

The strike price could also be below the current price of the stock. If the strike price is below the current price of the stock, it is said to be in the money. For example, if Gizmonics is trading at $38, a call option with a strike price of $35 would be considered in the money while a call option with a strike price of $40 would be out of the money.

Remembering the difference is simple: If the option expired today with the stock's current price valued below your option's strike price, you would be *out* the money you paid for the option. On the other hand, if the stock were valued above the strike price of your option, you would be able to buy the stock at the lower strike price and then sell it at the higher market price and put the difference *in* your pocket. (See Table 4.1.)

Premium Pricing

To entice someone to give you an option to buy his or her stock at a predetermined price, you have to pay that person a fee, known as the option's *premium*. The person selling you that option gets to keep the premium you pay regardless of whether you choose to exercise your option.

For example, let's assume you paid the call option seller a premium of $1.75 for a Gizmonics option with a $40 strike price. Later, when Gizmonics stock rose to $45, you could exercise your option to buy Gizmonics for $40. In this example the seller would get to keep the $1.75 you had already paid for the option and the $40 you would be paying for the stock, for a total of $41.75, and you would get the stock.

If, on the other hand, Gizmonics did not rise above $40 before the option expired, you would not exercise your call

TABLE 4.1

Out-of-the-Money Call	Option
Strike price	= $40
Current price	= $38
In-the-Money Call	**Option**
Strike price	= $35
Current price	= $38

option since you could buy the stock for less in the open market. The option seller would keep the $1.75 and the stock. The option seller could then sell another call option on the stock he or she owns.

Volatility of the Stock

The value of a *call* option and its premium price are determined by several factors. The most important ones are (1) the current price of the stock in relation to the option's strike price, (2) the time left before the option expires, and (3) the stock's volatility. *Volatility* refers to how much the stock price changes on a regular basis. Internet stocks, for example, move up and down dramatically (mostly down lately) and therefore are considered very volatile. Utility stocks, on the other hand, do not move very much, so they are not considered volatile.

Let's take a look at some call option prices for various stocks to see the difference volatility makes in option prices. So that we can focus on volatility, we will look at option strike prices near the current trading price of the stock and with about 14 months left before expiration.

On the day this was written, Broadcom (BRCM) was trading at about $46 a share. If you wanted to buy a call option that gave you the right to purchase Broadcom shares for $50 (the strike price) at any time over the next 14 months, that option would cost about $15 per share. That's a 30 percent *premium* percentage ($15 premium divided by $50 strike price). Broadcom is considered a volatile stock.

You also could have purchased an option to buy Dell Computer stock, which has been somewhat less volatile in the recent past. At the time of this writing, Dell stock was trading at about $26.30. A call option with a strike price of $30 costs $4.60 a share. The premium percentage is about 15 percent for the same amount of time.

Or you could buy a 14-month option to buy PepsiCo stock, which is considerably less volatile. As of this writing, PepsiCo is trading at $49 a share. A PepsiCo call option with a strike price of $50 would cost only $5.60 a share. The premium percentage is less than 12 percent. You can see from Table 4.2 that the

TABLE 4.2

Company Name	Strike Price	Option Premium	Premium Percentage
Broadcom	$50.00	$15.00	30.0%
Dell	$30.00	$4.60	15.3%
PepsiCo	$50.00	$5.60	11.3%

The more volatile the stock, the higher the option premium.

volatility of the underlying stock has a significant impact on the price of the option.

Time Value

The amount of time remaining on the option is also an important factor in its price (see Table 4.3). Let's take a quick look at how time impacts an option's price. The Dell $30 option we discussed above was priced at $4.60 a share for about a 14-month time frame. However, a call option at the same strike price but with an expiration date out 6 months instead of 14 months would cost only $2.25 a share. An option to buy Dell at the same $30 strike price but with 26 months to expiration would cost $7 a share.

As you can readily see, even though the premium for options goes up as the time to expiration increases, the price does not go up evenly. In other words, you will not have to pay four times as much for an option that will last four times

TABLE 4.3

Dell Computer Options (Current price = $26.30)

Strike Price	Months to Expiration	Option Premium	Annualized Premium Percentage
$30	6	$2.25	15.0%
$30	14	$4.60	13.1%
$30	26	$7.00	10.7%

The longer the time period to expiration, the larger the premium, but the smaller the annualized premium percentage.

as long. There are several reasons for this, but at this time it is important that you understand only that the *time decay* on option premiums accelerates as you get closer to the option's expiration date. In other words, the cost of an option decreases in value much more quickly as the option approaches its expiration date; therefore, shorter-term options produce higher annualized yields.

Proximity of Strike Price to Current Market Price

The last important factor in determining an option's premium is the strike price's proximity to the current stock price (see Table 4.4). For example, the 14-month Dell $30 call option quoted above was selling for $4.60.

However, you could buy the $35 Dell call option for just $3.10 a share or the $40 option for just $1.95 a share. Conversely, you would have to pay $6.70 for an option to buy Dell at $25 a share since, in this example, Dell is currently selling for more than that already.

Intrinsic Value versus Time Value

Option premiums are composed of two components: intrinsic value and time value. The *intrinsic value* is the actual in-the-money value of the option. For example, suppose IBM were trading at $100 a share and you wanted to buy a call option at a $95 strike price. Then the option price would include $5 of intrinsic value since IBM was already trading $5 higher than

TABLE 4.4

Dell Computer Options (Current price = $26.30)

Strike Price	Months to Expiration	Option Premium	Premium Percentage
$25	14	$6.70	26.8%
$30	14	$4.60	15.3%
$35	14	$3.10	8.8%
$40	14	$1.95	4.9%

Option premiums decrease as the strike price moves from in the money to out of the money and decreases further as the strike price moves further out of the money.

the call strike price. The difference between the actual option premium and the intrinsic value is called the *time value*.

So if the IBM $95 call option were trading at $8 a share, that would mean that there was $5 of the intrinsic value in the option and $3 of time value. The time value decays as time elapses while the intrinsic value changes based solely on the underlying stock's price. For instance, in the IBM example ($95 strike price), if IBM rose to $105 a share, the option's intrinsic value would go up to $10. There is no such thing as negative intrinsic value. Therefore, if an option is out of the money, the time value would be the entire premium.

One last important factor to remember is that the time value is a function of how close the strike price is to the stock's current price—whether or not the intrinsic value exists in the option. When you look at option charts, you will see that the time value on a $50 strike price is almost the same when the stock is trading at $53 or $47. It's only the intrinsic value that changes because in both cases the proximity to the strike price is the same.

OPTION CONTRACTS

Stocks are usually purchased in lots of 100, but it is also possible to buy a single share of stock, or any number of shares for that matter. Options, however, are sold in contracts that almost always represent lots of 100. In other words, you can usually buy or sell options only at a minimum of 100 shares of stock at a time. When you buy or sell 1 contract of options, you are buying or selling options on 100 shares of stock. The only exception is that sometimes, after a stock splits, the contracts written for those stocks before the split will be amended to reflect the appropriate number of shares those contracts represent after the split. For example, if a stock splits 3 for 2, that means the stockholder will receive 3 shares for every 2 he or she owned before the split; an option holder of 1 contract will own a "150-share contract" to account for the split. On the other hand, after 2-for-1 splits, the number of contracts is adjusted. In this case, an option holder that owned 1 contract before the split will own 2 100-share contracts after the split.

Option contracts always expire on the Saturday following the third Friday of the expiration month. Conventionally listed options can have an expiration date up to 9 months from the date the options are first listed for trading. *Long-term Equity Anticipation Securities* (LEAP) *option contracts*, have expiration dates up to 3 years from the date of the listing. However, equity LEAPS always expire in January. Stock options are written according to a preset quarterly calendar, but options may always be traded for the succeeding 2 months from the current date.

Appendix D lists all stocks that have tradable options and their quarterly trading cycle. Not all stocks listed on the options market have associated LEAPS.

LEVERAGE

Obviously, you would buy a call option for a stock only if you thought the stock's price was going to rise before the expiration of the option. One of the reasons traders buy an option instead of the stock itself is to increase trading leverage. For example, if you were to buy Dell stock for a price of $26.30 and it went up to $35, you would have made a $8.70 profit, or about a 33 percent ($8.70 profit divided by $26.30 investment) return on your investment. However, if you had purchased a 6-month Dell $30 call option for a premium of $2.25, you would have made $2.75. That's because you could have purchased Dell stock for the $30 strike price of your option and then sold it for $35, its current hypothetical price. Your $5 gain on the stock would have been reduced by the cost of the call option ($2.25), leaving you a net gain of $2.75, or a return of over 122 percent ($2.75 profit divided by $2.25 investment).

Of course, if the stock were to stay below $30 (the strike price), the option would expire as worthless and you would lose your entire investment.

It has generally held true that 80 percent of options expire worthless, which clearly shows that buying equity options is very risky and not something that I recommend except in very specific cases, which I will discuss later.

PUTS

What if you thought a stock was going to fall in price? You could buy the second type of option: a PUT. A *put* option gives its owner the right, but not the obligation, to sell a particular stock to someone at a predetermined price up to a predetermined date (the expiration date).

Just like call option premium, a put option premium is determined by (1) the strike price's proximity to the current stock price, (2) the length of time to the option's expiration date, and (3) the volatility of the underlying stock.

Options traders make money when they buy puts and the stock price falls. As with calls, they increase their leverage by using put options, but they could lose their entire investment if the stock does not fall below the put strike price before the option expires. Therefore, buying calls is a *bullish strategy*, and buying puts is a *bearish strategy*.

If traders felt reasonably sure a stock was going to drop in price, they could either sell the stock short, or they could buy a put option.

What's the difference?

If you sell a stock *short*, you are, in essence, borrowing stock from your broker to sell to someone else. Your broker will charge you interest for the use of the stock you are borrowing, and eventually you will have to purchase an equivalent amount of that stock to repay the broker. If you were correct and the price of the stock dropped, you could purchase it at the lower price to repay the broker. If, on the other hand, you were incorrect and the price of the stock rose, you would have to either hold on to your short position in the hopes that the stock will eventually fall (all the while paying interest) or liquidate the short position at a loss by purchasing the stock at the higher price.

Since it is entirely possible that the stock might never go down from the level at which you short sold and, in fact, could continue to rise indefinitely, your risk on that position is unlimited.

If you purchase a put option instead, your risk is limited to the amount of premium you paid for the put option. If the stock goes up instead of down, your option will eventually expire worthless, but you will have no further obligation.

Before you start getting ideas about making easy money buying puts on overvalued stocks, let's look at the downside of that strategy. To make a profit buying puts, the price of the underlying stock must drop substantially. A small drop in price will not suffice. That's because you must make up for the price you paid for the put—the *premium*.

Let's look at an example. Unfortunately, based on market movement over the past 2 years, not too many stocks look overvalued anymore. One stock that has held up well, however, is IBM. Let's say you think it is going to drop from a price of $115. You can buy a put that gives you the right to sell IBM for $105 within the next 9 months. You will have to pay about $7.50 for that option. If you're right and IBM falls to $100, you will still lose money. That's because if the stock drops from $115 to $100 before the option expires, you will recoup only $5 of the $7.50 you paid for the option ($105 strike price at which you can sell the stock minus the $100 price at expiration, after which you can buy it back to cover).

In other words, you were right, the stock *did* drop! And you still lost $2.50 per share. To make money on that trade, IBM would have had to drop below $97.50 ($105 strike price minus the $7.50 premium you paid).

Remember what I said earlier? I want to win in as many scenarios as possible. That won't happen buying options. If you buy puts, you make money only if the stock drops a lot. If you buy calls, you make money only if the stock goes up a lot, and only if it happens within a prescribed time frame, before the option expires. There are literally thousands of optionable stocks traded in the United States, as shown in Appendix D. Which of those are going to move enough to be profitable with options? When and in which direction are they making that move? I don't mind speculating as long as the odds of winning are at least even (preferably higher), but trying to guess which stocks are going to make a big move at a specific time and in a specific direction. . . . I gave up my subscription to the psychic hotline a long time ago!

SELLING OPTIONS

You don't have to be a psychic or a speculator or even a very good guesser to make money trading options because you don't have to buy an option to make money with options. You can be the one selling these options.

Writing Covered Calls

If you sell an option, you are called a *writer* because you are actually creating the option. One of the most conservative strategies using options is called *writing covered calls*. With this strategy, you purchase a particular stock and then sell calls against the stock.

Let's say you buy 100 shares of IBM for $100 each. That would be an investment of $10,000. (We'll ignore commissions for now.) Immediately after you make the purchase, you write or sell 1 call contract (1 contract equals 100 shares) for IBM shares, scheduled to expire in 1 year, at a strike price of $100. You might get $12 per share, or a total of $1200 for the 1 contract.

This reduces your investment by the amount of premium you received, in this case $1200, to a net cost of $8800. It also limits your potential gain for the year because you will have to sell the IBM shares for $100 next year if the stock goes above $100. If IBM shares stay level or go down, you keep the stock. (No one would exercise his or her right to buy the stock from you for more than they could purchase it for on the open market.) At that point, you are free to sell covered calls on those same shares all over again if you wish.

Although you have limited your potential gain to $1200, you have also protected your downside. You will not have a loss until IBM goes below $88 a share.

In summary, selling covered calls limits your upside potential while protecting your downside. But the upside isn't that bad. If IBM stays level, you actually make almost 14 percent on your investment ($1200 option premium divided by $8800 net investment) using absolutely no leverage—just for picking stocks that don't go down!

FIGURE 4.1

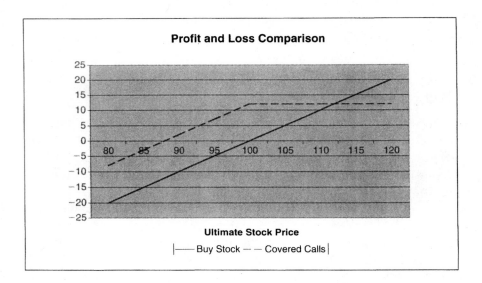

Take a look at Figure 4.1 to see how this approach compares to owning the stock outright. The risk in a covered-call position is similar in nature to the risk of owning the stock by itself, except that your downside risk is lower because the *premium* you received reduced your cost, or your breakeven point, and you make a profit even if the stock stays level.

You can make the position even more conservative by selling an in-the-money call. This means that you sell someone the option to buy IBM for less than its current price, say, $95 a share. In this example, you might get a premium of $14.50 per share. Now your downside is protected even further by the increased premium you receive. However, your upside is further limited because you now have to sell your shares at $95, and your net cost is $85.50 ($100 current price per share −$14.50 call premium received).

In this more conservative example (see Figure 4.2), you earn only 11 percent for the year, but the risk of loss is lower because the stock must go down over 14.5 percent in the year

FIGURE 4.2

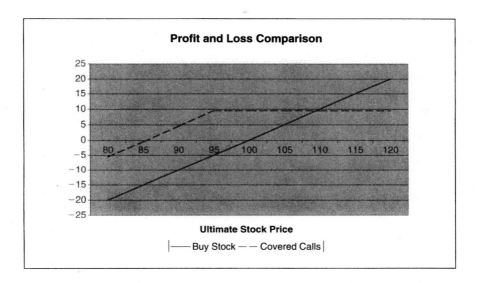

before you begin losing money. In fact, you make your 11 percent even if the stock drops 5 percent.

For some, this may be the first time you realized that it is possible to make a substantial profit in the stock market even when the stocks you thought were going up actually go down instead. Wait: It gets even better.

Writing Puts

A strategy similar to writing covered calls is *writing puts*. In spite of the fact that many investment professionals consider selling puts risky, this strategy has the exact same risk scenario as does selling covered calls. This strategy involves your selling puts for which you have no underlying stock position. (Some people call this *selling cash-secured puts*. It describes a situation in which you have enough capital in your account to purchase the stock if it is put to you.) With this strategy you would sell someone the right to sell you a stock at a particular price for a particular length of time.

The person buying that right would pay you a premium. For example, you may sell someone the right to sell to you IBM stock at $95 for the next year. If the stock were currently selling for $100, you might get a $9.50 premium. As you can see from Figure 4.3, the profit and loss potential is identical to the potential shown in Figure 4.2, which shows the profit and loss potential for in-the-money covered calls. That's because, if IBM goes below $95, you will be obligated to buy the stock for $95. With a covered call, you already bought the stock at $95. In both cases, you make your full profit even if the stock drops all the way down to your strike price. You will begin losing money only when the stock drops below the strike price by an amount that exceeds the premium you received.

Imagine for a minute that you took this position because you were bullish on IBM. You thought the stock was going to go up in value. But instead of going up, let's assume the stock went down $4 to $96. At the option's expiration, the put was still out of the money and expired worthless. You still made a $9.50

FIGURE 4.3

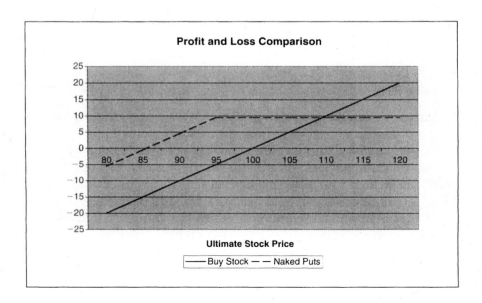

profit on a stock that went down when you thought it would go up. How's that for good odds? Even without using margin, that is, a fully cash secured position, you still earned an 11 percent annual return when you were wrong!

There are two basic differences between selling covered calls and selling puts. When you sell puts, you do not have to use your capital to acquire the stock, although you have to have capital available for margin requirements. (We will discuss margin requirements later.) The second difference is that, when you sell puts, you do not own the stock, so you will not receive any dividends. Instead, you can earn money market interest rates on the cash you need to keep in your portfolio to meet the margin requirements. In addition to those primary differences, it is important to note that when you sell covered calls, you have two commissions and two *spreads* (that is, the difference between the bid and ask prices on the security) to deal with. When you sell puts, you have only one commission and one spread.

Selling puts is a bullish strategy because you are hoping the stock will go up and that the premium will eventually decrease and ultimately expire worthless if the stock does not go down and stay below the strike price. Again, as with the covered calls, you can make a profit even if the stock you thought was going up actually goes down instead.

Selling puts that are out of the money (strike price below the current trading price) is more conservative because the stock will not be put to you unless the stock actually declines in value below the strike price. If the stock does not end up below the strike price on expiration day, you won't be required to buy the stock. In either case, you keep the premium you were paid when you sold the put.

I can't tell you how many old investment pros think selling puts is more risky than buying stock. Let's look at a specific example to prove the opposite. Let's say you buy IBM stock when it is at $105. If IBM goes down to $85, you will have a $20 loss in your account value ($105 − $85). On the other hand, if instead of buying the IBM shares for $105, you sell a put with a $100 strike price on IBM and receive a $10 premium, your loss will be only $5. That is calculated by assuming the stock was put to you at $100 (the strike price). You then subtract the strike price from the current price of $85 and then add back the premium received ($85 − $100 + $10 premium = $5 loss).

By purchasing the stock, you lost $20, but by selling the put, you lost only $5. There is absolutely no question that selling out-of-the-money puts is less risky than buying stock. In spite of what some may say, they will never be able to show you otherwise.

OPTION SYMBOLS

Option symbols are written in different formats for the same option. The long symbol is the easiest to understand. It is composed of the regular stock symbol followed by a space and then the first three letters of the expiration month, the strike price and the letter C or P designating whether the option is a *call* or *put*. For example, the long option symbol for a call option on IBM with a strike price of $120 and an expiration date in March would look like this:

IBM Mar120C

The short option symbol ("short" is referring to length, not taking a "short position") varies depending on which exchange the underlying stock is sold. NYSE stock options are easy to translate because the symbol usually starts with the stock symbol, which is then followed by a space and two more letters. The two letters represent the expiration month and the strike price, respectively. The code for these two letters can be found in Appendix B. The IBM Mar120C in a short form would look like this:

IBM CD

The short form for Amex and Nasdaq stocks is more difficult than for NYSE stocks because the first three letters of the short symbol are not the stock symbol letters. For example, the short option symbol for a Microsoft June 90 put would look like this:

MSQ FW

Another difficulty is that sometimes, because of how much the stock has moved in recent months or because of a stock split, there is more than one three-letter short option symbol for each underlying stock in order to accommodate all the different option prices. In addition, LEAPS (long-term options) have a completely different three-letter prefix for all stocks.

To see what I mean, go to yahoo.com. Click on the "Finance" section. Enter QCOM in the entry box, click on "Options" in the pulldown menu, and then click "Get." You should now be looking at what is commonly referred to as an *option chain*, or *option price chart*. By the time you read this, the Web site may have been redesigned, but the basic look and design of an option chain should remain relatively similar.

On the top of the chart is the stock's symbol (in this case, QCOM) and some current information. Below that, the chart begins. The chart is divided in half by a column showing different strike prices. On the left-hand side are calls, and on the right-hand side are puts. The first chart Yahoo! shows will represent the next option expiration month. You can choose a different expiration month by clicking on the appropriate option expiration date immediately above the chart.

The first column shows the short option symbol. The first three letters represent the stock. As I said before, options for Nasdaq and Amex stocks don't keep their regular symbols, so instead of saying QCOM, the short symbol begins with an arbitrary three-letter symbol. This is followed by two-letters that describe the option. Appendix B explains the letters used in the option's short symbol.

Some option chains (like this one) show an additional letter following a hyphen or period in an option series. This letter indicates the exchange(s) on which that option is traded. Appendix D shows on which exchanges the different options are traded.

Going back to the top of the option chain table, the first six column headings label their respective columns Last Trade, Chg (for "net change"), Bid, Ask, Vol (for "volume"), and Open Int (for "open interest"—that is, how many option contracts have been written so far at this particular strike price and expiration date). After the strike prices column, the right side represents puts. From here, looking to the right, you'll find the same data for puts that you found for calls.

While you're here, this would be a good time to take a few minutes to look at some current option prices. After looking over option prices for QCOM options, go back to the top of the page and type in another stock symbol. Take a minute to calculate the option premium percentages on various stocks to confirm what we've discussed.

MARGIN REQUIREMENTS

Let's talk briefly about margin requirements for options. Margin requirements will vary from broker to broker, but I will discuss the most common requirements. First of all, there are no margin requirements for selling covered-call options. This is because you already own the underlying stock, so if the stock goes above the call strike price, you can deliver to the option purchaser the stock you already own. Of course, you must have enough capital to purchase the underlying stock in the first place.

Writing or selling puts is a completely different story because you do not hold a position in the underlying security. When you sell a put, you must usually have the following margin requirements: 25 percent of the stock's current price minus the amount the put is out of the money plus the current option premium.

For example, the margin requirement for an IBM Feb100P when IBM is currently trading at $105 would be the following:

$$
\begin{array}{rl}
\$105 & \text{(the current price)} \\
\times\, 25\% & \\
\hline
\$26.25 & \\
-5.00 & \text{(amount out of the money)} \\
\hline
\$21.25 & \text{plus the option premium}
\end{array}
$$

This is the per share margin requirement. Remember, 1 option contract equals 100 shares.

One further note: Margin requirements vary from broker to broker, so you need to contact your brokerage firm for a complete explanation of its margin rules. When investors sell out-of-the-money puts, typically they are required to have in their portfolio cash or cash equivalents equal to only about 25 percent of the put's strike price to meet the margin requirement. However, I would never consider using maximum leverage when selling puts. I'll talk more about the use of margin a little later.

OPTIONS MARKET STRATEGIES FOR MAKING PROFITS

Numerous types of strategies exist for working the options market for potential profits. Some of the more common option strategies include taking advantage of bullish and bearish spreads, straddles, condors, and strangles, all of which have merit and can be useful under certain conditions.

However, there are also many options analysts who will, in my opinion, overplay the importance of analyzing the *Greeks* (deltas, thetas, and so on) in evaluating the current pricing of options. The theory they usually espouse is that you should sell overpriced options and buy underpriced ones. In contrast, I'm more concerned about properly evaluating the underlying security than the current fair price of the option. I would much rather sell underpriced puts on 50 stocks that go up (at which time the options expire worthless) than sell and receive too much money for overpriced puts on stocks that go down (at which time the stocks get put to me).

I also believe in keeping it as simple as possible, and I am convinced, after spending countless hours, days, weeks, months, and years searching for the optimum trading strategy, that the SafetyNet Trading System provides me the most conservative, potentially profitable approach to market investment.

ENTERING ORDERS

Although it is not paramount that you understand exactly how option orders are handled after you place them with your broker, it is worth a few minutes to become acquainted with the process. This process is quite different from purchasing stock. Unlike stock purchases, in option purchases, no certificates are transferred. The entire process is handled, recorded, and maintained by a computer at the Options Clearing Corporation (OCC).

When you place an order with your broker, you must provide the following information: (1) the number of contracts you want to transact, (2) whether you want to buy or sell the contracts, (3) the name of the underlying security (that is, IBM or MSFT), (4) the strike price, (5) the expiration month and year, (6) the type of contract (that is, put or call), and (7) whether you are closing or opening a position. This information is then transferred to the OCC, which records it in the name of your brokerage firm on its computer. It is common for brokerage firms to credit your account with the proceeds of put sales the next business day. Conversely, when you purchase options, you must pay for them by the next business day.

OPTIONS EXPIRATIONS

Options expire on the Saturday following the third Friday of the stated expiration month. If you hold short option positions that are out of the money, the options will expire worthless. In other words, if you were to sell a put on IBM with a $70 strike price and IBM ended up trading at expiration above $70, the put would expire worthless because no one would want to put IBM to you at $70 if they could get more for it by just selling it in the open market. However, if IBM were trading below $70, the stock may be put to you. I say "may be" because there is an automatic assignment rule that states that if the option is at least 75 cents in the money, it will be assigned automatically. Therefore, if IBM, in this example, were trading below $69.26, you could expect that the option would be assigned to you.

If, however, IBM were trading between $69.26 and $70, the option holder would have to elect to have the option assigned. Since not all option holders are likely to make that election, the OCC will randomly assign the options exercised among all short option writers. They do that by assigning the options to random brokerage firms holding short option positions. The brokerage firms receiving the random assignments must then assign them to one or more of their clients. They can do this either randomly or in the order the options were first sold by the client, first in, first out (FIFO). However, whichever choice the firms make, they must make it consistently every month. This random assignment may take place prior to expiration if an investor exercises an option contract early. This is not done too often since a person exercising an option early would be giving up the time value remaining in the option. The option holder could merely sell the option to close out the position and capture the profit generated by the stock moving in the right direction and thus receive the option's intrinsic value and the remaining time value.

The most important things to remember from this chapter are that (1) covered calls and naked puts are almost identical, (2) option prices are based primarily on the volatility of the underlying stock, the proximity of the stock's current price to the option strike price, and the remaining time to expiration, and (3) option premiums decay exponentially.

The next chapter utilizes this knowledge to begin implementing the SafetyNet Trading System.

CHAPTER 5

Implementing the System
The Devil Is in the Details

The SafetyNet Trading System is a strategy that is composed of two basic activities:

1. The sale of equity puts and
2. The purchase of puts on a relative index

In the system's most common application, an investor sells out-of-the-money puts on individual stocks to generate income and then uses some of that income to buy puts on a relevant index (typically the Nasdaq, S&P 500, or the Dow) for protection against a major market correction. I'll discuss these two components separately to show why this trading strategy has the potential to provide double-digit returns with less risk than other investment strategies.

SELLING PUTS

The first component of the system—selling puts—is the basic cornerstone of the SafetyNet Trading System. When we sell a put, we receive our profit up front in the form of the put option's premium. The maximum degree of profit we can receive on each put we sell is predetermined. In other words, we are agreeing to limit the profit we can receive in this trade to a specified amount, no matter how high this stock's value goes prior to the expiration of the option.

Why are we willing to do that?

We would do it for several reasons. First, because the premium provides us a profit of 10 to 15 percent per year—and even more if we use margin to leverage our account. Remember, we should always take the least risky approach to reach our financial goals.

The second reason we're willing to do it is because, in return, we receive assurance that our full profit is earned as long as the stock's value does not settle below the strike price at the option's expiration. In other words, even if the stock we choose doesn't go up, we make our profit.

As mentioned, there are five things a stock can do once I place a position. It can go up a lot, up a little, stay flat, go down a little, or go down a lot. I want a trading strategy that allows me to win in as many of those five scenarios as possible.

Selling out-of-the-money puts gets me pretty close. Since I make my profit from the sale of the put, I don't care if the stock goes up a lot. I make money if it goes up a little, goes up a lot, or if it stays level. If it drops down to my strike price, I still make my full profit. In fact, if it drops even more, to slightly below my strike price I still make money. It isn't until the stock drops well below my strike price that I begin losing money (see Figure 5.1). My breakeven point is the strike price minus the premium I received.

So the only time I lose money using this trading strategy is when the stock drops below that point. If the stock does fall below the breakeven point I do not have to close out a losing position. I can "roll" the option to a future expiration date and give the stock a chance to recover to my original strike price. Not only do I now have more time for the stock to recover but I also receive an additional time value premium when I repurchase the near term put and sell a longer-term put at the same strike price.

Five Things a Stock Can Do

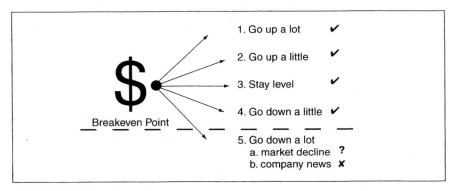

BUYING PUTS ON A RELATIVE INDEX

So far, out of all the things a stock can do after I place my position, I've shown you that I make money in four out of five possible scenarios. What can I do about the fifth possibility?

Assuming a stock is reasonably priced when I place my put position (I'll discuss that in a later chapter), there are typically two things that might cause that stock to drop substantially. The first is a drop by the entire market. During a major market correction (a drop of 20 percent or more), nearly everything goes down, although sometimes the correction is confined to certain sectors. I can, however, "insure" my portfolio against this type of event. Consequently, whether it's a Dow correction, a Nasdaq correction, or a total market meltdown, I no longer have serious worries. (Later in this chapter, I'll discuss the hedging component that prevents you from losing your shirt, even in a catastrophic market collapse. You might even make a profit.)

That leaves us with only half of that fifth scenario left: One of my stocks drops because the company experiences some fundamental problem, like a bad earnings report, a new competitor, a lawsuit, or government intervention. This is unexpected bad news that could not have been prepared for in advance. Even here, however, I want to try to minimize my potential losses as much as possible. One way I do that is by diversifying my portfolio. I never take a position that could result in one stock causing a loss of more than 5 percent of my portfolio. I will discuss diversification more fully in Chapter 11 covering The Rules.

The best way to minimize potential losses on individual companies' bad news is to limit your universe of stocks to really good companies—companies that have proven over time that they can recover from adverse circumstances. Of course, it is impossible to determine with certainty, in this new economy, which companies will be around for many years. But it is possible to pick companies that have the greatest likelihood of rebounding after bad news to properly established support levels.

For example, beginning in the middle of June 2002, when Johnson & Johnson (JNJ) was being investigated for possible problems with the manufacturing of an anemia drug in their Puerto Rico plant, their stock dropped from over $57 to $41 in less than a month. JNJ is a company that is here to stay, so I was not too concerned when it dropped that much. If news had been about a smaller company, however, I would have been very concerned because it might not recover for a year or more, if it all.

By choosing quality companies, you minimize the risk of a permanent decline in value due to unforeseen bad news. Now, let's see how you can protect yourself from a major market correction.

INSURING THE PORTFOLIO

So far, we've established that by selling out-of-the-money puts, we win if the stock price goes up a lot, up a little, stays level, or drops a little. We've explored ways to minimize losses if unexpected bad news causes the underlying stock to drop, and we know we will take positions only in solid companies that, when hit with bad news, will eventually go back up to at least their strike price.

The next step is to insure against losses due to a general market correction. As mentioned in Part 1, I do this by purchasing puts on a stock index. A stock index is a list of stocks that theoretically represents the overall movement of a certain group or type of stocks believed by the index compilers to represent the market at a particular time.

For instance, the S&P 500 index tracks the weighted compilation movement of the 500 stocks in the S&P 500. The Nasdaq-100 index (NDX) tracks the overall movement of the 100 largest Nasdaq stocks. These are two indexes along with the Dow index (DJX) I frequently use to protect against a market correction.

The idea behind this portion of the strategy is much simpler than it sounds. If you purchase index puts—that is, stocks that are listed on a particular index—and that index stays level or goes up, the most you can lose on that index put is the amount you paid for the index put: the premium. On the other hand, if the market goes down significantly and the index drops accordingly, the value of your index puts will increase.

You need to purchase enough puts on these indexes so that if the market drops substantially, your profit from the index puts will cover the losses on the individual stock puts you sold. On average, the cost of the index puts is about 20 to 25 percent of the premium you receive from the sale of the equity puts.

There are two reasons you can insure your entire put portfolio for only 20 to 25 percent of the premiums you receive: (1) because the volatility of the indexes is significantly less than the volatility of the individual stocks and, thus, the premiums are less, and (2) you can buy the index puts further out of the money because you can reduce the index put strike price as a result of the premium you receive when you sell the equity puts, as well as how far the equity puts are out of the money when you sell them. You are not trying to insure your profits, just your capital. As a result, if you take in a 12 percent premium on puts you sell 5 percent below the stock's current price, theoretically you don't start losing money until the market drops 17 percent. Buying index puts that far out of the money significantly reduces the cost of the index puts.

SUMMARY

Out of all the things a stock can do once we place our put position, we've seen that we can earn around 10 to 15 percent (more, using minimal leverage) profit per year in four out of five possible scenarios. We've also learned how to eliminate (or at least drastically reduce) the risk associated with a major market correction, and we've discussed ways to minimize losses when one of our companies suffers sudden bad news.

If you use a relatively conservative amount of margin leverage with this strategy, you can double your profits. After paying for the index put insurance, you can earn a net annual profit of between 12 percent and 20 percent, even taking into consideration a few losers. You'll have less risk than you would if you bought and held mutual funds or individual stocks.

Now that you have a basic understanding of the SafetyNet Trading System, let's explore how to set up your portfolio to begin implementing this strategy.

CHAPTER 6

Choosing Your Universe of Stocks

Stick with the Greats

Before you can sell puts, you need to know the answers to three key questions:

1. Which stocks?
2. When?
3. How many?

Determining *which stocks* to take a position in is one of the most crucial, subjective aspects of any investment program, including this one. Determining *when* to take the position is even more important. The *how many* question is easier to answer.

We will address the second and third questions in Chapter 8. Let's first address which companies. Over the past couple of years I've spent a lot of time with Jim Huguet, author of *Great Companies, Great Returns** and a large-cap fund manager. As

---

* Jim Huguet, *Great Companies, Great Returns: The Breakthrough Investment Strategy That Produces Great Returns Over the Long-Term Cycle of Bull and Bear Markets Based on the Twelve Traits of All Great Companies* (New York: Broadway Books, 1999).

result of his coaching and my natural inclination to use a more conservative investment approach, I've become persuaded that, especially in volatile markets, investors should restrict their investments to great companies.

Probably the most overused words on Wall Street are "This is a great company." This label is attached to companies that are hot for a day or week, companies that the speaker has fallen in love with, and/or companies that the analyst is hyping. While the strategy of investing in great companies is sound, in most cases the descriptor "great company" is undeserved.

The concept of investing in great companies has been around for years, and it has been embraced by some of the greatest investors of our time, Warren Buffett and Phil Carret. Warren Buffett, chairman and CEO of Berkshire Hathaway, has long touted the benefits of investing in great companies, while Philip L. Carret, founder of the Pioneer Fund, and a man Buffett refers to as the "greatest investor of the twentieth century," also embraced the strategy. Their thoughts on this topic are rather straightforward:

> Stocks are simple, all you do is buy shares in a great business for less than the business is intrinsically worth, with management of the highest integrity and ability. (*Forbes*, August 6, 1990).
>
> Metaphorically speaking, the phrase "Crown Jewels" is applied by an investor to those securities in his portfolio which he regards as particularly high-grade items. There is no substitute for buying quality assets and allowing them to compound over the long-term. Patience can produce uncommon profits. (*A Money Mind at Ninety*, 1995).

The challenge of course is to isolate the qualities that make companies great over time and then use these qualities to identify great companies that are worthy of your consideration. Jim Huguet's book provides the reader with an excellent insight into the qualities of great companies. His current fund, which is based upon the strategy of investing in great companies, ranks in the top 2 percent of all large-cap growth mutual funds during the period July 1, 2001, through July 31, 2002, one of the most difficult market periods in the past 70 years. (As a result of our conversations, funds utilizing Huguet's stock selection process combined with the SafetyNet Trading System are being developed for distribution through various mutual funds and insurance products.)

Huguet's short definition of a great company is as follows: "A great company is one that consistently increases its intrinsic value over time at a rate that exceeds the growth rate of the market." He notes that intrinsic value is based upon a company's discounted free cash flow and is impacted by a number of factors including revenue growth, margins, and taxes. Since he believes that P/E ratios are virtually meaningless in determining the value of a stock, Huguet disregards them in his analysis.

During the short term, Huguet believes that the market is highly emotional and that the price of an individual security is impacted more by emotion than detailed security analysis. In this environment some securities are priced well above their intrinsic values while others are priced far below. However, Huguet has found that the markets are rational over the long term and that intrinsic value and market price converge. With this knowledge, he searches for companies that are able to increase their intrinsic values over time, and he invests more heavily in securities that are selling at a price well below their intrinsic value. This is a philosophy embraced by Phil Carret who suggests in his book, *A Money Mind at Ninety*, that "the job of a security analyst, or money manager, is to determine relative values. If security X appears to be relatively cheaper, by a wide margin, than security Y, the holder of Y should sell it and buy X." In his book, Huguet demonstrates the positive impact that using intrinsic value has had on the performance of his Great Companies America Portfolio over time. From 1999 through 2001 the stocks in the Great American Portfolio performed approximately 16 percent higher by utilizing an intrinsic value analysis as opposed to using just an equal weighting analysis.

While it is critical to understand the strategic importance of intrinsic value in portfolio management, what is even more important is to understand the traits that companies must possess if they are to increase their intrinsic values over time. These qualities not only separate the great companies from other companies for today but will separate these great companies from well-managed companies for years to come. The qualities that are present in all great companies include those described through the rest of this chapter.

OUTSTANDING MANAGEMENT

Outstanding management is the most important trait, for without outstanding management a company will not remain great over time. In *The Tortoise Road to Wealth* (1963) Carret notes, "Good management is rare at best, it is difficult to appraise, and it is undoubtedly the single most important factor in security analysis." And as I had printed and displayed on the walls of my companies for years, "Good people are the foundation on which great companies are built."

Great companies are led by outstanding CEOs who create an environment in which people can succeed. They work hard to help the company get to and stay on the leading edge. These CEOs know what they're doing, where they're going, and how to get there. They can tell you why they are going to make money, and they do.

Many shareholders underestimate the importance of the CEO when evaluating a company for investment. More than anything or anyone else, the CEO is responsible for the success or failure of the enterprise and is therefore key to outstanding shareholder returns. Carret also recognized the importance of the CEO in saying, "Find the company whose boss is heart and soul dedicated to profitable operation, and even more interested in the profits of five years hence than those of today! If he has sound business judgment, skill in selecting the other members of his team, the rare ability to inspire them to superior performance as well, the company's stock is worth investigation."

Recently, the CEO's role in great companies has changed rather dramatically and taken on added importance. Historically, the CEO was a figurehead. Appointed to the job in their sixties, CEOs traveled the world as corporate ambassadors, making speeches, visiting hot shots on Wall Street and politicians in Washington, D.C. Jack Welch, more than anyone else, changed this profile. Welch was made CEO of GE in his early fifties. Over the next 15 years he molded GE into one of the great companies in the world. If he had had only 3 years to remake General Electric, I doubt seriously if he would have been anointed manager of the century.

The CEO is critical to any thorough analysis of a company for three reasons:

1. *The CEO is indeed the leader of the business.* In *A Money Mind at Ninety* Carret notes that "to serve its constituencies effectively, a business must have a leader, a chief executive who can decide. He will pay attention, greater or less according to his temperament, but he will make the decision." In a 2002 article in *Money* magazine, Jeff Immelt, chairman and CEO of General Electric, notes, "I think sometimes CEOs forget what their job really is, which is to serve investors, serve employees, and lead companies." While the CEO may give credit to the team, the buck stops at the CEO's desk, and the decisions that the CEO makes have both immediate and long-term ramifications on the success of the business. The CEO's values are shared by the organization, and they become imprinted on the company operating policies.

2. *The CEO builds the management team that drives the company forward into the future.* The executives that the CEO places in key positions within the organization will impact the successful implementation of the strategic plan. The CEO must be able to recruit, develop, and retain outstanding talent if the vision is to be realized.

3. *The CEO determines which businesses are worthy of investment, which should be sold, and which, if any, should be acquired.* These decisions have a profound short- and long-term impact on the business. Jeff Immelt believes that "nothing is ever going to protect investors from bad business models that don't work, whether it's energy trading or the dotcom phenomenon." The decisions that the CEO makes during the first 12 months on the job will tell a lot about how the CEO will

perform over the long term and the prospects for the company during the CEO's tenure.

The important qualities that a CEO must possess may be grouped into the following areas.

Integrity

Without integrity, nothing else matters. Phil Carret noted that "a company's directors . . . were looking for a chief executive who was profit minded, capable of making decisions, able to inspire the respect of subordinates, possessed of common sense, ambitious for the success of his company and himself. Integrity, of course! If that be lacking, nothing else matters." One has only to look at Tyco, Enron, and WorldCom to see how quickly an S&P leader can be reduced to bankruptcy by a CEO who lacks integrity. Integrity carries over to the quality of earnings, the composition of the board of directors, and virtually all aspects of the company. Shareholders will tolerate missing earnings estimates, and on occasion ineptness, but never dishonesty.

Emotional Intelligence

An article in the *Harvard Business Review* by a noted industrial psychologist concludes that the most effective leaders possess a high degree of "emotional intelligence." Specifically, these executives possessed a high degree of intellect and were particularly adept at creating the big-picture and long-term vision of the company. The importance of emotional intelligence was clearly highlighted in an interview that Jim Huguet conducted with the CEO of a leading technology company. After numerous attempts to question the CEO on his vision, Huguet realized that the CEO had absolutely no idea where the company was going, or how it would get there. He said they were working with a consultant and studying other companies, but it was clear that he didn't have a clue which path they should take. The CEO was subsequently fired and replaced by someone from the outside, but he had "blown" his company's chances for long-term success. Today this former industry-leading visionary company is a "hanger on."

Youthfulness

New CEOs should be no more than in their fifties and ideally in their forties. It takes new CEOs at least 3 years to really get their arms around the business, even if promoted internally. As previously quoted, Carret advises investors to "find the company whose boss is heart and soul dedicated to profitable operation, and even more interested in the profits of five years hence than those of today!" Therefore, the younger the CEO, within reason, the better, for the CEO will have more time to execute the vision and focus on the future. Consider Hank Greenberg, chairman and CEO of AIG since 1968. Appointed to the job at age 40, Greenberg has distinguished himself and his company during his tenure. He told Jim Huguet that it took him 20 years and numerous trips to build relationships with the leaders of China. To no one's surprise, AIG was the first foreign insurance company to sell insurance in China, the most populated country in the world. I wonder where AIG would be today if Mr. Greenberg had only been given 3 years as chairman.

Capacity to Lead

Jack Welch, although not without his critics, was and is a leader. He knew where he was going, why he was going there, and when he would arrive. He inspired people in GE to achieve goals they never thought possible. His courage and resolve were unshakeable.

Modesty

Avoid "Chainsaw Al" type CEOs. These people seldom last, and they are virtually incapable of building an organization. Al Dunlap cut costs at Scott Paper, unloaded inventory, and got a good return for himself and Scott shareholders when he sold the company to Kimberly Clark. Unfortunately he failed at Sunbeam because he had to build a company, something he was unable to do. The fact that the small appliance business is one of the most difficult businesses in the world didn't help; however, a shrewd CEO would have known this before taking the job. A *Financial Times* article titled "Beware the Celebrity CEO Trap," echoed these sentiments. The article warned that "come the bear market, it is the companies run by those same celebrity CEOs that tend to implode. Downturns expose overpayment, for assets bought at the peak of the cycle; they betray deal-maker CEOs ill-equipped to manage through a trough in profitability and liquidity; and they challenge the vanity of CEOs who cling to the empire they build."

The article goes on to note that "each of the big recent failures [Global Crossing, WorldCom, Adelphia, Qwest, Enron, and Tyco] was run by a CEO who presided over more than 86 percent of the revenue growth. Or, to put it another way, each CEO expanded his or her company—often through a series of acquisitions—by more than a factor of seven. Almost half the companies with a high tycoon index—more than 86 percent—have defaulted."

Level 5 Leaders

Jim Collins, the author of *Good to Great*, found that all companies that had transitioned from good companies to great companies had what the author refers to as a "Level 5 Leader," and that this person was indeed the catalyst for change. The author characterized a level 5 CEO as follows:

- *Company insider*: Of the 11 companies that the author found had transitioned from good to great, 10 of 11 CEOs came from inside the company.
- *Team-oriented*: These level 5 CEOs did an outstanding job of building their teams.
- *Market focused*: Most were focused on being market leaders. The CEOs had a strong resolve and were concerned about the long-term success of their company. The CEOs were skilled in organizing and analyzing feedback data, and adapting to a changing business environment.
- *Modest, humble, and fearless.*

The CEO transition is always a difficult time. A study conducted by Rakesh Khurana, a professor at the MIT Sloan School, found that CEOs appointed after 1985 are three times more likely to be fired than CEOs who were appointed before that date. Another study by the Center for Executive Options found that one-third of Fortune 100 companies have replaced their CEOs since 1995. An article in the *Harvard Business Review* reported that "a study found that more than 65% of CEOs were number twos before getting to the top. Sadly a terrific numero dos may turn out to be unsuited for the uno role. The problem is that outgoing CEOs often aren't good at the most unnatural leadership task: choosing their own successor. Surely developing talent is one of a CEO's key responsibilities, but choosing the next CEO is nobody's job but the board's."*

Typically the outgoing CEO has some "skeletons buried in the corporate closet," unpleasant issues that the CEO didn't deal with during his or her tenure. The new CEO wants to start from scratch, and therefore he or she exposes these rather unpleasant issues shortly after being appointed to the position. At best, this may lead to a short-term decline in the stock price. At worst, it might be years before the firm recovers. The disclosure of the "unpleasantries" might lead to animosity between the former CEO who was a "hero" to shareholders and the new CEO who is trying to set the record straight. This conflict can negatively impact the new CEO's chances for success.

There are numerous examples of new-CEO failures, an event that is particularly detrimental to shareholder value. Consider the impact of M. Douglas Ivester, the former CEO of Coca-Cola. Ivester had been heir apparent to Roberto Goizueta, a legend at Coca-Cola. When Goizueta unexpectedly died, Ivester took over. After mishandling several situations and seeing the stock price drop dramatically, he was replaced by Coca-Cola's board.

The new Coca-Cola CEO has faired much better, and the stock price is now reflective of the company's value. Whenever a marketing-oriented CEO (Goizueta) is replaced by a financial-oriented CEO (Ivester), it is more likely that the company will encounter a difficult transition period. The board of directors

---

* Warren G. Bennis and James O'Toole, "Don't Hire the Wrong CEO," *Harvard Business Review*, May–June, 2000.

plays a key role in the CEO selection process, which should be one of the safeguards for investors. The Coca-Cola situation clearly demonstrates the importance of an outside, objective board. Had the board been composed of Ivester's golfing buddies, he might still be the CEO.

Companies that have remained great overtime have done so because they successfully transitioned CEOs. This is one of the most difficult and risky personnel moves a company can make. It may be best to reduce positions in a company that is undergoing this transitional period.

In summary, successful CEOs are leaders who establish and implement sound long-term strategic plans, stay in touch with the needs of key customers, protect their businesses with "bullet-proof" protective barriers, build strong R&D capabilities, and work with the board to find the best successor. By doing this, their companies will remain great companies over time.

While vitally important, the CEO is only one element of a terrific management team. Another critical element of management is the company's board of directors. If the board is composed of golfing buddies of the CEO who are more interested in the benefits of remaining on the board than the best interests of shareholders, the company and its shareholders are sure to suffer. The best boards have a high percentage of outside directors and limit the terms of the board members.

TERRIFIC BUSINESS

The second most important element of a great company involves the quality of the company's business. *All great companies are in terrific businesses.* Warren Buffett demonstrated his conviction regarding the importance of a terrific business when he said at a Berkshire Hathaway stockholder meeting, "Ideally you want terrific management and a terrific business. And that's what we look for. But if you had to choose one, take the terrific business."

Qualities of a Good Business

Some companies are in good businesses, and some companies aren't. It is important to analyze the qualities of a good business and then select those companies that meet the requirements. The qualities of a good business are the following.

Permanency

The bottom line is, a terrific business is one that will be around for years to come. While the business may change and evolve, as all businesses do, the core business proposition will remain. People will continue to wash clothes, take baths, shave, buy insurance, get thirsty, ride in elevators, and invest in the stock market. Products that effectively cater to these needs will be around for years. The stock market has clearly shown that you don't want to buy businesses today that may become obsolete tomorrow.

High Consumption and Broad Market Appeal

Ideally, you want a business that has high consumption levels and broad market appeal. A strong sales velocity allows the company to enjoy the efficiencies of mass production and mass marketing. A business that has great appeal to a broad number of customers is extremely attractive. The fact that so many people drink a beverage several times a day, every day, means tremendous product velocity. If a company is able to capture a significant share of a market with a product that has these characteristics, the economics of the business can quickly become very attractive.

Excellent Return on Capital

Outstanding businesses require little capital to start, and as they mature, they internally generate the capital they need to operate and provide shareholders with outstanding returns. An example of this would be Coca-Cola, a company that generates more cash than the company needs. Contrast this to the paper business that requires a huge capital investment, is cyclical, and has relatively low margins. Because of the capital investment required, paper plants must operate around the clock at maximum capacity in order to turn a profit. A prolonged drop in volume destroys the economics of this business for the paper company and the investor.

A high return on invested capital gives a company numerous options. The company can repurchase shares, pass dividends along to the shareholders, invest in new businesses, expand globally, acquire other firms, and so on. The terrific businesses have a high return on invested capital.

Broad Global Appeal

As we move into a global economy, products or services that transcend cultures, countries, religions, and so on will be treasured. This greatly simplifies the business and allows a company to develop a worldwide brand franchise, thereby diversifying the company's revenue base. If one standardized product can be sold throughout the world, the economic advantage is huge. An example would be Microsoft's *Windows*, a truly universal brand.

Resiliency in Recession

Businesses that are recession proof offer a margin of safety for investors. When there is a downturn in the economy, the investor who is heavily invested in recession-sensitive businesses such as automobiles, airlines, or hotels will typically see their portfolios of recession-sensitive stocks decline more than the market drops. Conversely, investors who are invested in businesses that are recession proof (virtually no business is 100 percent recession proof) will typically experience much less of a decline. When you look at the Otis elevator business of United Technologies, you find an excellent example of a recession-proof business. While elevator sales may decline during a difficult business cycle, installed elevators must be maintained, and UTX collects a service fee on each elevator it maintains.

Streamlined Distribution System

Companies that have streamlined distribution systems—that is, they don't have to go through a multitiered distribution system— enjoy some advantages that companies with tiered distribution systems don't enjoy. For example, Dell's direct-to-the-consumer distribution system increases the company's productivity and reduces costs.

Low Labor Costs

Increasing revenues without increasing labor costs results in increased profits. Companies with low labor costs can typically increase sales revenues faster than they increase costs. This improves the overall profitability of the company and can also improve return on capital, which eventually results in increased intrinsic values.

Characteristics of Potentially Unprofitable Businesses

It's very important to understand not only the business models of companies in terrific businesses but also to understand the traits of unattractive businesses. Characteristics of bad businesses include some of the following.

Commodity Businesses

Warren Buffett seemed to cover the subject when he noted that "in a commodity business, it's very hard to be smarter than your dumbest competitor."

Commodity-oriented businesses include metals—steel and aluminum—commodity food products—flour, orange juice, tuna, produce, and so on—paper—which is often thought of as a commodity—and oil and gas. Some companies have tried to improve the commodity businesses that they are in by developing strong brand names and developing a point of difference. While branding improves the fundamentals of the business, the business's profitability remains a challenge subject to all of the factors that can negatively impact a commodity business.

High Labor Costs

Some businesses have extremely high labor costs. It is difficult for these businesses to increase sales without proportionately increasing costs—the optimum strategy for increasing returns on capital. The ideal business can increase sales while maintaining labor costs at or below current levels. The pharmaceutical industry works along these lines.

Capital-Intensive Operations

Unattractive businesses are capital intensive. It is far better to be in a business that is not capital intensive than to be in one that requires heavy infusions of capital. For example, would you rather own a company that returned $5 million in profit on a capital base of $2 million, or a business with the same growth characteristics but delivered $2 million in profit on a capital base of $15 million? You would undoubtedly opt for the first company. Why? Because your return on capital invested is so much higher. The airlines embrace all of the first three qualities. They are commodity oriented, have high labor costs, and are capital intensive.

Society-Harming Potential

Businesses that benefit society are better businesses than those that don't. Consider the cigarette business, for example. This business is dangerous to the people who consume the product. As a result, the cigarette companies are continually involved in litigation with consumers who claim the product caused them bodily harm. Fundamentally the business is very attractive because profit margins are good, production is highly mechanized, the product has a high level of consumption among users, branding builds loyalty, and a large segment of the population uses the product.

Rapidly Changing Industry

Businesses that change rapidly carry with them some inherent risks. Consider some of the high-tech businesses that were leaders one day and laggards the next. These companies can see their market caps dramatically reduced overnight. Investors who invest in these businesses must be aware of the risks that they face. For example, Corning Glass (GLW) moved into the fiber-optic cable business at a time when the business declined dramatically. Unfortunately, Corning investors have seen the company's share price drop from $113 on August 18, 2000, to under $2 as of this writing.

Occasionally management has successfully modified a difficult business in a manner that greatly improves the business. For example, GE modified its steam turbine business and dramatically changed the division's profit structure. GE did this by offering extensive service agreements to clients who owned steam turbines. GE will not only service the turbines that GE produces but it will also service turbines manufactured by any GE competitor. GE has changed the business model in turbines, locomotives, jet engines, and MRIs, and by doing so, it has changed the profit structure and nature of the business.

Dell Computer Corporation is a company that also changed its business model. In its start-up phase, Dell computers were sold through retail stores, and for the first five years of its existence Dell barely outperformed the S&P 500. Dell had to build computer inventories, then rely upon retailers who controlled the price and promotion of their product line to pay them. By changing the model and going directly to the consumer, Dell's inventories have been reduced, the company doesn't have to cover the costs of an intermediary, and it is building relationships with its consumers by providing them with made-to-order computers. Shareholder returns have improved dramatically.

Remember, not all businesses are created equal. Some businesses are far better than others, and few businesses are terrific in all areas. The really excellent businesses are few and far between.

In summary, the two most important elements in a company's success are

1. The quality of the business
2. The quality of its management

Classifying Companies by Their Characteristics

If we classify companies according to their management and business quality, we note that there are four possibilities as shown in Table 6.1. There are a few bad companies in bad businesses. Normally, these companies cannot overcome being in a bad business and being poorly managed. The combination is often fatal, and they quickly succumb to either their competition or their ineptness and are either acquired or enter bankruptcy. When you invest in a poorly run company in a difficult business, the company will surely underperform the S&P 500 index over the long term, which will often cost you a portion of your principal.

There are a number of poorly managed companies in good businesses. These companies are poorly managed, but they are in such good businesses that the quality of the business com-

TABLE 6.1

Four Categories of Companies

Difficult business Bad management Fail/acquired	Difficult business Good management Outperform sector/underperform market
Good business Bad management Acquired/merged	Good business Good management Solid returns over the long term

pensates for the lack of management ability over the short to mid-term. These companies seldom make major advances within their industry, and their market share and profits remain relatively flat. Because these companies fail to gain market share and increase their intrinsic value, over time their market price languishes. Often these companies are acquired by one of the well-managed companies within the industry.

Occasionally, a new management team is brought in to run the company, and they turn the company around, but this is the exception rather than the rule. Even when this turnaround occurs, the company often finds that it does not have the size to compete with the industry leaders, and it is eventually sold.

The third category is composed of well-managed companies in difficult businesses. It is a challenge to attract quality managers to difficult businesses. Most successful managers would prefer to spend their careers with companies that are in good businesses. However, occasionally a really outstanding manager emerges as head of a company that is in a difficult business. On these limited occasions, these companies will outperform the other companies in their sector, but they are seldom able to outperform the S&P 500 index over the long term.

There are also a number of good companies in good businesses. Many of these companies have grown and have done reasonably well over the years, and many are highly regarded by "the street." While these companies typically grow at or slightly above the S&P 500, they seldom report outstanding returns over time.

The rarest combination of all is the truly great company in a really great business. These are the true gems of the business world. They are the companies that are the best candidates for the SafetyNet Trading System. If one of these companies falls precipitously, it has the greatest potential to recover to your original support level.

PROTECTIVE BARRIERS

Another key quality that differentiates great companies from other companies is the breadth and depth of their protective barriers, or what Warren Buffett refers to as "moats." Buffett's description of the importance of a moat to protect the business model, as stated in a 1994 article in *U.S. News & World Report*, is as follows, "Look for the durability of the franchise. The most important thing to me is figuring out how big a moat there is around the business. What I love, of course, is a big castle and a big moat with piranhas and crocodiles."

There are a number of barriers that management can build to protect a business. These barriers might include the following.

A Strong Brand Franchise

Many companies seek to build a moat by creating superior brand franchises. The brand franchise or moat that is created provides these companies with a number of key benefits:

1. The great brand franchise creates value in the mind of the consumer, thereby allowing the company to charge and receive higher prices for its products than its competitors.
2. Once a franchise has been solidly established in the mind of the customer, it is very difficult to destroy the franchise.
3. The franchise provides the sales force with instant credibility and increases their odds of closing a sale.

4. Retail distributed brands typically pay less in promotional allowances and gain greater shelf space because of their brand power.

5. The efficiency of advertising increases as companies build huge franchises.

Long-Term Contracts and/or Agreements

Another tool for creating a protective barrier is a long-term agreement or contract. For example, insurance companies have their customers sign long-term agreements. These agreements protect the insured from risk, but they also protect the insurer from competitive threats. Companies in the real estate business who are leasing office space also rely on contracts. Signing long-term leases insures a steady flow of income for the lessor. These contracts and agreements serve to strengthen the protective moat that surrounds the business.

Geographic Barriers

Geography can also be used to strengthen the protective moat. Consider the Hilton at the O'Hare Airport. If you want to spend the night at the O'Hare Airport in Chicago and you don't want to take a shuttle to your hotel; you have one choice, the O'Hare Hilton. While the Marriott, Hyatt, and Westin are all nearby the airport along with at least 20 other hotels, there is only one hotel within walking distance, and you don't have to go outside to get to it (there is an underground tunnel from the terminal to the hotel). The O'Hare Hilton isn't necessarily the least expensive, the nicest, or the newest of the O'Hare hotels, but its location provides the Hilton with a moat that can be very powerful.

Other businesses like grocery stores, convenience stores, fast-food restaurants, car dealerships, and airlines with their hub systems try to use geographic location as a moat. If you have a one-of-a-kind location like the Hilton, this can be a powerful moat; however, if someone can open a business next door, your moat might serve to trap you in your castle as opposed to keeping the competitors out.

Patents

Securing patents can serve to strengthen your moat. If you have developed a new process or technology, a patent can keep your competitors from using the new technology. This can provide a very powerful moat, especially if your company has developed a breakthrough innovation.

Companies in the pharmaceutical industry are protected by securing patents on the new products that they develop. These patents make it very difficult if not impossible for competitors to replicate their successes for a 20-year period. Unfortunately, patents have a life of their own. Once the patent expires, the protection that they afford your company also expires.

Company-Owned Machinery

The machinery that a company uses to produce its products can serve as a barrier to competition. That is precisely why Gillette produces most of the equipment that it uses to manufacture many of its products. If Gillette purchased the machinery from a third-party provider, the provider could in turn sell the equipment to one of Gillette's competitors, thereby reducing Gillette's lead time on new products versus its key competitors. Gillette is quite willing to maintain the staff necessary to build this machinery because of the competitive advantage Gillette receives from doing so.

Reputation As a Low-Cost Producer

Being the low-cost producer can also strengthen the moat. Companies that have captured this advantage can price their products lower than the competition and still make a profit.

Reputation As a Low-Price Retailer

Wal-Mart uses low price as a barrier. The company can't necessarily be the low-cost producer, but it strives to be the low-cost distributor and merchandiser and to pass these savings along to the consumer in the form of low prices. Wal-Mart is able to do this because it has one of the most efficient distribution systems in retailing.

High-Quality Products

If a company is able to consistently produce a superior product that cannot be acquired at a lower cost, then quality can become a barrier to competitive entry.

GE's Six Sigma initiative is not only reducing costs and improving quality but it is also improving customer loyalty. In an interview with Jim Huguet, GE's quality goal was described by Jack Welch: "We want to make our quality so special, so valuable to our customers, so important to their success that our products become their real value of choice."

Customization Capability

Think of the custom shirt manufacturers that will tailor a shirt to fit and manufacture the shirt from any cloth you choose. Dell prides itself in building computers to order. When you call Dell, a sales associate will ask you questions about your computing needs. Dell will then design a computer that meets your needs. I recently read about a company, CD World, which sells kiosks called *Music Point*. For roughly $18 per CD, customers can choose from among 50,000 songs to design their own personal CD. A blank CD is actually "burned" right in the kiosk. I believe that we will see more and more of this mass customization, which will help companies build barriers around their businesses, while increasing customer satisfaction.

There are any number of ways to build barriers around a business. It's important to realize that some barriers are much stronger and more durable than others. For example, a good brand name is very powerful and typically much more difficult for competitors to attack than a barrier built of geography. Likewise, a patent is much stronger than a barrier built of price.

The great companies build their barriers of the strongest materials, brands, and patents. The moats of these great companies are getting wider and deeper as they continue to add more alligators and piranhas to the moat. These moats will become increasingly difficult and far more costly to broach with time. Frankly, I can't imagine trying to knock a brand like Coca-Cola from its worldwide position. Competitors that try to destroy the moats of the great companies will pay a heavy price.

OUTSTANDING EMPLOYEES

Great companies realize that it's not the brands or the machinery. It's the people that make the company great. They believe that their people are their most valuable asset. The CEOs of these companies believe that training and developing their people, instilling their values in their people, and providing for their people are the most important responsibilities that they have.

These companies leave little to chance in the human resources area. They begin the people process at the recruiting stage. They know the profiles of the people who will do well within their company, and they aggressively recruit at colleges and universities to bring only the best and brightest people into their companies.

As a result of their people development efforts, the CEOs of the great companies are able to promote people from within the company. They very seldom, if ever, go outside the company to fill a senior position.

The CEOs of the great companies reward their people who perform with bonus plans, stock option programs, or both. They offer 401(k) plans, outstanding medical coverage, and other benefits. They loathe unwanted turnover—that is, a person that they like and want to keep is lured away from the company. They measure turnover and constantly make adjustments to try and prevent turnover. I have always believed that employee turnover was the single biggest hidden cost of a corporation. Excessive turnover can destroy both profits and morale.

Because of the positives of keeping great people over the long term and the numerous negatives associated with turnover, these great companies view their people as their most valuable asset, and they do everything possible to protect those assets.

GREAT INNOVATORS

Richard Foster and Sarah Kaplan, the authors of *Creative Destruction*, note that "no more than a third of today's major corporations will survive in an economically important way over the next twenty-five years, and that the demise of these companies will come from a lack of competitive adaptiveness."

Great companies are great innovators. Rather than fear change, these companies relish change, for change provides them with new opportunities, and that means increased revenues and profits. These companies are organized to capitalize on new opportunities.

The companies that produce products have wonderful R&D divisions that create products of the future. These areas are staffed by some of the best and brightest people in the company. Their job is to stay out front and ahead of the changes. They search the globe for new technologies, products, or services, which could play a key role in the future of the company. They spread this learning to the operating divisions where these ideas are turned into new and better products. Innovation and research are key drivers of the success in every great company.

GLOBAL PRESENCE

A fully integrated global presence will be critical for future earnings growth as markets transition from national to global opportunities. It's important to distinguish a truly global company from a firm that sells product overseas. Five factors distinguish global companies:

1. Global is a business concept. A truly global company has a global strategy and a worldwide plan in terms of its products, marketing, manufacturing, logistics, and R&D.
2. A global company has no boundaries. Where a global company has its headquarters is transparent to the market or individual customer. The global company is prepared to do business anywhere in the world.
3. Not only does a global company serve its global customers with excellence but a global company has a

delivery system that is highly sensitive to local customer needs and cultures.

4. A global company balances those aspects of the company that must be viewed and planned as a global system with those aspects that must be highly sensitive to local requirements.

5. The global company takes a long-term perspective. It realizes that the globalization process takes time.

Having a viable global presence is critical for the following reasons:

- A company must be capable of competing for sophisticated customers in a variety of markets if it is to leverage its products and brands on a worldwide basis.
- Some huge international markets are critical for amortizing product development and marketing costs.
- Some of these megamarkets are strategic because of the enormous potential volume they could deliver.
- If a company can build a major presence in the competitor's home market, it can siphon off profits the competitor might use to defend or attack in another market.
- A strong global presence enables a company to significantly leverage future acquisitions.

Significant international experience and exposure provides a wonderful learning environment for the future.

OUTSTANDING SHAREHOLDER RETURNS

Companies are expected to create wealth for their shareholders through either dividends or share price increases, or both, over the long term. Companies that are truly great should provide returns that outperform the S&P 500 over the long term—at least 10 years.

It is important to analyze returns in two dimensions:

1. *Consistency of returns*: Did the company beat the S&P 500 year in and year out, or did the company have one

great year followed by a succession of poor to average
years? The fact that companies have delivered
consistent earnings is further reflected in their P/E
ratios.
2. *Level of returns*: What were the returns over the 10-
year period?

A PROVEN TRACK RECORD

Ideally, great companies have stood the test of time and have
prospered during recessions, improved as a result of strong
competition, flourished as the company developed, successfully
marketed new products, and built market share against all
odds. It takes time for a company to develop these attributes. At
a minimum, companies should not be viewed as great until they
have passed the 10-year mark.

LARGE MARKET CAPITALIZATION, IN EXCESS OF $5 BILLION

The market capitalization of a company is calculated by multi-
plying the number of shares of stock outstanding by the closing
price of the stock. For example, a company with 5 million shares
outstanding that closed at $20 per share the previous day would
have a market capitalization of $100 million. Normally the term
market capitalization is shortened to *market cap* or *cap*.

Companies that have market caps greater than $5 billion
are referred to as large-cap companies since they have a large
market capitalization. Large-cap stocks with market caps
greater than $5 billion provide the investor with a number of
key advantages:

1. Large companies have far greater resources than small
   companies. All truly great companies are large. The
   corollary is that if small companies are great, why
   aren't they big? Smaller companies are short the
   financial resources of the great companies. Most don't
   have a surplus of outstanding managers capable of
   leading the company to greatness. And very few
   possess the clout and resources required to take on
   megaopportunities in other parts of the world.

2. Obviously large companies with significant market shares and business franchises are at a significant competitive advantage in the increasing return arena. These market leaders have the potential for significant upside growth and have the opportunity to dominate the market. Rather than look at all large-cap stocks as lumbering dinosaurs, they should be viewed as potential King Kongs, capable of dominating the marketplace.

3. If a company is to compete aggressively on an international basis, a key to future success, the company must be capable of matching the resources and global distribution capabilities of other large international competitors. Establishing a defensible international beachhead is expensive and often requires more resources and time than the management of a small to medium-size company can muster.

4. Capitalizing on tomorrow's huge opportunities will require significant resources. The amount of money required to compete on a global basis is huge, and the costs will increase as the great companies grow bigger and stronger, making their fortresses virtually impenetrable to attack by competitors.

5. Large-cap companies afford the investor a much greater level of investment security. A great company with a large market cap affords additional security to the shareholder.

6. A well-run large-cap company will receive a high financial rating, and this is important when borrowing. Typically, the higher the credit rating, the lower the interest rate paid. Therefore, large, highly rated companies have access to large amounts of cash at relatively low interest rates.

7. The large cap can also be valuable when making major acquisitions. The large cap provides management with a resource against which it can borrow funds, or in a *pooling-of-interest transaction*—a transaction in which the acquiring company swaps its shares of its company

for ownership in the company being acquired—can leverage its market value to finalize the acquisition or merger.

SUMMARY

In summary, a well-managed company is often characterized by the following traits:

- *Predictable earnings growth*: Estimates are seldom revised.
- *An outstanding team*: Excellent managers who have been with the company over time. Typically the CEO is key in building and retaining the team.
- *Low personnel turnover*: Well-managed companies typically have turnover rates that are well below industry norms.
- *Market leaders*: They typically rank as first or second in the industry and/or sector in which they compete.
- *Focused on free cash flow*: They know that increases in free cash flow will result in increased shareholder values.
- *Innovative*: These companies know that they cannot remain stagnant and that they must change and evolve as industries and businesses change. In *Creative Destruction* the authors noted that "very few companies attempt to change at the pace and scale of the market. Yet only this kind of broad-based change can assure corporations that their long-term survival will not result in long-term underperformance of the market."

If you restrict your universe of stocks to these types of companies, you may reduce your potential yield from selling puts (many of these types of companies are less volatile), but you will simultaneously reduce the risk and still reach your financial goals.

CHAPTER

7

Establishing Support Levels

How Low Is Low Enough?

Now that we have developed a universe of potential stocks, we can begin doing the research needed to establish a *support level* for each stock in our universe.

SUPPORT LEVELS

For our purposes, *support level* refers to the price at which a stock is likely to become attractive to other market investors. If the stock drops below this price, we believe it will rebound and begin going up as "bottom-fishers" scoop up the undervalued stock. This is the price that will become our strike price if we choose to sell puts on this stock.

This step in the process is, by far, the most subjective. When you evaluate the support level, you must realize that it is this level that determines how much money you will make with the SafetyNet Trading System. Setting the level too low or too high will have a dramatic affect on your overall investment performance.

If you set the support levels too low, the option premiums you receive will be very low because, as I said earlier, option premiums decline as the difference between the current price and the strike price increases. If you set the support levels too high, you are in danger of having the stock put to you.

The ideal situation we are searching for is one in which the stock has already declined and is beginning to recover. If we catch it before it travels up too far from its support level, maybe even a little below it, the premium will be high enough to warrant taking the position. If we act too late, we will be forced to either settle for a smaller premium, forgo the trade entirely, or increase the risk involved by choosing a higher strike price, somewhere above support.

You are, therefore, challenged to find a support level for your universe of stocks that is the highest possible level without taking on substantial risk. Finding this particular point is easier for some stocks than it is for others. Take a look at the 3-year chart for Wal-Mart in Figure 7.1.

Notice that each time Wal-Mart's price dropped below $50, it rebounded. That indicates that, unless the company experiences a fundamental problem, investors will probably begin buying shares of Wal-Mart if it drops below $50 again.

In some cases you will find that a stock's price will actually drop below a support level and then begin its move back up. Most investors consider a support level acceptable as long as

FIGURE 7.1

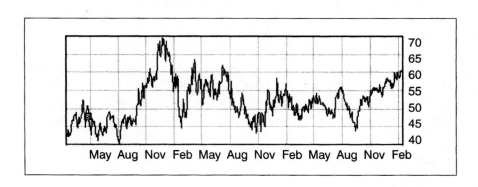

the price does not stay below support for more than a few days or a week at most.

Setting a support level for a stock that has been moving up in a continuous pattern is somewhat less obvious. Let's look at Procter & Gamble's 1-year chart in Figure 7.2. Determining a support level for Procter & Gamble is more challenging. Wal-Mart's stock price moved up and down several times, always rebounding at about the same price. It is relatively easy to set a support level in that scenario. However, Procter & Gamble's chart shows that its stock price has significant gains over an extended period of time. Setting a support level for this stock is much harder and much more subjective.

For a stock like this, it helps to add a moving average to the chart in order to establish support. The modified chart in Figure 7.3 shows Procter & Gamble's 50-day moving average. This line indicates what the average price of the stock was each day, going back 50 days. You can see that each time Procter & Gamble's share price dropped below its 50-day moving average, it bounced up. On the day this chart was created, Procter & Gamble's 50-day moving average was right around $80. That might be a good starting point for establishing the support level.

Of course, when a stock price has continually moved up, it's important to consider how far down it can drop if the market takes a tumble. Also, remember that no stock goes up in a straight line indefinitely. Eventually, it will flatten out for a

FIGURE 7.2

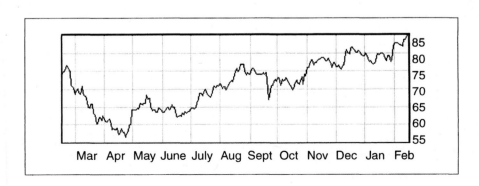

F I G U R E   7 . 3

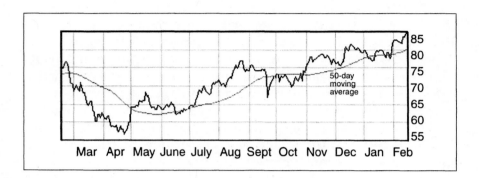

while, or possibly even decline when investors decide to take some profits.

It's a good idea to look more closely at these moving-average support levels. I usually like to compare several moving averages to determine my best estimate of a support level. Figure 7.4 shows Procter & Gamble's 200-day moving average. Until recently the stock stayed well above that average, so it is probably too conservative a position to consider, but I might consider something in between.

While looking at the charts, I also consider the level of the stock's recent price increases and the overall volatility of the stock before setting a specific support level. I'm not likely to

F I G U R E   7 . 4

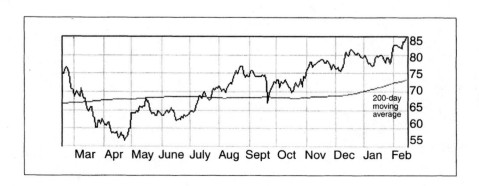

chase a rapidly increasing stock price but would rather wait for the stock to drop after some profit taking.

CONFIDENCE GRADES

To better define the integrity of my subjective support levels, I grade my support analysis between 1 and 5. In other words, I evaluate how confident I am with the support level. Average confidence will equal a 3. High confidence will equal a 5, and low confidence will equal a 1.

The Wal-Mart chart we looked at earlier made it easy to establish a good support level, so I would rank that support level a 5. The Procter & Gamble chart was much more difficult because of recent price movement, so it might rank as a 2.

If a stock is doing the opposite of what Procter & Gamble's did—if it has been continually trending downward—I will usually give that my lowest confidence level, and I rarely sell a put on a stock in that position. Let's look at a good example from 2001.

Cisco's (CSCO) stock had been trending downward since reaching a high of around $75 in early March 2001 (see Figure

FIGURE 7.5

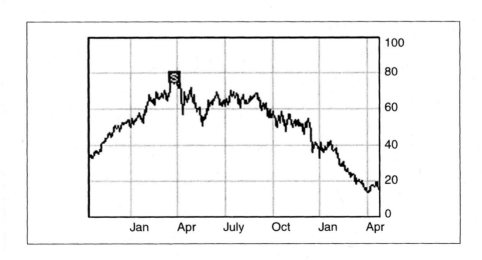

7.5). Notice that by June, the stock had already fallen to around $55. I can just hear those investors who bought it then: "It can't go below $55!" Notice that the price went back up over $60 within a week or so, at which point it began a slow, tortuous decent to the low $20 range. All along the way, at $40, at $35, at $30, and so on, someone bought the stock, absolutely convinced it couldn't go any lower.

When a stock has been trending down for a long time, set your support level conservatively and wait for it to prove, over at least a few weeks, that it has hit bottom before getting in.

ROUNDING

Another factor I take into consideration when ranking a support level is whether I rounded up or down. All support levels need to be set at a price that has a corresponding strike price available in the option market (see Table 7.1).

Strike prices under $40 are usually offered every $2.50, and strike prices above $40 are offered in $5 increments with $10 increments over $100. After stock splits there may be a lot of unusual strike prices available, especially after 3-for-2 stock splits. If I rounded down to a lower support level, I may increase my confidence grade. Conversely, if I round up to the next strike price, I would probably decrease my confidence grade.

REVIEWING SUPPORT LEVELS

Once you have established your support levels for each of the stocks in your universe, you will have to change only those that

TABLE 7.1

Round Off Support Levels Up or Down to Match Corresponding Strike Prices

Support levels under $40:	$2.50 increments
Support levels above $40:	$5.00 increments
Support levels above $100:	$10.00 increments

have made substantial moves. If, for example, a stock drops below your established support level and does not recover within a week or so, you may have set that support level too high (or, perhaps, something has affected the company's fundamentals). Take another look at the company's chart and consider another support level.

If, on the other hand, a stock moves up dramatically in price after you set a support level, you should not automatically chase it. While it is true that some stocks will rise steadily, with only a small amount of retracement, the majority of stocks do not go up in a straight line. Wait until a stock has sustained this new, higher level before raising its support level.

As you can see, the support level plays an important role in the process, and so it is important that you carefully select those levels not only to improve your profits but also to help insure against losses.

The next chapter discusses timing the placement of positions—that is, what you should look for to help you decide that it's time to sell a put on a particular stock, and how many contracts you should sell.

CHAPTER 8

Pulling the Trigger
When to Take a Position

Once you have established your universe of stocks and determined support levels for each of them, the real decision becomes when to take a position. Again, there is no shortage of advice in this area. The important point to remember is that when it comes to the when—nobody really knows.

Every single day, investors make predictions on which stocks are ready to make a move. Some investors base their opinions on fundamental data, things like earnings estimates, same store sales reports, and so on. Other investors base their decisions on technical analysis, which involves the review of a stock's price and volume trading. These data are typically reviewed in a chart to help determine trends and likely support levels, resistance levels, and turnaround points.

Some analysts' recommendations may sound convincing, and I believe that many of them truly believe they have the ability to predict the future movement of a stock. However, as I stated in the introduction, analysts often have other reasons for making certain stock calls. Never forget, regardless of the genuineness of their recommendation, it's just a prediction. Analysts don't really know for sure whether a stock will move in any particular direction at some precise time—unless they have some insider information that hasn't been made public yet. And, as I like to say—*If they really knew, they wouldn't tell you!* Just watch enough market news and you will find lots of occasions when the stock immediately does the opposite of an analyst's predictions.

Since selling puts is a bullish strategy, the obvious answer to the question of when to sell is:

When the stock is low!

But when is the stock low? I like to consider both fundamental and technical analyses when making this determination.

FUNDAMENTALS

Is the stock trading at a higher or lower P/E ratio than it has historically? Is the stock trading at a higher or lower P/E ratio than its peers in the same industry? Is the stock's intrinsic value higher or lower than its current market valuation? What is the stock's PEG ratio, and how does it compare to other companies? (The *PEG ratio* is the company's P/E ratio divided by its earnings per share growth rate.)

While a stock's price-earnings ratio may not be a good comparative tool across the entire market breadth, I believe it is still very important to compare P/E ratios of companies within similar industries. A higher P/E ratio than the industry average can be justified if the company is demonstrating higher earnings growth rates on a consistent basis. If, on the other hand, its P/E ratio is much higher than other companies within that industry and its growth rate is comparable or lower than its peers, I might be concerned that the stock is currently overvalued.

PEG ratios help us take growth into consideration. In general, if the PEG ratio is below 1 but greater than zero, the stock is more likely to be undervalued. For example, if XYZ company is trading at 20 times earnings and it is growing 20 percent a year, it has a PEG ratio of 1. If it is growing at 40 percent a year, its PEG ratio is ½. The higher the PEG ratio, the more likely that it is overvalued.

If a PEG ratio is a negative number, you should look closely at its P/E ratio and at its projected growth rate because one of them will be a negative number. In today's market it is not uncommon for a growth stock to have negative earnings (a loss instead of earnings) for several years. That would cause its P/E ratio to be a negative number. If its growth rate is reasonably high, its PEG ratio, while still a negative number, should be greater than -1 (negative one). If its PEG ratio is substantially below -1, I would be very cautious before placing a position and spend some time evaluating its future growth prospects.

If the PEG ratio is negative because the growth rate is negative, I might be reluctant to get involved in that company altogether, at least until it turns its earnings around and begins an upward trend again.

If a company has negative earnings and a negative growth rate, its PEG ratio might appear to be just fine (since a negative number divided by another negative number equals a positive number), but that is obviously a company you would want to avoid entirely.

An intrinsic value calculation may be the most important evaluator. As mentioned earlier, Warren Buffett popularized this indicator to help forecast stock movement and Jim Huguet of Great Companies has fine-tuned the process.

TECHNICAL INDICATORS

Technical analysts, using charts, review historical market data, including price, price averages, trading volume, market sentiment indicators, flow-of-funds indicators, and so on. They look for trends in the market and attempt to project support and resistance levels, among other things.

Unlike stock traders, who make a profit only when a stock rises (or falls if they take a short position), investors selling puts profit as long as the stock does not fall a lot. Therefore, we don't have to pick the bottom, and we don't have to sell at the top. We just have to pick stocks that will not fall dramatically after we sell a put or, if they do fall, are likely to rebound to the support level (strike price) before the expiration date.

The main technical indicators most investors look at, before considering a particular stock as a current trade candidate, are its previous price movements. For example, they calculate how much below its 52-week high the stock is currently trading and how much above the stock's "support level" it is trading.

I typically do not chase a stock up and place a position when that company is close to its 52-week high. I prefer to catch it after it has dipped closer to its support level and has demonstrated that it is moving back up. Obviously, it is advantageous to place the put position before the stock has risen too far above its support level. Once it is too high above support, the option premium is too low to make the trade worthwhile.

OPTION PREMIUMS

There's one more critical piece of information to review before taking a position in a particular stock. Analyze the amount of option premium available for the appropriate strike price. To do this, divide the option premium by the strike price to determine the potential percentage gain. Most investors expect to earn a minimum of 10 percent per year on each put position before considering leverage. If the option premium divided by the strike price is considerably more than 20 percent per year, you might want to consider choosing to lower the strike price slightly to provide an extra margin of safety.

If you can net a minimum of 10 percent per year on every put position you place, and if you utilize a relatively conservative amount of margin, I am confident you can earn 12 to 18 percent annual returns, even after paying for protective index puts and allowing for occasional losing positions.

CHOOSING BETWEEN STOCKS

There is almost always an assortment of positions that will return 10 to 15 percent premiums (before leverage) for puts sold at a strike price equal to or below the chosen support level. Therefore, I can usually pick and choose which positions to

Target Put Premium

$$\frac{\text{Option premium}}{\text{Put strike price}} > 10\% \text{ per year}$$

The option premium divided by the option's strike price must usually equal or exceed 10 percent per year before I will consider it as a potential candidate.

take. I do that by evaluating all the fundamental and technical data on each potential position, including the following:

- Confidence grade
- Percent current price is above support
- Percent current price would be above breakeven
- Percent current price is below 52-week high
- P/E relative to the industry
- Current P/E versus the historic P/E ratio
- PEG ratio
- Intrinsic value relative to the current market value

I prioritize the potential positions according to how favorably they compare to one another. I do this by assigning a weighted value to each piece of data. In other words, I decide which of the above factors are most important in evaluating the merits of the potential position and then assign a corresponding weighting factor to each. For example, I believe that a stock's current price relative to its intrinsic value is the most important factor, so I assign a higher weight to that factor when I score the positions. Each investor needs to determine which factors are most important to him or her. Technicians may place more importance on technical indicators, where value investors are more likely to consider fundamental data as better indicators of future market direction.

Let's go through an example of how you would evaluate a couple of potential positions. Let's assume companies ABC and

XYZ have the data attributable to their current condition as shown in Table 8.1. The first piece of data indicates that ABC is trading a little more above support (our proposed strike price) than XYZ. In other words, ABC could fall in price 4 percent before we would be required to purchase it as opposed to XYZ, which could only fall 2 percent. If everything else were exactly equal, we would be better off selling a put on ABC since that position would provide a little more cushion before the stock would be put to us. If that were the only data we had to analyze, this would be a very simple process. But, of course, it is just the beginning of our analysis.

The next factor shows us that ABC is trading 12 percent below its 52-week high, while XYZ is trading 26 percent below its 52-week high. A technician would consider this a significant positive for XYZ since the market has previously put a much higher value on XYZ. A value investor, on the other hand, may not see much value in this piece of information and place a very small weight to this factor. In any event, this would be a plus for XYZ, which begins to complicate the analysis process. ABC was a better candidate based on its current price in relation to the proposed strike price, but XYZ is a better candidate based on its historical price movement. Not only do we need to consider the relative importance of each factor but also the degree to which each factor is more favorable for the different compa-

TABLE 8.1

ABC		XYZ
4%	Percent current price is above support	2%
12%	Percent current price is below 52-week high	26%
1.2	P/E relative to industry	1.4
1.3	Current P/E versus historic P/E	0.9
1.0	PEG ratio	2.2
1.4	Intrinsic value/relative price	0.92
15%	Option premium percent	13%

nies we are comparing. This gets even more complicated as we analyze more data.

For example, let's look at the next data provided in our example. Company ABC has a current P/E ratio relative to industry of 1.2. That means that ABC's price-earnings ratio is 20 percent higher than its peers. In and of itself, most investors would find that a negative; however, company XYZ has a current P/E ratio of 1.4. That means it is trading at a price-earnings ratio 40 percent higher than its peers. By this comparison, ABC looks more attractive. However, we still need to take into account the other factors we have already analyzed. Remember, ABC was trading a little higher above support than XYZ, giving us a little more cushion, but it was trading closer to its 52-week high. Now we find that it is trading at a lower relative P/E ratio. Once again, your ultimate decision will be swayed by the factors you find more important. But, alas, we have much more data to complicate our decision process.

The next factor compares the companies' current price-earnings ratio to its historical P/E ratio. ABC is trading at a 1.3 ratio to its historical earnings. That means that it is currently trading 30 percent higher than it has historically traded based solely on its earnings. This is an indication that the stock may be a little overvalued. In contrast, XYZ is trading at a 0.9 ratio to its historical earnings. In other words, XYZ is trading 10 percent below its historical valuation based solely on earnings. Many investors, especially value investors, will find this an important difference and place a higher weight on this factor when making the ultimate investment decision. However, there may be a legitimate reason that ABC is trading at a higher P/E ratio, which leads us to our next piece of data.

This next factor has us considering the companies' PEG ratios. The PEG ratio is the company's price-earnings ratio divided by its estimated growth rate. For example, if a company is trading at a P/E ratio of 20 and it is estimated to grow those earnings at a 20 percent annual rate, its PEG ratio would be 1.0. On the other hand, if it were trading at a P/E ratio of 30 with the same estimated growth rate, the PEG ratio would equal 1.5. Therefore, the lower the ratio, the better.

In our example, ABC has a PEG ratio of 1.0. Most investors consider anything below a PEG ratio of 1 very good. This may be an indication of why ABC is trading at a higher-than-usual price-earnings ratio. XYZ, on the other hand, has a current PEG Ratio of 2.2. This is much worse than ABC and once again complicates our decision making process. At this point we have three factors favoring ABC and two favoring XYZ.

The next indicator is a comparison of the companies' intrinsic values. As you will recall, a company's intrinsic value represents a discounting of the company's future anticipated earnings to arrive at a current valuation. This is one method appraisers use to value private companies. In this example, ABC has an intrinsic value relative to its current price of 1.4. That means the company is currently trading at a value that is 40 percent higher than its discounted future earnings, while XYZ is currently priced 8 percent below its future discounted earnings. Many, like Warren Buffett, would find this an important distinction.

The last piece of data we will evaluate is the option premium. In our example, ABC provides us an annualized option yield (without the use of leverage) of 15 percent, while XYZ provides us a 13 percent yield. By itself, this would lead us to sell a put on ABC, but we have to consider all the relevant data, not just one indicator.

As you can see, we have a real dilemma. Several factors point to ABC as the best investment candidate, while several other factors point to XYZ. The only way to objectively solve this dilemma is to weight each factor and develop a score based on the relative weighting and the degree to which each company fares better than the other on the individual factors. For example, if ABC were a better choice on the most important factors but better on those factors only by a slight margin, and XYZ were better on the least important factors but better by a wide margin, that might shift the ultimate decision to XYZ.

You are probably beginning to see the problem. Not only will you have to analyze two potential companies but you will have to analyze your entire universe of potential companies at the same time in order to determine, on a completely objective basis, the best investment decision at any particular time. You should, in fact, employ this kind of analysis for any investment strategy. But even employing this type of thorough, objective analysis does not guarantee success. As I continue to implore—it is impossible to know the future direction of any stock or the market, in general. This type of analysis can make you only a better guesser, so we should always employ a strategy that rewards us even when we're wrong.

But back to our problem. How do we analyze 50 or 100 companies at the same time? It is impossible to do manually since by the time you assimilate all the relevant data for just 10 companies, the numbers have changed for the first one. Consequently, I went looking for a solution. Finding none, I created the solution. Over a period of 3 years I paid a software development company to develop a tool that performed the entire task automatically. The goal was to develop a program that would allow investors to enter a universe of potential stocks along with suggested support levels and a proposed expiration date for the put options. From there the computer was to take off on its own and retrieve relevant fundamental and technical data about those stocks. It would also determine the appropriate option symbol based on the company name, expiration date, and proposed support level. It would then submit the option symbol and retrieve the current option premiums as well.

Investors would then enter scoring weights for each factor, and based upon those scoring weights, the computer would analyze and score each position in seconds. Investors could then sort the potential stock list by score, bringing the best scoring positions to the top. Not only would this significantly reduce the amount of time needed to effectively evaluate and compare many different investment opportunities, but it also actually makes what has been heretofore impossible, a simple task.

Of course, once I got started building the automated system, I couldn't stop there. As I'll mention below, it is important to properly diversify your portfolio to make sure one bad dog doesn't severely impact your overall portfolio. By entering a minimum diversification requirement in the program's Profile section, the computer will automatically indicate how many puts an investor should sell for any one particular stock.

We also added an alert system that allows the investor to establish any number of different alerts based on any of the retrievable data. In this way, an investor can just turn on the program and be alerted to a particular circumstance he or she thinks merits special consideration. For example, let's say you have been following Home Depot and want to know when it drops below $30. You can set an individual alert that lets you know when Home Depot drops below $30. That's an example of an *individual alert*. You can also set alerts that are universal to every potential position. For instance, you could set an alert that lets you know when a particular position has an annual yield that exceeds 25 percent and a breakeven point that is at least 30 percent below its current price.

We also developed a Monitor module that performs three basic functions. First, it allows you to monitor your existing positions on an individual basis, as well as on a total portfolio basis. Second, it automatically computes the amount of index puts to buy, on which market indexes, and at what strike prices to appropriately insure your portfolio. And third, it allows you to establish alerts that indicate when you should close out an existing position early to capture a higher annualized yield based on analyzing the current profitability of the position, the anticipated profitability at inception, and the position's remaining profitability. We will talk more about buying index puts and properly monitoring your portfolio in subsequent chapters.

THE FINAL STEP

The last step in the process is to take the stocks from my prioritized "scored" list one by one and look up the latest news related to each company and industry. I look for any indication that this company might have a problem in the near term. Again, I'm not concerned about whether this company's stock will be going up in the near future; I just want to avoid it if I think it might go down substantially.

I take into consideration the date the next earnings report is due out. I try not to place a position if the company is scheduled to announce its earnings within a week or so. If its earnings report is questionable, I would rather wait to see if there are any surprises.

I review the stock's chart one more time, to confirm that the support level is reasonable and that the price is not trending down but is instead headed up, away from its support level. I also check my existing portfolio to ensure that this position will not cause me to be overly invested in any one market sector. If everything appears positive, I will then sell puts on that stock.

HOW MANY PUTS TO SELL

After you have determined what stock you want to sell puts on and when to establish the position, you need to determine how large a position to take (that is, how many puts to sell). You can do this with an objective analysis based on predetermined diversification requirements.

All investment programs need to be properly diversified to protect against a major portfolio loss resulting from a bad decision. You never know when what looked like a great opportunity will turn into a disaster.

For my own portfolio, I want at least 30 different positions so that no one position represents more than about 3 percent of my portfolio. Depending on the size of your portfolio, that may or may not be an appropriate number of positions for you. However, I strongly recommend that you split your holdings among a minimum of at least 15 positions.

I also want to use only a conservative amount of leverage. The average margin requirement for an out-of-the-money put is about 25 percent of the strike price. Therefore, I could sell up to four times the value of my capital in puts. I prefer to take a more conservative approach. I limit my sales to two times my

---

Always diversify your portfolio by spreading your investment dollars among at least 15 different stocks.

I personally prefer at least 30 different positions so that no one position represents more than about 3 percent of my portfolio.

Determining the Number of Put Contracts to Sell

Total portfolio value	$150,000
Times 200 percent leverage	× 2
Equals maximum portfolio exposure	$300,000
Divided by number of positions	÷ 30
Equals max exposure per position	$ 10,000
Divided by position's strike price	÷ 50
Equals number of put shares to sell	200
Divided by 100	÷ 100
Equals number of put contracts to sell	2

capital, so I will always have enough money to cover stocks that could be put to me. A more complete discussion about leverage follows in a later chapter.

Therefore, I multiply my account value by 2* and then divide that by 30 to establish the maximum dollar amount I might be required to pay to purchase stocks that are put to me for that position.

For example, let's say I have $150,000 in my investment account. I multiply the $150,000 by 2 and divide the $300,000 product by 30 to get a maximum of $10,000 exposure for each of the 30 put positions.

That means that if a stock drops below my strike price and settles there on expiration day, the most I want to have to pay to own that stock is $10,000.

If the put I want to sell has a support level (and hence a strike price) of $50, I would sell 200 put shares, or 2 contracts. Since $50 times 200 shares equals my maximum exposure of $10,000, this is the maximum number of contracts I should sell for this stock.

---

* *Special note:* Investors wishing to take an even more conservative approach can consider using less margin or no margin at all. In addition to reducing your risk, however, this would also, of course, reduce the annual return you could expect to earn.

WHICH MONTH TO SELL

Over the last 3 years, I have come to the conclusion that it makes sense to sell puts, in most cases, that have a long-term expiration date. Long-term puts are generally referred to as LEAPS.

As I previously mentioned, option premiums decay exponentially. In other words, option premiums go down more slowly further away from the expiration date, and the decay accelerates significantly as the expiration date gets nearer. As a result, selling short-term options dramatically increases the annual yield achieved from option trading. Annualized yields on short-term options (using minimal leverage) would normally run between 40 to 80 percent while similar long-term options would yield half of that.

In spite of the lower yield, I now recommend the use of longer-term, more conservative options. There are two reasons for that recommendation. First, most investors are looking for only 10 to 15 percent annual returns, and it is possible to achieve more than that goal by using the more conservative long-term options.

The main reason long-term options are more conservative is that you receive a higher dollar premium even though the annualized yield is lower. This higher premium reduces the breakeven price on the trade. In most cases, the stock can lose up to 20 percent in value without incurring a loss. For example, you could sell a 1-month put on IBM and receive $1.50 in premium. However, you could sell a 12-month put and receive $9. Although the annualized yield would be significantly lower by selling the longer-term put, your breakeven point would go down $7.50 because you had received that much more in premium when you opened the position.

Second, the long-term option gives us a longer window for the stock to go up in price and thus provide us, through proper monitoring of the position, an opportunity to close out the position before expiration, at a higher annualized yield with no more risk. Take a look at several stock charts to help you understand this point.

Most stocks go up and down over and over again. The problem is that you never really know when the stock is actually low, except in hindsight by looking at one of these charts. One thing we do know is that the stock prices of quality companies do go up and down.

Let's assume that we sell a 1-year put option (LEAP) on a stock that provides a premium that gives us a 30 percent annual return if we hold it till expiration (using minimal leverage). We think that the stock is low when we sell the put, but of course, we don't really know. Over the next year it is extremely likely that the stock is going to go up and down. We may have been right when we took the position and the stock goes up first. Or we may have been wrong and the stock goes down first.

If we are wrong and the stock goes down, we would hold onto the position. We hope that, by the end of the year, the stock will recover. But even if the stock goes down and stays down around 20 percent, we will still break even. If the stock does recover at or near the end of the year, we can close out the position at that time and realize a profit as a result of the time value decay or just wait for the option to expire worthless.

On the other hand, if we are right and the stock goes up shortly after we take a position in it, we have the option to close out the position for a smaller dollar profit but a much higher annualized yield. For example, let's say we received an $8 premium for a $50 strike price on a 1-year put. Remember, this position only requires, using our more conservative approach, a cash deposit of only $25 as collateral. If we hold the position to expiration and the stock does not go down, the put will expire worthless, and we will earn more than 32 percent on our investment, taking into account the interest earnings on the cash collateral and the premium received.

However, if the stock goes up $8 in the next month, the value of the put we sold will drop in price by about $3. We could then close out the position by repurchasing the put we sold originally for $8, for about $5. That would be a $3 profit in 1 month, which works out to an annualized return of over 140 percent.

We may not be quite that lucky, and the stock may take 4 months to go up $8 in price. We could choose to close out the position then and make a little more than $4 because the put has diminished in value not only because the stock has gone up in price but also because some of the option's time value has expired. At this point we can buy the put back for $4, giving us a $4 profit in 4 months. That works out to about a 50 percent annualized return.

The point is that any time during the year when the stock goes up a reasonable amount above where it was when we initially placed the position, we have the option to close out the position and achieve, in most cases, a higher annualized return than we anticipated at the time we entered the original put position. We can then take another position on another stock and wait for the same thing to happen again.

Of course, sometimes the stock will not go up and you will have to be satisfied with the originally designed return based only on the decay of the time value. As long as the stock does not go down and stay down more than about 20 percent, you will, in most cases, not lose any money on the trade.

But even if the stock does go down and stays down the entire year, you can still keep the entire original premium as profit and avoid having the stock put to you. Remember, option premiums consist of two components: intrinsic value and time value.

If you originally sold a $50 strike price put and the stock is trading at $40 near expiration, the put option premium is probably around $10.75. That's 75 cents of time value and $10 of intrinsic value. You could buy back the put for around $11 and immediately sell another long-term put at a $50 strike price for about $14 ($10 of intrinsic value and $4 of time value. The time value is higher on the new put because you are extending the expiration date). This is called *rolling the put forward*.

You now have taken in another $3 of premium and have another year for the stock to recover to a price you once thought of as low. Note that this year you receive only $4 of time value versus the $8 you received the previous year. That is because at this time the strike price is further away from the stock's price, and that results in a lower time value.

So let's summarize how we monitor our portfolio. First, we watch our positions to see if a stock has risen noticeably and consider closing out the position for a higher annualized yield and starting another one.

Second, if the stock is below the strike price near expiration, we merely repurchase the put and immediately sell another put further into the future to capture some more time value and give us more time for the stock to rebound.

SUMMARY

I have discussed developing a universe of stocks that you will track. You've established support levels for those companies, and you've gathered some fundamental and technical data. Then you calculated the option premiums for each position based on selling puts with a strike price equal to or below your support level.

After discarding any trade that would result in a premium with less than 10 percent annualized return (using no leverage), you compare all of your collected data on each remaining position, based on a weighted value system that reflects the degree to which you feel each piece of technical and fundamental data rates in importance.

This results in a relatively short prioritized list of possible positions. Beginning at the top of the list, you check on recent news events affecting each company. You double-check the stock's chart to ensure that the support level is still appropriate and take into consideration whether this trade will cause your portfolio to become overly exposed in any one market sector.

You then calculate the number of contracts you should sell for your chosen positions, based on the amount of diversification you have selected for your overall portfolio. You then sell each put. Then you monitor your portfolio as discussed above.

You're probably thinking that you could spend every waking hour doing this analysis. Fortunately, you don't have to. The automated toolkit I developed will allow most investors to properly analyze and monitor their investment portfolio in less than 30 minutes a day.

CHAPTER 9

Insuring against a Market Crash

Protection to Help You Sleep at Night

Immediately after placing your put positions, you should buy index puts to protect your portfolio from a major market correction. This is especially important when the market is volatile. When purchasing the index puts, you need to evaluate the following:

1. Which index puts to buy
2. How many index puts to buy
3. At what strike price to buy the index puts

These are basically objective decisions. Let's take them one at a time.

WHICH INDEX PUTS TO BUY

First, investors need to match their purchase of index puts to the types of stocks on which they sold puts. The goal is to match as closely as possible the movement of the stocks on which puts were sold to the index movement.

If the index chosen does not move in a direction and to the degree substantially similar to the stocks in the portfolio, that index will not provide optimum protection. For example, if most of the positions are in Nasdaq stocks, an index on the Dow probably won't provide adequate protection.

There are two approaches you can use to determine which index more closely correlates to the equity put position you are intending to insure. The first approach would be to use the index with which the company has traditionally been aligned. For example, if you sold a put on Citibank, you might use the Dow index.

The second approach is to compare the stock's recent price movement to various indexes to see if the stock has recently been moving more in line with another index. You can do this by looking at charts at various Web sites like Quicken.com. With these charts, you can add multiple indexes to see which one more closely correlates to the current trading activity.

For instance, in March 2000, Goldman Sachs had been tracking closely to the NDX index in spite of the fact that this company would normally be associated with the Dow or S&P index. There is no perfect answer. Few stocks move closely with any particular index. However, the purpose of using the index puts is to protect against a major market correction when almost every stock goes down.

As we discussed in the last chapter, part of your ongoing maintenance with this trading system requires you to track the performance of your portfolio. You can do this manually or by using the automated system that monitors your existing positions.

When you set up a manual spreadsheet to monitor your positions, one of the bits of information you will need for each put you sell is which index the underlying stock trades on or is more closely associated with. Keep in mind that many stocks are associated with more than one index. For example, Microsoft is part of the Nasdaq, the Nasdaq-100, the S&P 500, the S&P 100, and the Dow.

Also keep in mind that there is sometimes more than one way to trade a particular index. For example, you can protect your portfolio against a decline in the Nasdaq-100 by purchasing puts either on the index itself (NDX) or on a fund that attempts to mirror the index (QQQ). Further details on these index options are in the appendices. Using QQQ allows you to insure a much smaller portfolio since QQQ trades at about 1/40th of the NDX index value. Please refer to Appendix C for a complete explanation of QQQ.

HOW MANY INDEX PUTS TO BUY

Determining how many index puts to buy is a simple division problem. Divide the value of the puts (total put shares times their strike price) sold, which match a particular index by the current index value to find out how many index puts you need to buy.

For example, let's say you sold puts with a potential cost, if put to you, of $200,000 (strike price times number of shares of puts sold) on stocks that match up to the Dow index (DJX). If the Dow index were currently at 100 (the DJX trades at 1/100th of the Dow), you would divide the $200,000 by 100, so you would need to buy 2000 puts, or 20 contracts.

DETERMINING THE STRIKE PRICE

The next thing to do is to determine at what strike price to buy the index puts. Most investors will buy an out-of-the-money index put because it provides ample protection against a major market correction and it costs substantially less than an in-the-money or an at-the-money put. Keep in mind that many of the individual stock puts sold are out of the money, which means the stock can drop down to the strike price by expiration and still produce the full anticipated profit. In addition, investors receive premiums when they sell the puts. That reduces the breakeven point, or the at-risk point, even further.

The purpose of the insurance should not be to insure your potential profits but to insure your principal. That means the stock can drop all the way to your breakeven price (strike price minus premium amount) before you need the index puts you purchased to begin generating a profit to offset losses on the equity puts you sold.

Why do most investors buy index puts with as low a strike price as is practical? Simply because the higher the strike price, the more the puts will cost. Since investors use the index put strictly as an insurance policy against a major market downturn, they don't expect to make money on the index put. In fact, they expect and hope to lose the entire premium they paid for the index put. Look at it the way you would a term life insurance policy on your life. With your term life insurance policy, you want to pay as little as possible for the right amount of protection, and you hope you never make a profit on it! This is the same principal.

I determine the strike price of the index put by reducing the current index by the average out-of-the-money position plus about 75 percent of the option premium received (see Table 9.1).

In other words, if my average equity put sale were 6 percent out of the money and my average premium were 12 percent, I would buy index puts at a strike price 15 percent [6 percent + (12 percent × 75 percent)] below the index's current price. Although we use an objective approach to derive the correct number of index puts and the appropriate strike price for those puts, the results will not always be perfect. That is because, during a market correction, the index will not drop by the exact same percentage as the stocks represented by our put positions.

If the index drops by a greater percentage than your underlying stock positions drop, the index puts will increase in value by a greater percentage than your equity puts value will decline. In other words, you will make more money on the index puts than you will lose on your individual equity puts. On the

TABLE 9.1

Determining the Strike Price of the Index Puts

Average percentage your puts are out of the money	6%
Average put premium times 75%	9%
Total	15%
Current index level	1500
Minus 15% = strike price	1275

other hand, if the individual stocks go down by a greater percentage than the index does, you will lose more money on your individual equity puts than you will earn on the index puts.

If you started out with stocks that were somewhat overpriced to begin with, when the market corrects, those stocks could drop further, as a percentage, than the index. If you start out with stocks that had already been "beaten up" when you placed the position, it's reasonable to assume that they will drop by a smaller degree than will the index during a major market correction.

There are no guarantees in life or investing. Your portfolio may not track appropriately with the underlying index you used to protect yourself in a market decline. But it is true that *dispersion* (the difference in portfolio movement to index movement) is less during major corrections. In any event, an imperfect hedge is better than no hedge at all.

MONITORING YOUR INDEX PUTS

Unless the market has dropped dramatically by the time your index puts are close to expiration, there will be no value left in those options. They should be left to expire worthless. Keep in mind that we look at these index puts as we would a term life insurance policy: We need insurance for protection, but we hope we never have the opportunity to cash it in! The value of this kind of insurance comes with the peace of mind we receive, knowing we are protected from the potential of a devastating loss due to a stock market crash.

There will be times when the market will go through a minor correction and our index puts will become more valuable. While the market is dropping, we will be grateful we have those index puts, but once the market begins to turn around and head higher again, we will be tempted to sell them before the profit disappears.

Do not sell those puts and take the profit unless there has been a significant market correction. The purpose of the index puts is to provide insurance against a major market correction. The most conservative investor would never close out the insurance position. However, if there has been a major correction and the market has retested its lows on several occasions, you may decide to take your index put profits. Remember, even though you think the market can't go any lower, it still can.

One of the reasons to consider closing them out after a significant correction is because at that time the put positions should be in the money and have a high time value and some intrinsic value. Remember, the closer the option's strike price is to its current price, the more time value will be in the option. If you do close out the index puts, the cash you receive for selling the time value of the index puts will still offset a further loss in case the market retreats a little further. For example, let's assume you purchased index puts on the S&P 500 index at a 1000 strike price for $50. At the time of the purchase, the S&P was trading around 1150. As I previously suggested, you purchased the lower strike price because of the premium you received and the fact that the equity puts you sold were also out of the money.

Two months later the market has dropped about 20 percent to the point that the S&P 500 is trading at about 950. As a result, the index puts have gone up in value significantly. They currently have an intrinsic value of $50 (1000 strike price minus 950 current price) and a substantial time value. Even though a couple of months has elapsed since their original purchase, the time value will have increased because the index is now closer to its strike price and the extreme market correction will likely have caused an increase in market volatility that also increases time value.

As a result, the current time value has risen to $90. If you sell the index puts, you will receive $140 ($50 intrinsic value plus $90 time value). You have of course, two options: (1) You can take the more conservative approach and hold the index positions as insurance against a further market correction, or (2) you can take the index put profits.

By taking the profits, you have assumed that the S&P 500 will be trading no lower than 860 by the time the puts would have expired. That's because by selling the puts now, you will receive $90 in time value, which will expire when the puts do. At expiration, the intrinsic value will have to equal $140 in order to get the same price for the index puts as you would get for selling them now. Therefore, the index would have to be trading at 860 (1000 strike price minus 860 equals 140 intrinsic value).

In other words, taking the index put profits now would still have been a good decision even if the market drops another 10 percent before the puts would have expired. In fact, the market may still drop another 10 percent, but then recover. Obviously, it is impossible to pick the bottom of any market decline, and retested lows do not insure that another breakthrough is not eminent. You need to determine for yourself when it may be appropriate to close out profitable index put positions.

One note of warning: If you close out your index put positions, you will be exposing your portfolio to potentially large losses, especially if you have utilized any amount of leverage. Consequently, you should only consider doing this if (1) the market has incurred a significant decline, (2) the market has successfully retested lows on several occasions, and (3) the market, in general, is considered substantially oversold. Once you sell the index puts, you should be prepared to repurchase them, at a lower price, as the market recovers.

Remember, always SafetyNet your stocks. The purpose of the insurance is not to earn a short-term profit. The index puts are there to make sure you can meet a margin call if the bottom drops out of the market.

CHAPTER

10

Managing Your Portfolio
To Maximize Your Profits

One of the aspects of this trading strategy that many investors appreciate is that they don't have to be great stock pickers or market timers to make steady profits in the market.

As shown in previous chapters, investors don't have to get in each trade at the bottom and get out at the top. As long as the stock settles at or above their strike price, they make their full profit. Even if the stock does drop a little below their strike price, they make a profit (albeit reduced from their original profit expectation). It isn't until the stock crosses below their breakeven point that they begin to lose money. And even then, if it's a company that they are confident will eventually rebound, they don't lose money unless they decide to sell out of the position before it makes its recovery.

So the only time investors using the SafetyNet Trading System lose money is when:

1. The stock drops well below their strike price,
   AND

2. It settles well below their strike price by expiration day,
   AND
3. They close the position before it has a chance to recover.

Why would you close a position with a loss instead of waiting for it to rebound back up to its support level? The answer is: You would do that only if you lost confidence in that stock's ability to rebound to its original support level. That happens. Fortunately, it doesn't happen very often, but it has happened to me, and it will happen to you too.

In most cases, if you have done your homework right, you will have few stocks put to you at expiration that result in an actual loss. Doing your homework right means that you have accomplished the following:

- Carefully chosen your universe of stocks
- Set reasonable support levels
- Thoroughly evaluated fundamental data, technical indicators, and option premiums
- Checked for any news that might adversely affect the positions you're considering
- Maximized your profits by timing the sale of your puts properly (stock was close to support, trending up when position was placed)
- Purchased the correct index puts at the appropriate strike price (your safety net)

If you have done all of that, the majority of the puts you sold should expire worthless and you won't have to buy the underlying stock, or at least the stocks will not have fallen to a price worse than your breakeven point (strike price − premium − interest).

Eventually, however, a stock *may* be put to you. It might be because you chose the wrong support level or because you did not bail out when the earnings report came out below expectations or because that particular industry is simply out of favor with the market at the moment. Whatever the reason, you will end up owning the stock if you don't take some action. Now what should you do?

You have three choices. First, if the stock is close to the strike price, you can just let the stock be put to you and sell it for a small loss, but one that is more than made up for by the premium you originally received.

Second, you can roll the put out to a future date. As mentioned in a previous chapter, you will receive more for selling a new put than you will pay to buy the old one back. This rolling technique can be used when the stock is near the strike price or further out of the money. Rolling a slightly in-the-money put is an excellent choice when you still have confidence in the stock. At this point it has a lot of time value due to its proximity to the stock price. Even puts that are way in the money provide some additional time value premium and another year for the stock to recover to its original support level.

The third choice is to punt. On occasion, even when choosing among only high-quality companies, bad news may impact the long-term prospects of a company. In these cases you may choose to have the stock put to you and then sell it immediately. If you had been properly monitoring the position, you may very well have closed out the position already.

KNOW WHEN TO TAKE THE MONEY AND RUN

As mentioned in Chapter 8, always watch positive stock price movements as well. These are excellent opportunities to close out positions early for high annualized gains. You can then take new, promising positions that may result in similar gains down the road.

You may want to set up models that suggest when it is time to exit a position early. These models would take into account the original intended yield, the amount of profit not yet realized and the amount of annualized profit already realized on the transaction.

For example, you may decide to exit a transaction that has a 15 percent remaining annualized yield but will result in a 125 percent annualized yield if it is closed out. This would be especially appealing if you knew of a really good new potential position that would provide a 35 percent annual return.

REVIEW SUPPORT LEVELS

Part of the job of managing your portfolio is reviewing your support levels. Periodically, before placing new positions, go through your universe of stocks and look for those stocks that are currently trading either below your support level or considerably higher than your support level.

Below Support

Stocks that are trading below support should be watched over a period of time (a week or so) to see if they recover and move back up above support within a short period of time. Keep in mind my definition of *support level*: the price at which a stock is likely to become attractive to other market investors. If the stock drops below this price, it will rebound and begin going up as bottom-fishers scoop up the undervalued stock.

If a stock drops below support and rebounds quickly, you might want to increase your confidence grade for that stock. That might be a good current candidate. On the other hand, if a stock drops below support and fails to rebound within a week or so, you should drop your support level to a new, more appropriate level. Don't trade that stock for now until you see whether it stops dropping and settles in above this new support level.

Above Support

Stocks that are trading well above support might warrant a higher support level, but don't assume that to be true. Before you raise the support, evaluate the chart, just as you did when you originally set the support level.

I'm very cautious about selling puts on stocks that have moved up dramatically. Eventually, the momentum carrying this stock higher could reverse if investors decide to take profits. I'd rather wait until after that's happened and the stock's on its way up again. Proceed with caution.

REVIEW MARGIN AND DIVERSIFICATION

Once you have been using this strategy for a while, you should recalculate the number of contracts you sell per position based on your new, higher-valued portfolio. In Chapter 8, I showed you how to calculate the appropriate number of contracts to sell for each position. If you continue to base that amount on your original portfolio value, you'll miss out on the "compounding effect." After a few years, this compounding effect can make a dramatic difference in your net worth.

You should also continue to monitor your diversification. Make sure you do not end up overly exposed to one industry or market sector.

USING LEVERAGE

Leverage is an important consideration in every investment program. In its most common application, *leverage* means the borrowing of money to increase the amount of investments you can buy. For instance, your broker will allow you to buy $1000 worth of IBM stock by just depositing $500 with the brokerage firm. That example represents the use of 200 percent leverage. In other words, you have purchased two times your cash deposit in stock. Of course, when you use leverage in this way, you have to pay interest to your broker for the money you borrowed to buy the stock. This is referred to as *margin interest*, and it is one of the brokerage firm's most profitable activities. Their loan to you is fully secured by liquid assets, and they charge you a rate, which significantly exceeds their cost of borrowing money to lend to you. In many cases, that spread produces the lion share of the brokerage firms' profits.

There is a way, however, to use leverage without borrowing money. You can do that when you sell puts! Leverage is employed when the value of the put contracts you sell exceeds your cash investment. If it does not exceed your cash investment, the puts are considered "cash secured." For example, let's say you deposit $100,000 with your broker and then you sell 10 put contracts with a $100 strike price. Remember, each contract represents 100 shares, so the 1000 shares (100 shares times 10 contracts) times the $100 strike price represents $100,000 in stock. In other words, you are now obligated to buy $100,000 of stock if the stock drops and stays below the $100 strike price. By depositing $100,000 with your broker, you have sufficient cash to cover that obligation, so the puts are considered cash secured.

However, your broker will not require you to deposit $100,000 to sell those 10 put contracts. In fact, with most brokers you would be required to deposit only around $25,000. By only depositing $25,000 you are using leverage, but since you are not actually borrowing money from your broker, you do not have to pay interest. You actually earn interest because your deposit and the premium you receive for selling the puts are not being used to buy the stock and can be invested in an interest-earning vehicle like Treasury bills.

The key question is, Should I use leverage, and if so, how much? Most investors should not use any of the typical forms of leverage. They should not borrow money to buy more stock because (1) they have to pay interest on the borrowed funds and (2) a drop in the price of their stocks will double their losses, in addition to their interest costs.

But what about using leverage when you sell puts? A reasonable amount of leverage is appropriate when selling puts for the following reasons. First, you have no interest cost. You actually earn interest on your deposit and the extra premium you receive from selling more puts. Second, any loss incurred as a result of falling stock prices is offset by the premium you received for selling the puts and the amount the stock was above the strike price when you sold the put. In most instances, when selling long-term puts, your breakeven point will be 15 to 20 percent below the stock's price at the inception of the trade.

If you had purchased stock on leverage and it fell 15 percent, you would have lost 30 percent plus the interest paid on the margin loan. By selling the put using the same 200 percent leverage, you will actually break even if the stock falls 15 percent. And third, by using some of the put premium you receive to purchase index puts as a hedge, you further protect the leveraged position in case of a significant market correction.

Some investors believe that having this type of downside protection allows them to use even more leverage, but I continue to recommend a maximum leverage of about 200 percent. We will discuss the use of leverage further in a subsequent chapter as it relates to other risk parameters.

11

Learning from My Costly Mistakes

Eight Rules That Will Save You Money and Frustration

Most of the things I've learned about investing, I learned from mistakes. As a result, this chapter may be the most important. I'm going to share my most humbling moments in the hopes that you can learn from my costly mistakes rather than from your own.

RULE 1. DIVERSIFY YOUR PORTFOLIO.

About 8 months into this program, I started getting a little cocky. I had only one losing trade out of well over a hundred. I felt extremely confident about several new trading opportunities. I did not yet have my fully automated system, and I got lazy. Instead of doing more research to uncover new positions, I doubled and tripled up my favorite trades.

Well, you can imagine what happened. A couple of the positions went drastically south. Bad news had come out about the companies that drove the stock price significantly lower. Had I invested only my normal amount per position, it would not have had a major impact on my portfolio, but because I had tripled up as a result of my laziness and overconfidence, my portfolio incurred a major loss. One of the stocks ultimately came back, but I had to dump one for a big loss.

Since then, I never fail to properly diversify my portfolio even when I am extremely confident about a particular stock. Once in a while, I may double up on one position, but that's the maximum exposure I am willing to take on a particular company, and I don't do that often. You just never know what will happen to jeopardize the valuation of even the best of companies.

I like to have at least 30 positions in my portfolio so that no one position can impact more than about 3 percent of the overall portfolio. I understand that many of you reading this book may not be starting with enough capital to enjoy that kind of diversification. Just make sure you diversify as much as possible. With less diversification, you must do more research to ensure, as best as possible, that you are making the right investment choices. You may also want to limit your positions to more conservative plays until you increase your capital enough to get proper diversification.

I not only diversify my portfolio by stocks but also by industry and sector. In other words, I will not invest more than 30 percent in any one industry at any one time or more than 50 percent in any one sector.

Lesson: Always properly diversify your portfolio to make sure no single position can have too dramatic an impact on your overall portfolio.

RULE 2. NEVER SAY NEVER.

It is absolutely amazing to me that I could have been making over 20 percent a year with a conservative strategy and I still failed to stick to it. At the end of 1999, I saw QUALCOMM go up over 200 percent in a couple of months. I just knew QUALCOMM would NEVER go up any further, at least not in the short term. I was convinced there were major overvaluations on popular tech stocks. So I sold it short. I took a relatively small position, so it wouldn't have a big impact on my overall portfolio. But then it began to run much higher. I said, "It will NEVER go higher than this." Well, it did.

Now, I'm not going to tell you the rest of the story until we get to another rule, so for now, remember: Anything in the stock market is possible. I've seen great earnings reported and the stock tanks. I've seen bad earnings reported and the stock goes up. I've seen good stocks tank for missing earnings by 1 percent. And I've seen no-revenue companies go up 400 percent in 2 days.

Don't get caught thinking you know what will happen next because of extreme things that have just happened. You can't out-guess the market.

Lesson: Don't think you really know what the market is going to do—ever!

RULE 3. DON'T DOUBLE DOWN.

Back to QUALCOMM. I was so sure QUALCOMM would not go up further that I doubled my "short" position as it rose, so that I would average up my "sell" price. Unfortunately, it kept going up. So, guess what? I doubled up again, right before an analyst came out saying that the stock was going to go up another 60 percent!

I took a minor position and turned it into a major position and a very substantial loss before I bailed. (Obviously, hindsight showed us that I was right, just a little early.) No matter how confident you are about a position that has turned sour, don't double it up in order to catch up. This makes you violate the first rule of diversification. Take a minor loss. It won't affect your long-term performance.

Lesson: Don't try to make up for a bad choice by violating another principle, that is, proper diversification.

RULE 4. DON'T STAND IN FRONT OF THE TRAIN.

I had sold puts on Intuit, and it dropped pretty substantially very quickly. So, to reduce my loss, I turned around and sold

calls on Intuit (before the stock was put to me) at the same
strike price I had used when I sold the puts. I figured that with
as much as it had dropped, it would never go up that high before
expiration day. I was wrong! In about a week Intuit started
turning around. When it got back to the strike price, I bought
the stock to cover my naked-call position (naked as opposed to
covered because I sold calls on a stock that I didn't own). Then
the stock started to fall again, so I sold the stock. The stock
price hovered around my strike price for a while. Then I had to
go away on a business trip, and I wasn't able to watch the market for a few days. Sure enough, Intuit made a quick bounce
over the strike price by about $3.

    When I got home, I realized that I then had an in-the-
money, naked-call position. In other words, if the stock expired
up this high, I would have to buy it at this higher price in order
to honor my commitment to sell it at the lower price. Instead of
buying the stock to immediately cover my naked-call position, I
decided to wait it out and let it fall back again before I covered
it. Unfortunately for me, the stock started a run. I kept thinking it had to correct. So I stayed right in the middle of the track
as the train charged forward. You don't want to know how much
money I lost on that position.

    Lesson: Don't get caught on the wrong side of a momentum
play—which leads us to the next rule.

RULE 5. CHECK THE NEWS BEFORE YOU TRADE.

This rule is very simple. I had been selling puts on United
Airlines for some time. Never once was the stock put to me. The
stock had been on a steady rise for several months, so I eventually did not have a position because the stock appeared to be too
high over its support level. (This was back when I sold short-
term puts.)

    Then oil prices began to rise, and United's stock price
began to fall along with the other airline stocks. When it got
close to my original support level, I dove in headfirst. I forgot to
check the news first. United Airlines had just been downgraded
for an expected earnings warning. The stock dropped 10 percent
in 2 days while I was left wondering what happened.

Lesson: Always check recent news before placing a trade, no matter how much you have been watching a position.

RULE 6. DON'T TRADE ON EMOTION.

Another one of my out-of-the-system trades: Near the end of 1999 I sold Yahoo! short. My feeling: The Nasdaq was over-valued, and Yahoo! was highly overvalued. My plan was to sell it short and watch the profits roll in. Then reality hit me right between the eyes. The market went nuts over high-techs and Internet stocks, and Yahoo! shot up over 100 points. Ouch!!!!

I just knew Yahoo! would fall. Logically, it could not sustain that incredibly overvalued price. A correction was imminent. But my losses were mounting, and I finally bailed out on emo-tion—just one day before Yahoo! began its 150-point descent.

Even when things look their bleakest, if your position is well founded and researched, if you still have sound reason to believe in the stock's direction, don't trade on emotion. Close your position if it makes sense, but don't trade on emotion.

Lesson: Don't allow your emotions to get the best of you... or your money.

RULE 7. RESIST THE BIG GAINS.

As you can see from some of my previous mistakes, I have at times gotten tired of hitting singles and have gone for the home run. I've watched some investors make gigantic short-term profits, and I've wanted to join the party.

Almost every time I join the party, the party fizzles. I am not a stock picker. I should not go for the home run. If I want to gamble, I should go to Las Vegas where they will at least give me some free food, drinks, and entertainment to console me in my losses. You all know the story about the tortoise and the hare. It applies to investing, as well. Some hotshot traders will make 100 percent gains every now and then, but over the long term, after spending many sleepless nights worrying about their risky trading positions, the vast majority of those hotshots won't earn more than anyone else, and some will even go broke in the process. I've decided to be an investor turtle, and I suggest you be one too. And that means . . .

RULE 8. STICK TO THE SYSTEM.

1. Let me recap just what the basic system is:
2. Sell puts at or below a stock's support level on companies you wouldn't mind owning for the long term.
3. Sell a maximum of two times your portfolio value in puts.
4. Buy puts on the appropriate index to protect against a significant market correction.
5. If a stock is below the strike price near expiration, consider rolling it forward by repurchasing the existing put position and selling a new one at the same strike price out further into the future.

The potential results from using the SafetyNet Trading System are 12 to 20 percent annual returns. This comes from selling long-term puts with annual yields averaging 12 percent and using minimal leverage, doubling that yield to 24 percent. Then reducing that yield by one-fourth to cover the cost of the index put insurance. Then add 3 to 5 percent a year in interest income from the underlying cash portfolio. Of course, some of the positions will end up with either no profit or a potential loss. Others, however, with proper monitoring, will be closed out early with higher annualized gains. In the end, whether you make the low or high end of that range will depend on the overall market movement and how good a job you do in choosing and monitoring your individual positions.

12

About Those Critics

Selling Puts Is Safer Than Buying Stock—Despite What Your Broker Says

Nobody can claim that you can invest your money yourself and make 15 to 20 percent a year with less risk than a mutual fund without some critics surfacing. And not too many advisors will be happy that I suggest their recommendations to buy stocks and traditional mutual funds are unsuitable for most investors. Too many people are impacted by those kinds of claims. So, what will they say?

TOO RISKY?

First, some will say, out of ignorance, that selling puts is too risky. Let's review what we demonstrated earlier in the options chapter when we compared the risk and reward of selling a put versus buying the stock itself.

On the day this was written, you could have bought a share of Microsoft for $65.10. If Microsoft falls to $53 and you sell it, you will lose $12.10.

Consider what would happen if, instead, you sold a Microsoft put with a $65 strike price and you received a $9.70

premium, which was the premium available for a 14-month put on the day this was written.

Assuming the very same scenario (the stock price started at $65.10 and dropped to $53), you would only lose $2.30. That's because, when your put expired you would subtract from your $65 cost the $9.70 that you earned in premium when you sold the put. That would leave you with a net cost of only $55.30. If you sold the Microsoft stock for $53, you would incur a loss of only $2.30, and that would not take into account the interest you would have earned on the cash collateral.

Buying the stock results in a $12.10 loss, while selling a put results in losing only $2.30 (see Table 12.1). Which one is more risky? The answer is obvious: Selling out-of-the-money puts is less risky than buying the stock.

So why do so many investment professionals think it is risky? It's because they are only repeating what they have been told by others who don't know any better either. It's absolutely and mathematically impossible to prove that selling out-of-the-money puts is more risky than buying stocks. Challenge anyone who claims otherwise to show you the numbers. Let him or her prove under what possible scenario it is more risky. He or she simply won't be able to.

In fact, on my Web site I make a $1 million challenge. If anyone can show me even one example in which an investor

TABLE 12.1

Which Is Riskier: Selling Puts or Buying Stocks?

Buy Microsoft		Sell MSFT Jan65 Put	
Current price	$65.10	Strike price	$65.00
Premium	None	Premium	$9.70
Net cost	$65.10	Net cost	$55.30
Sold for	$53.00	Sold For	$53.00
Loss	$12.10	Loss	$2.30

If you bought MSFT when it was selling for $65.10 and it dropped to $53, you would lose $12.10.

If, instead, you sold an MSFT 65 Put when MSFT was at $65.10, and the stock dropped to $53, you would only have to pay $65 at expiration. Subtract from that the $9.70 premium you received when you sold the put, and your loss would be only $2.30.

Same starting price—same ending price—less loss!!!

loses more money by selling an out-of-the-money put than by buying the same stock, at the same time, in the same amount, I will give that person $1 million. In over 3 years I have had no takers.

WHAT ABOUT 1987?

What the critics might do is use criticism number 2. They will tell you that, in October 1987, many investors selling puts lost all their money.

What they won't tell you is why those investors lost so much:

1. They used excessive margins.
2. They sold deep-in-the-money puts.
3. They had not bought insurance (hedges) against the market correction.

Excessive use of leverage can make any trading strategy risky. But the truth is, if you use the exact same amount of leverage with a buy-hold-sell strategy and a put selling strategy, and the stocks you pick go down, you would lose more with the buy-hold-sell strategy than you would lose with the put-selling strategy. That's because, as we repeated above, you always lose more money buying stocks in the same amount, at the same time, than you would by selling out-of-the-money puts on the same stocks in the same amounts.

No matter what trading strategy you use, incorporating an excessive margin increases your risk. That's why I recommend that you never sell more than two times your portfolio value in puts, and why it is absolutely imperative that you use some of the put premium to purchase puts on the appropriate indexes to offset the impact of a major market correction.

If those 1987 investors had purchased the insurance puts as a hedge, they might not have lost anything.

HAS THE SYSTEM BEEN BACK TESTED?

Potential critics of the program may ask, "Has the system been back tested?" This clearly indicates that they have missed the point. First, I do not claim that this investment approach produces the highest returns. To the contrary, in a significant bull market, it does not. The objective is to produce a greater probability of success with less downside risk. That does not need to be back tested because the evidence is empirical. In other words, you can readily see from the facts that, with the SafetyNet Trading System, you make winning trades more often because you make your full profit in four out of five scenarios and do not necessarily lose money in the fifth possible scenario. In addition, you are substantially protected in case of a major market correction. This result does not need to be back tested. It is self-evident. In spite of this, I present a back test of the entire Dow Jones Industrial index in Chapter 17 that should provide even the harshest critic the necessary evidence to support my position.

On the other hand, your approach to picking which stocks to take a position in is subjective and could be back tested. I do not claim to be an exceptional stock picker. That is why the software program I developed gives the individual investor the flexibility to customize the investment criteria used in determining which companies to invest in. Or the investor can choose a fund manager who employs this strategy to do it for him or her. The good news is that with the SafetyNet Trading System, you can be wrong and still make a good profit. I know because I am frequently wrong, and I still make profits.

LIMITED GAIN—UNLIMITED RISK

The last criticism will look something like this: Selling puts results in an investment scenario in which you have limited gains but unlimited losses. At first, that type of criticism sounds like it makes some sense, especially when the basic comment is almost completely correct. When selling puts, you do have a limited amount of gain and a large potential loss.

The criticism, however, does not consider the *probabilities* involved. What is the probability that the underlying stock will go down to zero or even significantly down without coming back? What is the probability that a stock will fall below and stay below its reasonably established support level? Do they realize that 80 percent of options expire worthless?

Let me give you an analogy in the real world about probabilities. Most people who visit Las Vegas go there with a preset loss limit. They say, "I'm willing to lose $300." At the same time, they are hoping to hit the jackpot and take home millions. In other words, they are going to Las Vegas with the idea that they will have a limited loss but that the possibility exists for them to have unlimited gains.

The house, on the other hand, realizes that the individual gamblers have that perspective. The house has the other side. It knows that, with each gambler, it has a limited potential gain (the gambler's $300 loss limit) and an unlimited loss potential. Which side of that equation do you want to be on?

As for me, I want the probabilities for gain on my side. Any casino executive will tell you that probabilities are much more important than possibilities. And I'm satisfied making 15 to 20 percent a year as my "limited" upside, an upside I can make even when the market is flat.

It is actually option buyers that are taking all the risk, even though many writers suggest the contrary. Buying an option is like buying a lottery ticket. If you win, you win a lot, but the likelihood is that you will lose the entire investment. Many writers suggest that because your losses are limited to the amount you use to buy the option, this approach has less risk. At the same time they will tell you that you should use only a limited amount of your capital to buy options. Why, if this is so "less risky"? It's because it is not less risky. No one would suggest that you use your entire retirement account to buy lottery tickets, and no one in his or her right mind would suggest you use it to buy options. The reason is clear: Buying options is risky! To win when you buy an option, the stock must move in the right direction, enough to cover the option premium and do it in a timely fashion (before the option expires).

When you buy options, you can actually be right about the stock's direction and still lose money. In contrast, when you sell options, you can be wrong about a stock's direction and still make a nice profit. Which one of these approaches really sounds less risky? True, you're profit potential is less when you sell options, but your likelihood of success is extraordinarily higher.

So just call me a turtle, and I'll be happy watching my little gains while the gamblers keep buying my puts in hopes of a windfall. I always wanted to be the house. Now I am. And you can be too.

It's interesting to read what other authors write about options, especially the ones who are not experts in the field. For instance, I just finished reading a book about the stock market written by an attorney. Much of the book was accurate until she got to the part about options. Here are some of the things she said: (1) "Stockbrokers love options because they are so commission intensive." (2) "The term conservative does not properly describe any kind of option transaction." (3) "Covered calls are not necessarily conservative, you own the stock, and it can go down a lot further than the premium you received." (4) "Covered-call writing can be one of the stupidest investment strategies there is." (5) "Selling an option contract without owning the underlying security is one of the riskiest transactions you can make."

Well, let's analyze those statements one by one. Is option trading really "commission intensive"? Let's say you wanted to buy 1000 shares of stock. Obviously, the commission will vary dramatically depending on which broker you use. But it would not be difficult to find a broker who would make the trade for about a penny a share ($10). On the other hand, if you sold puts on 10 contracts of the same stock, which equals 1000 shares

Would You Rather Be the Gambler or the House?

Gambler	House
Limited loss:	**Unlimited loss:**
Gamblers show up with preset loss limit.	Gamblers could hit the jackpot and house must pay up.
Unlimited gains:	**Limited gains:**
They might hit the jackpot.	Gamblers show up with preset loss limit.
Low probability of gain:	**Low probability of loss:**
Most gamblers lose.	The house rarely loses.

since there are 100 shares in each contract, you would pay about $15. That equals about 1.5 cents per share. That doesn't look too commission intensive to me.

Next the author suggests that "conservative" does not properly describe option trading. I wonder to what criteria she applies the label "conservative"? I've always used conservative to mean "less risk." As I have previously mentioned, there are only two types of risk when it comes to the financial marketplace: severity and frequency. When you sell a put, you always lose less than if you bought the stock. And since the breakeven point is lower with put selling, you lose less often. True, as the author points out, you have limited your upside, but you always reduce your upside when choosing a more "conservative" approach. How could a strategy that reduces both the severity and frequency of losing be considered less conservative than buying stock?

According to our attorney-author, covered calls are "not necessarily" conservative. I'm not exactly sure what she means by "not necessarily" conservative. Maybe she isn't sure. And that would be a good thing because she can't be more wrong. In her book she says that it's risky because you own the stock and it can go down. I wonder what she thinks happens when you buy the stock and don't sell a covered call? If you don't sell the covered call, does that mean the stock won't go down? Hardly. If the stock goes down, by selling the covered call, you offset your loss. Offsetting your loss is the conservative, less risky approach. Sure, you cap your upside. But you always reduce your potential gain when you take a more conservative investment approach.

She then suggests that this strategy (covered-call writing) can be one of the stupidest investment strategies there is. Since covered calls and naked puts are almost identical approaches, I take issue with her opinion. So let's take a minute to see how stupid this strategy is. Let's assume that our goal is to earn 10 to 15 percent a year on our investments. Of course, we want to take the least risky approach to accomplishing that objective. We can't earn that type of return with bank CDs or safe government or corporate bonds. Consequently, we are relegated to some form of equity investing.

If we buy stocks, we are subject to losing money if they fall in price, and they must go up at least 10 to 15 percent every year to reach our goal. However, if we sell covered calls (or naked puts), our losses, if the stocks drop, will be reduced by the premium we receive. Since we recommend selling naked puts that are out of the money, we would also recommend selling in-the-money covered calls. For instance if XYZ were trading at $52, we would sell a covered call at $50. As a result, we would receive more premium since the option would have an intrinsic value of $2 in addition to its time value. In most cases, we would not lose any money unless the stock dropped over 15 to 20 percent. In addition, we would make our full anticipated profit of over 15 percent even if the stock were to stay level. So, in summary, by using the option strategy, we reduce our losses if the stock goes down, and we accomplish our goal if the stock stays flat, goes up, or even goes down a little. In contrast, if we buy the stock instead, we have no limit on our losses and we only make our goal if the stock goes up 10 to 15 percent. Which one of those strategies sounds stupid to you?

And last, our author suggests that selling naked options is the riskiest transaction of all. By now you know that you always lose less when you sell a naked put that you would lose if you bought the same stock. Someone must have told her that if you sell a naked put and the stock goes to zero, as Enron did, you will lose a lot of money. What they didn't tell her is that if she had sold an out-of-the-money naked put, she would have lost a lot of money minus what she received in premium and minus how far out of the money the strike price was and minus how much she received in interest on her cash collateral. If she had bought the stock instead, she would have lost a lot of money period—with no offset! Buying stock is much riskier than selling puts even if 500 authors say otherwise.

Another author who wrote a book teaching people about options wrote the following: (1) "One of the basic tenets of the option market is [that] purchasing long options is a limited risk endeavor." And (2), "Selling put options has unlimited risk." These statements certainly imply that the more conservative approach would be to buy options, not to sell them. And this is coming from a purported expert!

His first position is based on the theory that when you buy an option, you can lose only the amount of money you invest. That is true, but it's still 100 percent of your investment. Now if by that he means that you shouldn't or wouldn't invest all your money that way, the logical question then is: If this is such a nonrisky way to invest, why wouldn't you invest all your money this way? The answer: It is risky. Both the severity and frequency of losing is much higher with this approach. Consider that when you buy a call option, you profit only if the stock goes up and goes up within the time frame of the option. And further, it has to go up enough to cover the premium you paid for the option. If you paid $5 for a 1-year option on XYZ at a strike price of $50 when XYZ was currently trading at $48, XYZ would have to rise to over $55 before you make any money. And it would have to do it before the end of the year. You will lose money if the stock goes up only a little, stays flat, or goes down. Eighty percent of options expire worthless. The frequency of losing is significantly higher when you buy options. And the severity is worse since you lose 100 percent of your investment if the stock stays flat! How can an "expert" in options suggest that a basic tenet of the options market describes a "limited-risk endeavor" strategy as one that will result in you losing 100 percent of your investment if the stock stays level?

To make matters worse he describes naked-put selling as a strategy with "unlimited risk." One of the problems in his line of reasoning is that he fails to take into consideration probabilities. What are the odds that IBM will go to zero? It could happen, but the odds are low. That's why you should always properly diversify with any investment strategy.

And then I have a little problem with his term "unlimited risk." Since we always lose less when we sell puts than we lose when we buy stock, what kind of risk do we incur when we buy stock? Unlimited risk *plus*! The risk is always reduced when you sell puts by the amount of premium you receive and the amount for which you sell the put out of the money. Of course, as I previously stated, any strategy can be risky depending on how you implement it. If you sell highly leveraged, in-the-money naked puts with no hedge, you can lose a lot of money. And as many investors have experienced over the past few years, you can lose a lot of money investing in name-brand mutual funds like Janus.

And then there is my favorite book, which purports to teach people how the option market works. In this book, the author first describes buying options as a "conservative approach" and then says, "Writing uncovered options is always a dangerous strategy." I just can't quite understand what criteria these authors are using to define what is risky and what is conservative. Let's first take a look at this author's conservative approach.

The author suggests that buying options is conservative because your loss is limited to what you have invested. If that is the criterion for determining a conservative investment, then buying a lottery ticket would be a conservative investment. Or buying an interest in a space hotel limited partnership that does not require additional capital contributions would be a conservative investment. Or going to Las Vegas and playing roulette with a predetermined amount of money would be a conservative investment. None of these examples would be considered conservative investments and in fact, all would be considered very risky even though your loss would be limited to the amount you had invested. Of course, the author would argue, "You shouldn't invest a large portion of your assets in options." Once again, why not, if they are conservative? Shouldn't you invest a large portion of your assets in conservative investments? The reason you shouldn't: Buying options is risky!

Taking the converse of his argument, a risky investment is defined as one through which you can lose more than the amount you invested. Well, if you put 20 percent down on a house and borrow the rest, you could lose five times what you invested if your house ends up worth nothing. By his definition, this would be a risky investment because you could lose a lot more than you invested. Is buying a house really a risky investment? I don't think so. In fact, many financial planners suggest it should be the first investment you make.

Now what about the author's claim that selling naked puts is always a dangerous strategy. He must think buying stock is always a really dangerous strategy because by selling naked puts, all you are doing is promising to buy those stocks at a price lower than you would buy them today. If you sell a naked put today on IBM at a $65 strike price ($4 below its current price of $69) and receive a $7 premium, in effect, you are promising to buy IBM for $58 ($65 strike price minus the $7 premium received). If it is dangerous to promise to buy IBM for $58, how dangerous is it to actually buy it at today's price of $69? It would have to be at least $11 more dangerous. I don't care if you put up the entire $69 today or not. Whether you pay for the stock today or borrow money today to buy it, you will some day have to pay for it.

Again, all our critics would say that we have limited our upside by selling the put. And they are right, we do. But as long as the upside allows us to reach our financial goals, why should we take additional risk to make more? And even more importantly, we will achieve our financial goals more often because we can achieve them even if the stock stays flat or goes down a little, which is impossible to do when you buy stock or call options.

My suggestion: Use a conservative investment strategy that reduces your risk but allows you to accomplish your financial goals on the upside. Selling naked puts allows you to accomplish that even in a flat or slightly down market.

CHAPTER 13

Choose Your Own Risk Tolerance

More Risk, More Reward— The Choice Is Yours

By now you know that selling puts is less risky than buying stock. It's a mathematical certainty. The question becomes, How much less risky? And the answer depends on how you use the strategy. Like any investment approach, it can be used in a way that is less or more risky. You have to decide for yourself how much risk you want to assume. There are several factors that determine the amount of risk involved in using the SafetyNet Trading System. This chapter discusses and quantifies those risks. Remember, most people should take the least risky approach to accomplish their financial objective.

STOCK CHOICES

The first factor that impacts risk is the stocks on which you choose to sell puts. There are over 5000 stocks on which you can sell puts. Some have very high volatility and command very high premiums, while others have low volatility and provide relatively low premiums. Obviously, you increase your risk and potential reward by selling puts on volatile companies. You may want to revisit a Web site that shows options prices to compare different companies. By doing so, you will see that some puts (using no leverage) will produce annualized returns of over 30 percent, while others produce less than 10 percent returns.

STRIKE PRICES

The second factor impacting risk is what type of strike price you use. If you sell puts that are further out of the money, you will receive lower premiums. In other words, if there is less chance that the stock will be put to you, you will receive a lower premium. We know that the further you sell the put out of the money, the less chance the stock will be put to you. By taking the lower risk, you reduce the premium and the corresponding yield. One of the reasons so many people think selling puts is risky is that in the late 1980s, a lot of investors sold in-the-money puts, with no hedge, and lost their shirts as the market dropped precipitously. As I've said, it is possible to implement any strategy in a risky way. If you want to minimize your risk, you should sell puts that are further out of the money so that it is less likely that the stock will be put to you.

HEDGING

The third factor *impacting* risk involves the use of hedging. You will remember that with the SafetyNet Trading System, we take some of the premium we receive from selling puts on individual stocks and use it to buy puts on the entire market by purchasing index puts. The idea is that if the market drops and we lose money on the individual puts we sold, we will make money on the index puts we bought. The amount of risk varies depending on how much hedge we buy and how "tight" we buy it.

Typically, we buy an amount of index puts that equals the amount of equity puts we sold. If, for instance, we sold puts on $100,000 worth of individual stocks (calculated by multiplying the strike prices of the puts sold by the number of puts sold), we would purchase $100,000 worth of index puts. We can decrease our risk by actually buying more index puts than we sold in equity puts. This is something we may consider doing if we think the market is going to go down. Conversely, we increase our risk if we buy fewer index puts than we have sold in individual stock puts.

How tight we buy the index puts is an even more important factor when it comes to risk. Again, typically we reduce the strike price of the index puts we purchase by some factor that relates to how much premium we received when we sold the equity puts and how far out of the money the equity puts were sold. For example, if our average put premium received equaled 10 percent of the stock's current price and the average individual stock put was sold 15 percent out of the money, we might purchase index puts that were 25 percent out of the money since *theoretically* the market could fall 25 percent before we would lose any money. I emphasize the word "theoretically" because there is no perfect hedge. The stocks we sell puts on will never react, as a whole, exactly the same as any market index unless the entire market goes to zero. The difference between how our stocks react and the market reacts is called *dispersion*. If our stocks do better than the market, it is called *positive dispersion*, and if our stocks do worse, it is called *negative dispersion*.

To help offset the effects of potential negative dispersion, you may wish to buy index puts that are tighter. In other words, using our previous example, although you may be justified in purchasing index puts 25 percent out of the money because theoretically the market could fall 25 percent before you started losing money, you buy index puts that are just 18 percent out of the money in case there is negative dispersion. Purchasing the tighter insurance will cost more and reduce your overall portfolio profitability, but it will reduce the risk.

TIME FRAMES

The next factor that impacts risk is the length of the put sales. You reduce risk by selling puts that have a longer time frame because you receive a higher premium. This higher premium reduces the breakeven point and thus reduces the position's overall risk. Of course, as I have previously mentioned, an option premium declines exponentially; therefore, even though you receive higher premiums for selling longer-term puts, your annualized yield is actually lower. Conversely, you will increase your potential yield by selling shorter-term puts.

DIVERSIFICATION

Another factor that impacts risk is diversification. It is extremely important that you properly diversify your portfolio. By increasing the number of positions in your account, you reduce the negative impact of one stock going south forever. Imagine the impact of having 20 percent of your portfolio in WorldCom. But by properly diversifying your portfolio, you can minimize the effect of a poor pick. By the way, it is highly likely that you will sooner or later have a bad apple in your account, and minimizing its negative effect is important no matter which investment strategy you use.

LEVERAGE

The last factor that impacts risk is leverage. How many puts do you sell based on the size of your portfolio? Based on most brokerage firm margin requirements, you would be permitted to sell puts equal to over 400 percent of your starting capital. Margin requirements usually provide that you have cash collateral equal to 25 percent of the stock's current price plus 100 percent of the option's current premium minus the amount the position is out of the money, if any. For example, if you sold 5 contracts of XYZ company puts at a $50 strike price when the stock was trading at $52 and received a $3 premium your margin requirements would be calculated as follows:

> 5 contracts × 100 shares per contract = 500 shares
>
> 500 shares × $52 × 25% (margin requirement) = $6500
>
> $3 premium × 500 shares = $1500
>
> $52 current price − $50 strike price = $2 per share out of the money
>
> $2 per share out of the money × 500 shares = $1000
>
> $6500 (25 percent of stock value) + $1500 (current option premium) − $1000 (out of the money) = $7000 capital requirement

Since you would have received $1500 in premium, your beginning capital requirement would have been just $5500 to sell puts on $25,000 (500 shares times $50 strike price) worth of stock.

The real question, though, is not how much leverage you can employ but rather how much you should use. Throughout the book I have recommended using no more than 200 percent leverage. You would, of course, reduce your risk by using less. However, as long as you sell puts that are out of the money, sell long-term puts, properly diversify your portfolio, purchase an adequate insurance hedge, and do not use overly volatile stocks in your portfolio, I believe the use of up to 200 percent leverage is justified.

Some may suggest that using this amount of leverage actually increases your risk above that assumed by purchasing stocks without leverage; however, although that is theoretically correct, it does not take into account the probabilities that weigh in your favor by using this approach. For example, it does not consider the likelihood of your stocks going down past their breakeven point, usually 20 to 30 percent below their current prices. When you purchase stock, you begin losing money as soon as the stock drops just 1 percent, but with selling puts, it must go down substantially before you lose money. It also does not take into account the index put hedge. For you to lose more money using 200 percent leverage, a preponderance of your stocks would have to fall significantly at the same time the market was not falling. What are the probabilities of that happening, especially if you have limited your stock universe to truly great companies?

Obviously, these factors are not interdependent, so you can structure your portfolio by considering the amount of risk assumed by each. For instance, you may wish to sell puts on more volatile stocks because you feel that the technology sector is primed for a rebound, but you choose to use less leverage to offset the risk. You may choose to use more leverage, but purchase more insurance hedge to offset the increased leverage risk. Or you may not have enough capital to properly diversify your portfolio, so you reduce the risk on all the other factors to compensate for the reduced diversification. By changing the amount of risk you use, you can end up with a portfolio with little risk and the potential for 8 to 10 percent annual returns or one with a lot more risk but potential returns above 30 percent. The choice is yours, but remember, always take the least amount of risk necessary to accomplish your financial goals.

THE ROLLERCOASTER RISK FACTOR

One last risk factor that few investors consider is the impact a volatile market has on their portfolio over time. I can't even count the times during my 30 years in the financial services industry that I have heard the advice, "just buy and hold. The market will always come back." It is the mantra of the investment advisory world. And to be honest, with the exception of the current period, which may not have had a chance yet, it always has come back. The problem is how long it sometimes takes.

The "buy 'em hold 'em" crowd never tells you the historical record. Let's take a quick look at five modern-day bear markets starting with the Great Depression. It took the S&P 500 index 25 years to return to its September 1929 high. That's holding 'em for a really long time! In December 1968 the S&P 500 hit 106 before starting to fall. It didn't reach 106 again until March 1972. Then there was the bear market that began in January 1973 when the S&P 500 was at 118. It took over 7 years to get back to 118 in July 1980.

Two shorter-term bear markets took place in the 1980s. The S&P 500 was at 135 in November 1980, and it took 2 years to recover. In September 1987 the market took another 2-year hiatus. And, of course, we still haven't recovered from the S&P 500 fall from 1485, its high in August 2000. How long will we have to wait to get back there? Most analysts don't even have price targets that high for any time in the foreseeable future.

However, with the SafetyNet Trading System, it is possible to avoid the dips. How much more comfortable would it be not having to wait for the market to come back? More importantly, for those living off those assets, how essential is it not to have to withdraw assets when your portfolio is down in value? Table 13.1 shows the impact of investing in a rollercoaster market as opposed to investing in a strategy that provides limited but more consistent returns. In this example we have assumed that we find ourselves at retirement with \$1 million and that we need \$100,000 a year to live. The chart compares the results of these two different investment approaches—the more volatile investment strategy of buying stocks and the more consistent strategy of selling puts—that produce the same average annual return over time but in an entirely different manner.

In the first approach the investor rides the market roller-coaster and averages 12 percent a year but achieves that by earning 38 percent the first year and losing 14 percent the next. This pattern continues for the 20 years. In the second approach,

TABLE 13.1

Assumptions: Good Year Earnings, 38.00%. Bad Year Earnings, −14.00%. Average Earnings, 12.00%. Required Income, \$100,000.

Up and Down Returns		Year	Average Returns	
Beg Balance	End Balance		Beg Balance	End Balance
\$1,000,000	\$1,242,000	1	\$1,000,000	\$1,008,000
1,242,000	982,120	2	1,008,000	1,016,960
982,120	1,217,326	3	1,016,960	1,026,995
1,217,326	960,900	4	1,026,995	1,038,235
960,900	1,188,042	5	1,038,235	1,050,823
1,188,042	935,716	6	1,050,823	1,064,922
935,716	1,153,288	7	1,064,922	1,080,712
1,153,288	905,828	8	1,080,712	1,098,398
905,828	1,112,043	9	1,098,398	1,118,205
1,112,043	870,357	10	1,118,205	1,140,390
870,357	1,063,092	11	1,140,390	1,165,237
1,063,092	828,259	12	1,165,237	1,193,065
828,259	1,004,998	13	1,193,065	1,224,233
1,004,998	778,298	14	1,224,233	1,259,141
778,298	936,051	15	1,259,141	1,298,238
936,051	719,004	16	1,298,238	1,342,026
719,004	854,226	17	1,342,026	1,391,069
854,226	648,634	18	1,391,069	1,445,998
648,634	757,115	19	1,445,998	1,507,517
757,115	565,119	20	1,507,517	1,576,420

the investor utilizes a strategy that produces more consistent returns of 12 percent each year. As you can see, with both approaches the investor earns an average of 12 percent returns. (I have exaggerated the example in order to make the point clearer; however, the same result with less differential would occur with less exaggerated assumptions.)

As you can see by looking at the chart, by the end of the second year, the rollercoaster approach is already losing capital. It is down to $982,120, but because of the great returns in the third year, it is back up again to $1,217,326. However, like a stock that can't find long-term buyers, we keep getting lower highs and lower lows until by the end of the twentieth year, our capital has been reduced to only $565,119. Conversely, by achieving equal but consistent returns, our capital continues to grow each year until at the end of the twentieth year, we have $1,576,420. That is over a million dollars' difference even though the average returns were identical!

The point is that achieving consistent returns is almost as important as reducing overall risk in your portfolio, especially in years when you may be withdrawing funds for some purpose. That purpose may be for living expenses or, as we will be discussing later, to cover costs associated with some types of tax-favored investment vehicles.

14

Best Sources for Stock Research

The Internet Can Help You Be a Better Guesser

When it comes to stock research, the Internet has certainly leveled the playing field. No matter what you are looking for, you can find it there. In fact, I would go as far as to say that if you are investing your own money and you do not have access to the Internet, you should stop now! Not that I believe that any information you find will be definitive by itself as to the direction of the market or any particular stock, but the information should make you a better guesser. And that's all we can hope for in this crazy market.

So where do you look? There are a number of choices depending on what you are trying to find. One of the best sites is Morningstar.com. My favorite section of the Web site is its QuickTake Reports. The site provides access to analysts covering over 1000 stocks, and in this section you can get an entire overview of the company in just a couple of minutes. First, you get an overview of the company from the Morningstar staff. They don't have any axes to grind, so you get a straight dose of objectivity. They'll even admit when they've been wrong in previous forecasts. Then they point out the company's primary business strategy. Following that they provide a brief update on company management and a brief profile of the company's overall business. After the company profile they list the company's largest competitors and allow you to compare them from several different perspectives including, growth rates, valuation, and stock performance.

In addition, Morningstar provides you a summary of their take on the company's valuation, growth prospects, profitability, and overall financial health. Then they provide you their current stock price valuation along with links to current articles about the company. Last, they provide an unbiased analysis of what both bullish and bearish analysts say about the company and its future prospects. There is probably no other site that provides you such a quick summary of a company's current position and what the street is thinking about it.

If you want to delve into the details, the Morningstar Web site provides quick links to almost any kind of financial information you want. In their Morningstar Grades section you will find growth and profitability figures for the past 5 years including sales growth, earnings-per-share growth, book-value-per-share growth, and dividend growth. This section also provides a profitability analysis, including, the last 5 years' returns on assets and return-on-equity numbers. There's also a link to a summary financial statement with graphs and charts.

Another section worth looking at is their Ownership section. Here you can quickly see which institutions own the greatest percentage of the company, which mutual funds have made recent purchases, and whether the "insiders" are currently buying or selling the stock. I've listed my favorite sections, but the site has a lot more for those that have time to explore all its features. The site provides a great way to quickly get an overall feel for a company and its future prospects. On the downside, however, all this information is not free. At the time of this writing, Morningstar was charging $109 a year for access to their premium services. However, in my opinion, that's a small price to pay for their excellent compilation of information and objective analysis.

On the other hand, much of this information can be found free, if not as handily, on other Web sites. For example, at Quicken.com you can get all of a company's technical and fundamental data, insider trading activity, current news, and a brief company profile. Although not as in-depth and without the analysis, the information is free. For late-breaking news, CBSMarketwatch.com is a great site. The site also provides basic information about individual stocks and like most financial sites, allows you to establish your own portfolio. However, the information is more limited and less user friendly.

Another interesting site is Validea.com. The Web site is a database covering hundreds of analysts, market pundits, newsletter jockeys, and media figures. Each one has touted stocks through investment magazines, TV channels like CNBC, or well-known investor Web sites. Validea.com records each recommendation, then tracks how the stock does in the following weeks and months. Those results are combined, yielding average return figures for each expert. In addition, you can search the site for top-performing prognosticators over the last 12 months. The site also displays each expert's most recent stock selections, his or her most successful picks and biggest losers. Although hundreds of stock pundits are included, obviously not all are included in their listings. Validea covers only those recommendations that show up in nationally known media.

It's possible to customize your access to the site by weeding out stock pickers in high-risk fields, or you can get an early warning about stock touts who have poor records. You can also register for reports on new stock picks by your chosen specialists. There's also a daily update of new stock picks from all the experts, and you can start tracking how recommended stocks performed in the week after they were named. That might indicate which experts really impact stock prices. Like Morningstar, there is a charge for access to this information.

Obviously, this is just a short list of all the incredible research available via the Internet.

PART THREE

HISTORICAL EXAMPLES AND CURRENT TRADING OPPORTUNITIES

CHAPTER 15

History Doesn't Lie

Indisputable Proof That Investors Can Lower Their Risk

The best way to prove if something works or not is to use hindsight because hindsight is always 20/20. With that thought in mind, I decided to look back at five different times in 2000 and 2001 when the market had significant losses in a relatively short period of time. I wanted to verify that using our approach would indeed reduce or eliminate the losses associated with significant market drops.

The evidence is conclusive: Using the SafetyNet Trading System will significantly reduce losses in a down market. The charts in this chapter prove it, once and for all. The examples illustrate the use of short-term options even though longer-term options would be even more conservative.

The first period I evaluated started on November 7, 2000—Election Day, or rather as they call it in Florida, the beginning of election quarter! I chose this period because it demonstrates so well how little anybody really knows about the market. You probably remember what all the analysts, stock market pundits, and talking heads on CNBC were saying just before the election.

I remember three distinct reasons they gave for loading up on high-tech stocks. First, tech stocks had already been hammered and were due for a turnaround. Second, there is always a rally after a presidential election. And third, Alan Greenspan, Federal Reserve chairman, was about to reduce interest rates, which would have a positive impact on the market. Well, if you had taken their advice and bought a million dollars' worth of popular tech stocks on Election Day, 4 weeks later you would not have been happy. As you can see from the Table 15.1, you would have lost $195,811.

On the other hand, if you had sold puts on the exact same stocks, in the exact same amounts on the exact same days, you would have lost only $80,660. And if you had used some of the premiums to buy the appropriate amount of index puts, you would have made $78,780 on the index puts. Last, you would

TABLE 15.1

November 7 through December 4, 2000

Company	Stock Price, Nov. 7	Stock Price, Dec. 4	Total Loss on Puts	Loss If Bought Stock
MSFT	$69.00	$56.00	$ 8,455	$ 19,500
ORCL	28.00	26.25	−480	7,000
CSCO	55.25	46.25	5,500	18,000
JDSU	77.50	59.00	10,322	25,900
EMC	94.37	79.75	12,375	16,082
ALTR	33.12	27.94	825	17,094
MOT	24.50	18.37	17,415	27,585
TXN	47.12	40.37	3,948	14,175
PALM	61.00	44.50	13,300	31,350
NSM	24.00	19.75	9,000	19,125
Total			$80,660	$195,811

Index Puts	Index Price, Nov. 7	Index Price, Dec. 4	Total Gain on Puts	
QQQ	$83.00	$64.00	$78,780	
Interest earned			$5,403	
Net result			$3,523	Gain

have earned $5403 on the cash collateral for the positions, net-ting you $3523 in profit for the month.

History doesn't lie. Using the SafetyNet approach would have provided you a real safety net against a falling market.

A similar result occurred from February 8 to March 8, 2001. Using a fresh million dollars and the same tech stocks, you would have lost $204,475 in 1 month if you had **bought** the stocks (see Table 15.2). Conversely, with the SafetyNet System you would have lost only $82,264 on the individual stock puts, made $67,000 on the index puts, and offset that net loss with $4885 of interest on the cash collateral. The bottom line would have been a $10,379 loss instead of a $204,475 loss. Not perfect, but much better than buying the stock.

Once again, history proves my point from March 8 to April 3, 2001. Obviously, the market was already severely down or we

TABLE 15.2

February 8 through March 8, 2001

Company	Stock Price, Feb. 8	Stock Price, Mar. 8	Total Loss on Puts	Loss If Bought Stock
MSFT $62.12	$57.18	$ 1,200	$ 7,904	
ORCL 27.25	16.82	26,344	38,591	
CSCO 30.00	20.75	11,458	31,450	
JDSU 45.00	27.25	19,800	39,050	
EMC 59.75	35.35	26,571	41,480	
ALTR 27.00	26.37	−6,697	2,331	
MOT 19.88	15.75	6,222	21,063	
TXN 38.25	32.78	2,730	14,222	
PALM 22.06	20.00	−1,794	9,476	
NSM 23.75	24.01	−3,570	−1,092	
Total			$82,264	$204,475

Index Puts	Index Price, Feb. 8	Index Price, Mar. 8	Total Gain on Puts	
QQQ	$58.75	$45.85	$67,000	
Interest earned			$4,885	
Net result			**−$10,379**	**Loss**

TABLE 15.3

March 8 through April 3, 2001

Company	Stock Price, Mar. 8	Stock Price, Apr. 3	Total Loss on Puts	Loss If Bought Stock
MSFT	$57.18	$53.37	$ 1,566	$ 6,858
ORCL	16.82	13.25	8,520	21,420
CSCO	20.75	13.75	22,800	33,600
JDSU	27.25	14.16	36,815	48,433
EMC	35.35	25.10	12,740	28,700
ALTR	26.37	19.66	14,744	25,498
MOT	15.75	13.70	5,440	13,120
TXN	32.78	27.50	5,890	16,368
PALM	20.00	6.25	53,150	68,750
NSM	24.01	24.20	−3,570	−798
Total			$158,095	$261,949

Index Puts	Index Price, Mar. 8	Index Price, Apr. 3	Total Gain on Puts
QQQ	$45.85	$34.66	$132,500
Interest earned			$4,890
Net result			**−$20,705** Loss

would not have had such a big loss for the prior period just evaluated. This market has to be at the bottom by now.

Not yet. Using a fresh million dollars and buying the same 10 stocks, we lose $261,949 in 4 weeks. But, as you can see, with the SafetyNet Trading System (see Table 15.3) we lose only $20,705. As we always say, there is no perfect hedge, but an imperfect one is much better than none at all.

The next period we examined was right before the World Trade Center disaster. From August 7 to September 6, 2001, you would have lost $251,604 in 1 month buying the same 10 stocks. In contrast, using the SafetyNet Trading System, you would have lost only $32,694 (see Table 15.4).

And the last period I looked at was right after the attack on the World Trade Center. I had to stop using PALM as one of the stocks because there were no option premiums available, so

TABLE 15.4

August 7 through September 6, 2001

Company	Stock Price, Aug. 7	Stock Price, Sept. 6	Total Loss on Puts	Loss If Bought Stock
MSFT	$66.30	$56.02	$ 8,804	$ 15,934
ORCL	17.25	10.92	22,214	36,714
CSCO	19.29	14.40	12,480	25,428
JDSU	9.62	6.25	10,920	35,048
EMC	19.58	13.88	15,912	29,070
ALTR	31.50	26.98	3,104	14,464
MOT	18.58	13.94	13,284	25,056
TXN	36.00	29.50	8,260	18,200
PALM	5.25	3.00	25,650	42,750
NSM	33.50	30.52	−2,700	8,940
Total			$117,928	$251,604

Index Puts	Index Price, Aug. 7	Index Price, Sept. 6	Total Gain on Puts	
QQQ	$42.35	$33.90	$80,400	
Interest earned			$4,834	
Net result			**−$32,694**	**Loss**

we divided the million-dollar investment among the remaining 9 stocks. In the 2 weeks following the disaster, the stock buyer lost $203,713. The SafetyNet investor lost only $3894 (see Table 15.5).

The preceding examples assume that in each period we started fresh with a new million dollars. However, if the investor had continued to reduce the pot by the prior period losses, he or she would have ended up with about $279,000 of the original $1 million investment. The SafetyNet investor would have ended up with over $935,000. This analysis was performed during a time that the Nasdaq-100 Composite Index fell around 65 percent. You might be saying, "Yes, but you looked at only down markets."

That's right, because we are trying to prove that this approach reduces risk. However, if the market and these stocks

TABLE 15.5

September 6 through September 21, 2001

Company	Stock Price, Sept. 6	Stock Price, Sept. 21	Total Loss on Puts	Loss If Bought Stock
MSFT	$56.02	$49.71	$ 6,688	$ 13,882
ORCL	10.92	10.78	−6,630	1,428
CSCO	14.40	12.09	−2,639	21,021
JDSU	6.25	5.36	−9,225	18,245
EMC	13.88	11.15	4,455	27,027
ALTR	26.98	17.92	35,563	55,266
MOT	13.94	14.88	−4,440	−6,956
TXN	29.50	23.00	16,320	31,200
PALM	3.00	1.77	0	0
NSM	30.52	22.00	31,250	42,600
Total			$72,342	$203,713

Index Puts	Index Price, Sept. 6	Index Price, Sept. 21	Total Gain on Puts	
QQQ	$33.90	$28.19	$63,504	
Interest earned			$3,944	
Net result			−**$3,894**	**Loss**

had just remained level, the SafetyNet strategy would have produced over 30 percent annualized gains. The stock buyer makes **no** profit unless his or her stocks go up.

Of course, had the market had a splendid recovery, the stock buyer may very well have done better, but at what risk? If your financial goals are to earn 10 to 15 percent a year, why take the additional risk associated with buying stocks and traditional mutual funds when you can achieve those goals with a lot less risk?

CHAPTER 16

Examples from Today's Market
The Truth Never Changes

In this chapter we will establish a small sample portfolio based on the closing numbers on July 19, 2002. We'll go through the entire process of picking stocks to sell puts on, and then we'll purchase index puts to insure the portfolio from a further fall in the market. We would, of course, usually place 25 to 30 positions for a portfolio, but for purposes of illustration we will establish just 10 positions. Each example shown will also compare selling puts (with an expiration out about 6 months) to buying the same stock. We will provide a summary page for each example, which contains a 1-year chart of the stock in the lower left-hand corner. Above the stock chart is a minispreadsheet that shows the financial results of the trade given different price movements of the underlying stock.

The first column in the spreadsheet represents the ultimate stock price. In other words, it lists the various prices at which the stock may end up trading at on the option expiration date. In the middle of the first column is the stock's price at the inception of the position. That price is then increased and decreased in 5 percent increments up and down the column. Columns 2 through 5 show the potential results based on the various stock prices depending on whether stocks are bought or puts are sold.

Column 2 shows how much a stock buyer would make or lose in dollars per share as the stock price goes up or down. Column 3 shows the annualized profit percentage based on the gains or losses when buying the stock.

Column 4 shows the dollar amount per share that an investor who sold a put would make, based on the ultimate stock price. In these examples we have sold 2 puts for every dollar of stock we would have purchased, and we have assumed a 2.5 percent interest rate on the cash collateral and premium received.

Column 5 shows the annualized percentage gain or loss based on selling the puts.

To the right of the spreadsheet is a graph that illustrates and compares the potential annualized percentage gain or loss of the two strategies based on the varying ultimate stock prices.

As you will see, selling puts can easily achieve the desired financial goals of most investors with significantly less risk. We will use the following assumptions for our portfolio: (1) We will start with $200,000 in cash, (2) we will use 200 percent leverage, which means we will sell puts on $400,000 worth of stock (based on the selected strike price), and (3) we will earn 2.5 percent interest on our cash. After taking our put positions, we will analyze the composite positions and purchase index puts as a hedge based on reducing the current index strike price by 100 percent of the out-of-the-money delta and 75 percent of the premium we received. In other words, when we decide what strike price to use when we buy the index puts, we will arrive at the strike price by reducing the current index price by the amount, on average, that the put positions we sold were out of the money and 75 percent of the average premium we received when we sold the equity puts.

I will begin each portfolio position with a brief commentary about the stock, and at times may quote various analysts. The quoted analysts' opinions are not meant to imply that I trust without question the analysts' recommendations or points of view. Rather, the opinions are mentioned to give you some idea of the street's prevailing view of the stock.

Okay, let's put together our own portfolio. As I have previously stated, I restrict my universe of stocks to large-cap industry leaders. So I'll start with one of the largest: General Electric (GE).

GENERAL ELECTRIC

This company encompasses a broad array of industries. It manufactures aircraft engines, trains and other transportation equipment, appliances (kitchen and laundry equipment), lighting, generators and turbines, nuclear reactors, medical imaging equipment, electric distribution and control equipment, and plastics. Its financial division, GE Capital Services, accounts for about 50 percent of the company's sales, and it is one of the largest financial services companies in the United States. It also owns the NBC television network.

Along with the rest of the market, GE took a bath during 2002. On July 19, 2002, it closed at $26.52 a share (see Figure 16.1). That represents about a 35 percent drop in just 4 months. Part of the problem seems to be a carryover from the mess at Tyco (TYC). Accounting concerns with conglomerates like TYC have spread over the market. And corporate governance issues smack down one stock after another. It was recently reported that GE owns four apartments in the Trump International Hotel & Tower in New York City. GE admitted that one of the apartments, for which it paid over $2 million, is used by the NBC chairman and CEO, Robert Wright, and his wife, and that Mr. Wright is not obligated to declare the value of the apartment home on his income taxes. This type of news, which should in my opinion have little effect on the stock's price, tends to be exaggerated in this jittery market.

GE is currently trading at a price-earnings (P/E) ratio of just 18.14, well below the S&P average. It has a PEG ratio of just 1.2, very respectable for a mature company. And its dividend yield is about 2.4 percent, exceeding the rates available from short-term Treasuries. GE was quick to lower its cost structure and lighten inventories in response to a global economic slowdown. The result has been higher profit margins on smaller sales volume. According to Morgan Stanley research, the company is trading below its historical averages and below the average S&P 500 company for the first time since 1993. Morgan Stanley's 1-year price to target for GE is $36. Morningstar, which also has a bullish call on GE, has a $34 value on the shares. GE is also one of only nine U.S. firms that have a AAA credit rating. All of these factors lead me to the conclusion that GE is a good candidate for a put sale, so let's take a look at the available premium.

The option premium for a put with a strike price of $25 and a January 2003 expiration date is $2.55 per share. When you take into account the interest earned on the cash collateral and the premium, the breakeven price for the position is $22.31, or almost 16 percent below its current price. In other words, GE could drop another 16 percent and you wouldn't lose any money on this trade. In fact, GE could drop 5.7 percent and it would not be put to you, meaning you would keep the entire $2.55 premium as profit. Selling the put, of course, would be much safer than buying the stock, since the breakeven price is 16 percent lower. And even though this position is much safer, it still yields over 43 percent in annualized profit. You could reach your goal by taking an even safer position by selling a $20 strike price on GE. That would still produce an annualized yield of over 24 percent while protecting you against a loss if the stock drops 29 percent to $18.81. Because I feel especially confident that GE, even if it drops below $25, will eventually recover to at least that price, I would sell the $25 strike price put.

The next question is, How many puts should we sell? Based on our original assumptions and the desire to diversify this portfolio among 10 positions, we should sell 16 contracts. As a result, we will add $4080 to our portfolio ($2.55 premium times 16 contracts times 100 shares per contract). Figure 16.1 illustrates and summarizes the trade and compares it to buying the stock outright.

As you can see from Figure 16.1, your potential gain is much larger if you buy the stock. However, you still make over 43 percent by selling the puts, and at the same time, you dramatically reduce your downside risk. You will note that by using 200 percent leverage with your put sales, it is possible to lose more money selling the puts than buying the stock if GE falls

FIGURE 16.1

Company: GE
Gain or Loss

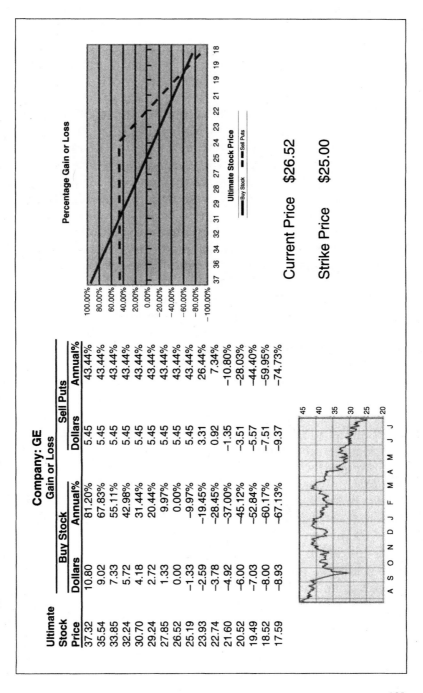

Ultimate Stock Price	Buy Stock		Sell Puts	
	Dollars	Annual%	Dollars	Annual%
37.32	10.80	81.20%	5.45	43.44%
35.54	9.02	67.83%	5.45	43.44%
33.85	7.33	55.11%	5.45	43.44%
32.24	5.72	42.98%	5.45	43.44%
30.70	4.18	31.44%	5.45	43.44%
29.24	2.72	20.44%	5.45	43.44%
27.85	1.33	9.97%	5.45	43.44%
26.52	0.00	0.00%	5.45	43.44%
25.19	-1.33	-9.97%	5.45	43.44%
23.93	-2.59	-19.45%	3.31	26.44%
22.74	-3.78	-28.45%	0.92	7.34%
21.60	-4.92	-37.00%	-1.35	-10.80%
20.52	-6.00	-45.12%	-3.51	-28.03%
19.49	-7.03	-52.84%	-5.57	-44.40%
18.52	-8.00	-60.17%	-7.51	-59.95%
17.59	-8.93	-67.13%	-9.37	-74.73%

Percentage Gain or Loss

Ultimate Stock Price
— Buy Stock   ■ ■ Sell Puts

Current Price $26.52

Strike Price $25.00

and stays below $18 a share. That, of course, assumes that you would not have used leverage when buying the stock.

AMGEN

The next stock we'll add to our portfolio is Amgen (AMGN). Amgen, the country's largest biotech firm, recently purchased Immunex, the maker of leukemia and rheumatoid arthritis medications. Prior to its Immunex purchase, Amgen's primary drugs were Epogen, an antianemia drug, and Neupogen, a white blood cell immune system stimulator. These two drugs accounted for about 90 percent of its sales. However, there appears to remain a strong, growing market for these drugs. In addition, Amgen has a strong pipeline of additional drugs to exploit in the coming years, including discoveries as a result of stem cell research and its recently approved anemia drug—Aranesp. According to Morgan Stanley research, sales of Aranesp should grow to $2.9 billion by 2006.

The company operates commercial manufacturing facilities located in the United States and Puerto Rico, and a packaging and distribution center in The Netherlands. A sales and marketing force is maintained in the United States, the European Union, Canada, Australia, and New Zealand. In addition, Amgen has entered into licensing and/or copromotion agreements to market certain of its products including Epogen, Neupogen, and Aranesp in other geographic areas.

Amgen has strong institutional support since 61 percent of its outstanding shares are held by large institutions or mutual funds. In spite of this, like most other stocks, it has been hammered. (See Figure 16.2.) It is currently trading at $35.46, more than 74 percent off its high, and Morgan Stanley has a 1-year price target on the stock of $75, over double its current price. The company trades at a relatively high 33.2 price-earnings ratio, but not unusually high for a biotech stock.

Amgen's ability to successfully raise $2.5 billion in convertible notes in February 2002, second in size only to Ford's $5 billion offering in 2001, further validates analysts' belief that it will generate plenty of cash flow. In addition, Standard & Poor's recently upgraded Amgen's credit rating to A plus, an unusual

Company: AMGN

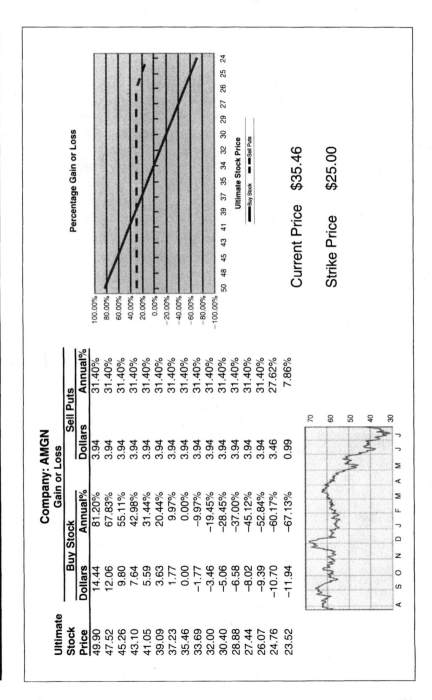

Ultimate Stock Price	Buy Stock		Sell Puts	
	Gain or Loss			
	Dollars	Annual%	Dollars	Annual%
49.90	14.44	81.20%	3.94	31.40%
47.52	12.06	67.83%	3.94	31.40%
45.26	9.80	55.11%	3.94	31.40%
43.10	7.64	42.98%	3.94	31.40%
41.05	5.59	31.44%	3.94	31.40%
39.09	3.63	20.44%	3.94	31.40%
37.23	1.77	9.97%	3.94	31.40%
35.46	0.00	0.00%	3.94	31.40%
33.69	−1.77	−9.97%	3.94	31.40%
32.00	−3.46	−19.45%	3.94	31.40%
30.40	−5.06	−28.45%	3.94	31.40%
28.88	−6.58	−37.00%	3.94	31.40%
27.44	−8.02	−45.12%	3.94	31.40%
26.07	−9.39	−52.84%	3.94	31.40%
24.76	−10.70	−60.17%	3.94	31.40%
23.52	−11.94	−67.13%	3.46	27.62%
			0.99	7.86%

Current Price $35.46

Strike Price $25.00

step these days among all the other credit downgrades. In doing so, they said, "The ratings and outlook reflect Standard & Poor's assumption that Amgen will not experience any significant issues in its merger with Immunex and that manufacturing capacity constraints, which have limited Enbrel's sales growth, will be resolved quickly. The significant cash balances and strong cash flow prospects also provide Amgen with adequate financial flexibility to conduct significant periodic share repurchases."

Based on the current high volatility in the stock, we can take a significantly out-of-the-money position and still receive a high yield. Based on a $25 strike price, we can receive a $1.80 premium for selling January 2003 puts. That results in an annualized yield, as long as the stock stays above $25, of 31.4 percent. That means that the stock can go down another 29 percent and we will still make a 33 percent annualized gain. Our breakeven price for this trade is $23.02, which means the stock can fall over 35 percent before we would incur a loss, even though Morningstar's current valuation of the company is $55 per share. Based on our diversification requirement, we will sell 16 contracts of the January 2003 AMGN puts. This sale will add $2880 ($1.80 premium × 16 contracts × 100 shares per contract) to our portfolio.

As you can see from Figure 16.2, your potential gain is much larger if you buy the stock. However, you still make over 31 percent by selling the puts and at the same time, dramatically reduce your downside risk.

AOL TIME WARNER

For our next position we'll look at a stock that is substantially out of favor with the market but retains significant assets and important franchises—AOL Time Warner. This company reflects the merger of Internet giant AOL and entertainment conglomerate Time Warner. The combined companies hold major franchises in the Internet and entertainment world, including its flagship America Online Internet service, CompuServe, Netscape, major film and TV studios, and cable networks such as CNN, TCM, and TNT. Unfortunately, the market has not treated this marriage kindly. The stock has fallen almost 72 percent since the merger. It appears the combined companies have not yet effectively found a way to capitalize on their apparent synergies. However, a recent reshuffling of executives has made some analysts more confident in their future.

For example, Blaylock & Partners' equity analysts John Tinker and Mark Zadell have raised their stock rating for AOL Time Warner to "buy" from "hold" and set a target price of $21 per common share. The upgraded recommendation reflected the analysts' confidence in the executive management changes that they believe will positively impact declining profitability in the AOL division as well as remedy AOL's lack of integration to date with stronger Time Warner divisions. Another key factor cited for the favorable stock rating is the anticipated 30 percent annual growth of free cash flow per share between 2002 and 2004.

In a July 2002 *Multichannel News* article, Tinker said, "Promoting Time Warner executives Don Logan and Jeff Bewkes to Chairman of the Media & Communications Group and Entertainment & Media Group, respectively, will result in a stronger penetration of content from the company's other divisions into the AOL network. Such changes would enable the company to better leverage its assets and enhance the appeal of AOL across other possible distribution channels. Now that the Time Warner folks have effectively wrestled back control of the company, we expect less negative publicity and more of a focus on the managing of the businesses."

Although the company has reported current losses, partly as a result of restructuring costs, its first-year projected earnings will result in the company's stock trading at a 14.2 price-earnings ratio. More importantly, the company is currently trading at steep discount to its book value. The current book value per share is over $22 compared to its current stock price of $11.58. It also has strong institutional support with over 59 percent of its outstanding shares being held by large institutions. Morgan Stanley research has a 1-year price target on the company of $30.

Once again, the current high volatility provides us an excellent put selling opportunity. (See Figure 16.3.) By selling a

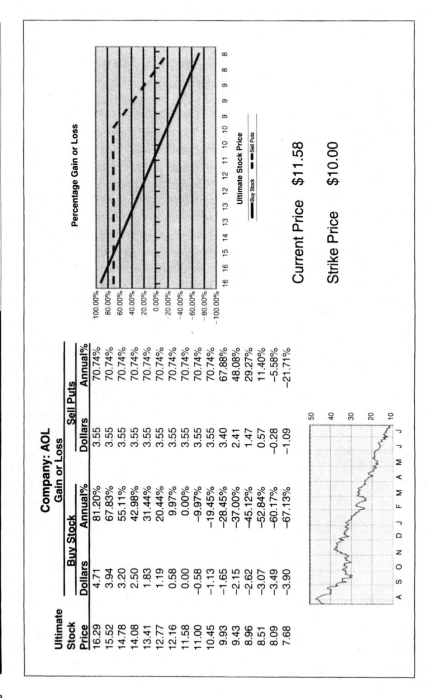

FIGURE 16.3

Company: AOL
Gain or Loss

Ultimate Stock Price	Buy Stock		Sell Puts	
	Dollars	Annual%	Dollars	Annual%
16.29	4.71	81.20%	3.55	70.74%
15.52	3.94	67.83%	3.55	70.74%
14.78	3.20	55.11%	3.55	70.74%
14.08	2.50	42.98%	3.55	70.74%
13.41	1.83	31.44%	3.55	70.74%
12.77	1.19	20.44%	3.55	70.74%
12.16	0.58	9.97%	3.55	70.74%
11.58	0.00	0.00%	3.55	70.74%
11.00	−0.58	−9.97%	3.55	70.74%
10.45	−1.13	−19.45%	3.55	70.74%
9.93	−1.65	−28.45%	3.40	67.88%
9.43	−2.15	−37.00%	2.41	48.08%
8.96	−2.62	−45.12%	1.47	29.27%
8.51	−3.07	−52.84%	0.57	11.40%
8.09	−3.49	−60.17%	−0.28	−5.58%
7.68	−3.90	−67.13%	−1.09	−21.71%

Percentage Gain or Loss

Current Price $11.58

Strike Price $10.00

put with a $10 strike price and a January 2003 expiration date, we will receive a $1.70 premium per share. That computes to a whopping annualized yield of 70.74 percent! That yield will be achieved even if AOL drops in price another 13 percent to $10. In other words, we can be wrong in our thinking that AOL will go up in price and still make over 72 percent annualized profit even if the stock ends up going down 13 percent. In addition, based on this trade, we will not lose money unless AOL ends up trading below $8.22, a 29 percent drop in price and well below analysts price targets, including Morningstar's conservative $13 per share valuation. Based on our diversification requirement, we will sell 40 contracts of the January 2003 AOL puts. This sale will add $6800 ($1.70 premium × 40 contracts × 100 shares per contract) to our portfolio.

INTERNATIONAL BUSINESS MACHINES

Our next company will be the software and hardware behemoth IBM. In addition to manufacturing hardware and software, the company also provides financing services in support of its computer business. The company's major operations comprise a global services division, three hardware product divisions, and a software division.

The global services segment provides supporting computer hardware and software products and professional services to help customers realize the full value of their information technology (IT) department. The division provides value through three primary lines of business: strategic outsourcing services, business intelligence services (BIS), and integrated technology services. Strategic outsourcing services creates business value through long-term strategic partnerships with customers, by taking on the responsibility for their processes and systems. BIS provides business and industry consulting and end-to-end e-business implementation of such offerings as supply chain management, customer relationship management, enterprise resource planning and business intelligence. Integrated technology services offers customers a single source with which to manage multivendor IT systems' complexity in an e-business environment including such traditional offerings as product support, business recovery services, site and connectivity services, and systems management and networking services.

The hardware division produces multipurpose computer servers that operate many open-network-based applications simultaneously for multiple users. They perform high-volume transaction processing and serve data to personal systems and other end-user devices. This segment also includes system-level product businesses such as the company's disk storage products.

The software division delivers operating systems for the company's servers and e-business enabling software for IBM and non-IBM platforms. In addition to its own development, product, and marketing effort, the segment supports 56,000 business partners to ensure that the company's software and hardware offerings are included in their solutions. Licensing and maintenance agreements provide a major source of ongoing revenue for the company.

IBM offers its products through its global sales and distribution organizations and also offers its products through a variety of third-party distributors and resellers. The company operates in more than 150 countries worldwide and derives more than half of its revenues from sales outside the United States.

Like most technology-based companies, IBM has been laying off employees and cutting costs to improve its bottom line. However, unlike many technology companies, it is actually making money. (See Figure 16.4.) The company is currently trading at a 22.81 price-earnings ratio, and based on the average earnings estimate for next year, it would be trading at a P/E of about 17. In spite of relatively strong earnings, the company has not avoided the recent sell-off. The stock is currently trading at $72 a share, 40 percent off its highs of the year. As you might expect, IBM has institutional support with over 53 percent of its shares held by large institutions, but with this lower percentage there is a potential for additional buying by those institutions as IBM's prospects improve.

We can sell puts on IBM with a strike price all the way down to $60 and still receive a $3.60 premium. That computes to a 27.13 percent annualized return. We will earn that return even if IBM falls another 16.7 percent to $60 (our proposed

FIGURE 16.4

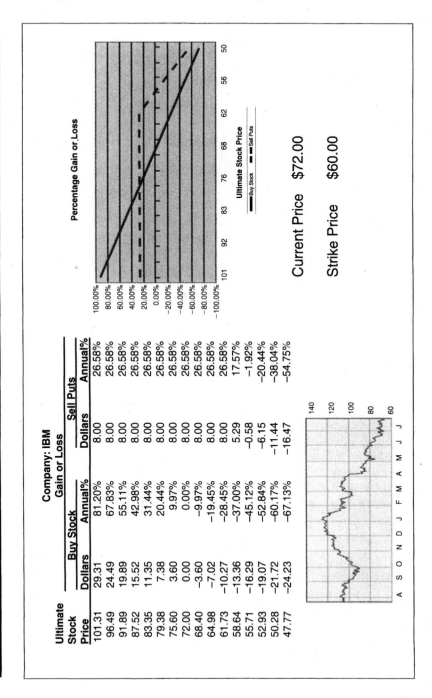

Company: IBM
Gain or Loss

Ultimate Stock Price	Buy Stock		Sell Puts	
	Dollars	Annual%	Dollars	Annual%
101.31	29.31	81.20%	8.00	26.58%
96.49	24.49	67.83%	8.00	26.58%
91.89	19.89	55.11%	8.00	26.58%
87.52	15.52	42.98%	8.00	26.58%
83.35	11.35	31.44%	8.00	26.58%
79.38	7.38	20.44%	8.00	26.58%
75.60	3.60	9.97%	8.00	26.58%
72.00	0.00	0.00%	8.00	26.58%
68.40	-3.60	-9.97%	8.00	26.58%
64.98	-7.02	-19.45%	8.00	26.58%
61.73	-10.27	-28.45%	8.00	26.58%
58.64	-13.36	-37.00%	5.29	17.57%
55.71	-16.29	-45.12%	-0.58	-1.92%
52.93	-19.07	-52.84%	-6.15	-20.44%
50.28	-21.72	-60.17%	-11.44	-38.04%
47.77	-24.23	-67.13%	-16.47	-54.75%

Percentage Gain or Loss

Ultimate Stock Price
— Buy Stock ▪▪ Sell Puts

Current Price $72.00

Strike Price $60.00

191

strike price). More importantly, we will not lose money on this trade unless IBM falls over 22 percent, to below $56. Based on our diversification requirements, we will sell 6 put contracts on IBM. This sale will add $2160 ($3.60 premium × 6 contracts × 100 shares per contract) to our portfolio.

WAL-MART

Our next company is Wal-Mart (WMT). Wal-Mart Stores, Inc., which incorporated in October 1969, operates mass-merchandising stores. The company operates 1647 discount stores, 1066 supercenters, 500 SAM'S CLUBs, and 31 neighborhood markets in the United States. Internationally, the company operates stores in Argentina (11), Brazil (22), Canada (196), Germany (95), South Korea (9), Mexico (551), Puerto Rico (17), and the United Kingdom (250), and, under joint-venture agreements, manages 19 stores in China. The company operates through three separate business divisions, the Wal-Mart Stores division, the SAM'S CLUB division, and the International division. Last year, the company officially overtook ExxonMobil as the largest company in the world based on sales. Total revenue for the year rose 13.7 percent on square-footage growth of 10.5 percent, which indicates that Wal-Mart is continuing to boost returns on invested capital. Comparable-store sales for the year rose 6.6 percent, which shows that shoppers like what they see and keep coming back for more.

Wal-Mart discount stores and the general merchandise area of the supercenters offer a wide variety of merchandise, including apparel for women, girls, men, boys, and infants. Each store also carries domestics, fabrics and notions, stationery and books, shoes, housewares, hardware, electronics, home furnishings, small appliances, automotive accessories, horticulture supplies and accessories, sporting goods, toys, pet food and accessories, cameras and supplies, health and beauty aids, pharmaceuticals, and jewelry. In addition, the stores offer an assortment of grocery merchandise, with the grocery assortment in the supercenters being broader, including meat, produce, deli, bakery, dairy, frozen foods, and dry grocery. The company markets lines of merchandise under private-label brands, including SAM's American Choice, One Source, Great Value, Ol' Roy, Puritan, and Equate. The company also markets lines of merchandise under licensed brands, some of which include Faded Glory, General Electric, Stanley, White Stag, Catalina, and McKids.

Wal-Mart operates SAM'S CLUBs in 48 states. The average size of a SAM'S CLUB is approximately 123,558 square feet. SAM'S CLUBs offer bulk displays of name-brand hard-goods merchandise, some soft goods and institutional-size grocery items, and selected items under the Member's Mark store brand. Generally, each SAM'S CLUB also carries software, electronic goods, jewelry, sporting goods, toys, tires, stationery, and books. Most clubs have fresh-food departments, which include bakery, meat, and produce. In addition, some clubs offer 1-hour photo services, embroidery departments, pharmaceuticals, optical departments, and gas stations.

The company's international segment comprises its operations through wholly owned subsidiaries in various countries. The merchandising strategy for the international operating segment is similar to that of domestic segments. While brand-name merchandise accounts for a majority of sales, several store brands not found in the United States have been developed to serve customers in the different markets in which the international division operates.

The recent bankruptcy filing of Kmart, a key competitor, should improve Wal-Mart's position since many of its stores overlap with Kmart. This should improve same-store sales and help increase gross profit margins with less competitive pressures.

Many retailers, until recently, have performed well in this tough market. In fact, the consumer has been the one bright spot in this economic decline. However, recent consumer spending and sentiment numbers have suggested that the average consumer may finally be curtailing his or her robust spending. As a result, retail stocks have also hit the skids. Even industry leader Wal-Mart, which recently announced higher quarter- and full-year earnings estimates, has not avoided the deluge. Its stock price has dropped $12 in the last month to $46.50. (See Figure 16.5.)

FIGURE 16.5

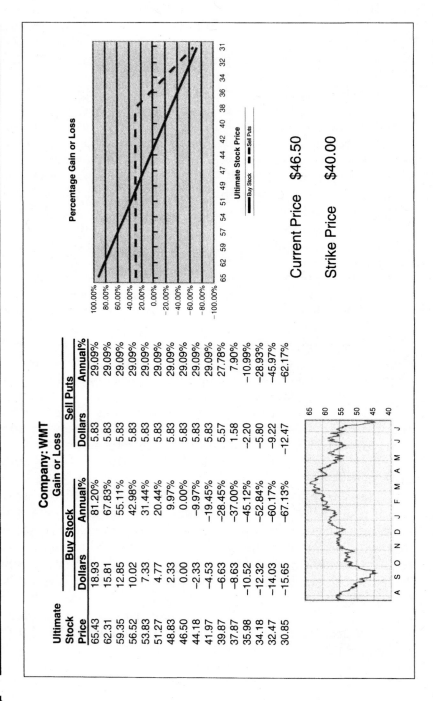

Company: WMT
Gain or Loss

Ultimate Stock Price	Buy Stock		Sell Puts	
	Dollars	Annual%	Dollars	Annual%
65.43	18.93	81.20%	5.83	29.09%
62.31	15.81	67.83%	5.83	29.09%
59.35	12.85	55.11%	5.83	29.09%
56.52	10.02	42.98%	5.83	29.09%
53.83	7.33	31.44%	5.83	29.09%
51.27	4.77	20.44%	5.83	29.09%
48.83	2.33	9.97%	5.83	29.09%
46.50	0.00	0.00%	5.83	29.09%
44.18	−2.33	−9.97%	5.83	29.09%
41.97	−4.53	−19.45%	5.83	29.09%
39.87	−6.63	−28.45%	5.57	27.78%
37.87	−8.63	−37.00%	1.58	7.90%
35.98	−10.52	−45.12%	−2.20	−10.99%
34.18	−12.32	−52.84%	−5.80	−28.93%
32.47	−14.03	−60.17%	−9.22	−45.97%
30.85	−15.65	−67.13%	−12.47	−62.17%

Percentage Gain or Loss

Ultimate Stock Price

Buy Stock   Sell Puts

Current Price $46.50

Strike Price $40.00

Although it still trades at a healthy 30 price-earnings ratio, the company has traditionally traded at high multiples because (1) it consistently makes money, (2) it pays a dividend, (3) it has significant growth, and (4) investors are willing to pay a premium for quality. For the last 3 years the company has traded between the low 40s and the high 60s. At its current price, it is a good candidate for our portfolio, especially if we sell puts with a strike price at $40, a price Wal-Mart hasn't fallen below in the last 3 years.

Morgan Stanley research calls Wal-Mart a "core holding," and it has established a 1-year price target for the stock at $70. Morningstar also sees Wal-Mart as a core-holding and has a current valuation on the stock of $60.

The January 2003 put, at a $40 strike price, provides us a $2.65 premium. That works out to a 29 percent annualized return—return we will realize as long as Wal-Mart doesn't fall and stay down more than 14 percent. Our breakeven price on this trade is $37.07, a full 20 percent below the stock's current price. Based on our diversification requirements, we will sell 10 put contracts on Wal-Mart. This sale will add $2650 ($2.65 premium × 10 contracts × 100 shares per contract) to our portfolio.

MORGAN STANLEY

Our next portfolio candidate is Morgan Stanley (MWD). Morgan Stanley, until recently known as Morgan Stanley Dean Witter & Co., is a global financial services firm that maintains market positions in three business divisions: securities, investment management, and credit services. Morgan Stanley operates its security business through approximately 550 securities branch offices around the world. The company also has total assets of $459 billion under management or supervision. It has approximately 45.7 million general-purpose credit card accounts, primarily under the Discover Card franchise.

The company's securities business includes investment banking, which includes securities underwriting and distribution, and financial advisory services, which includes advice on mergers and acquisitions, restructurings, real estate, and project finance. The securities business also includes financing and investing and financial advisory services for high-net-worth clients and other businesses, including aircraft financing activities.

The company's investment management business segment includes global asset management products and services for individual and institutional investors. Morgan Stanley has three principal distribution channels for asset management products and services: Morgan Stanley's financial advisors and investment representatives; a nonproprietary channel consisting of third-party broker-dealers, banks, financial planners, and other intermediaries; and Morgan Stanley's institutional channel.

The company provides worldwide financial advisory and capital-raising services to a diverse group of domestic and international corporate clients, primarily through Morgan Stanley & Co., Incorporated, Morgan Stanley & Co. International Limited, Morgan Stanley Japan Limited, and Morgan Stanley Dean Witter Asia Limited. These subsidiaries conduct sales and trading activities worldwide, as principal and agent, and provide related financing services on behalf of institutional investors.

Morgan Stanley manages and participates in public offerings and private placements of debt, equity, and other securities worldwide. The company is an underwriter of common stock, preferred stock, and other equity-related securities, including convertible securities. Morgan Stanley is also an underwriter of fixed income securities, including investment-grade debt, high-yield securities (debt issued by non-investment-grade issuers), mortgage-related and other asset-backed securities, tax-exempt securities, and commercial paper and other short-term securities.

Morgan Stanley may be better positioned than others in the brokerage industry because the firm is a leader in mergers and acquisitions and has a heavy presence in Europe. Many analysts anticipate that demand for M&A services will outpace the weak equities underwriting market in the near term, and they believe that Europe is likely to offer better prospects than the United States for the next several years. The firm also has been more aggressive than its rivals at slashing costs. So although Morgan Stanley's top line has suffered from the indus-

FIGURE 16.6

Company: MWD
Gain or Loss

Ultimate Stock Price	Buy Stock		Sell Puts	
	Dollars	Annual%	Dollars	Annual%
54.38	15.73	81.20%	4.53	30.10%
51.79	13.14	67.83%	4.53	30.10%
49.33	10.68	55.11%	4.53	30.10%
46.98	8.33	42.98%	4.53	30.10%
44.74	6.09	31.44%	4.53	30.10%
42.61	3.96	20.44%	4.53	30.10%
40.58	1.93	9.97%	4.53	30.10%
38.65	0.00	0.00%	4.53	30.10%
36.72	-1.93	-9.97%	4.53	30.10%
34.88	-3.77	-19.45%	4.53	30.10%
33.14	-5.51	-28.45%	4.53	30.10%
31.48	-7.17	-37.00%	4.53	30.10%
29.91	-8.74	-45.12%	4.34	28.86%
28.41	-10.24	-52.84%	1.35	8.98%
26.99	-11.66	-60.17%	-1.49	-9.91%
25.64	-13.01	-67.13%	-4.19	-27.86%

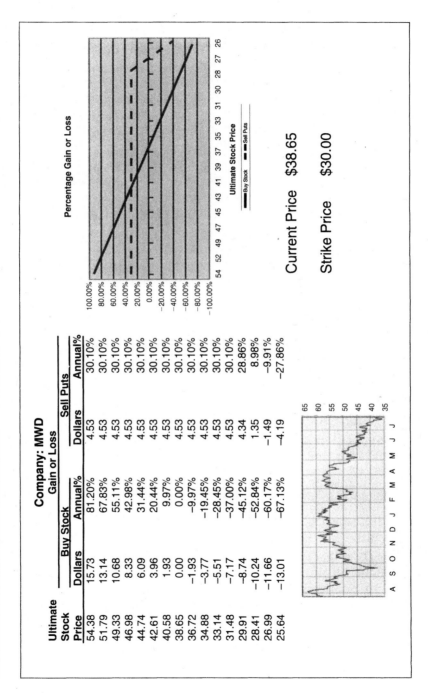

Percentage Gain or Loss

Buy Stock — ■ — Sell Puts

Ultimate Stock Price

Current Price $38.65

Strike Price $30.00

trywide drop-off in trading and investment banking services, the firm's return on equity of 16 percent in the first quarter was just shy of its long-term goal of maintaining at least an 18 percent return on earnings (ROE).

In spite of this, the incredibly poor stock market performance over the past 3 years has left its mark on the brokerage firms' stock prices. (See Figure 16.6.) Morgan Stanley is no exception. It is off over 30 percent in 2002 and down almost 50 percent from its high in 2001. In spite of the recent hard times, the company maintains its 0.92 dividend, and it is currently trading at a low 13.31 price-earnings ratio. Even more impressive, its PEG ratio is under 1, an incredible number for a profitable, mature company. It also enjoys strong institutional support with over 62 percent of its shares held by large institutions.

The high volatility in the brokerage sector provides us an excellent put selling opportunity in Morgan Stanley. We can receive a $2.05 premium for a January 2003 put, with a strike price of just $30, well below Morningstar's $58 current valuation of the company. This computes to an annualized gain of 30.1 percent—gain we will realize even if Morgan Stanley drops all the way down to $30 (a 22.4 percent drop in price). We won't lose any money on this trade unless Morgan Stanley drops over 28 percent. Based on our diversification requirements, we will sell 13 put contracts on Morgan Stanley. This sale will add $2665 ($2.05 premium × 13 contracts × 100 shares per contract) to our portfolio.

DISNEY

Our next portfolio candidate is Disney (DIS). The Walt Disney Company is a diversified entertainment company with operations in four business areas: television and radio networks, amusement parks and resorts, movie and television studios entertainment, and consumer products. The company acquired Fox Family Worldwide, which included the Fox Family Channel, which was renamed ABC Family, ownership interests in Fox, Fox Kids channel in foreign countries, and the television rights to Major League Baseball games two nights a week during the regular season, plus several first-round playoff games.

The Walt Disney Company operates the ABC Television Network, which has 226 primary affiliated stations reaching 99.9 percent of all U.S. television households. The company operates the ABC Radio Networks, which reaches more than 126 million domestic listeners weekly and consists of more than 8900 program affiliations on more than 4600 radio stations. In addition, the ABC Radio Networks produce and operate Radio Disney, which is carried on 48 stations that cover more than 54 percent of the U.S. market.

Disney owns 10 television stations, half of which are located in the top 10 markets in the United States, 36 AM radio stations, and 17 FM radio stations. All of the television stations are affiliated with the ABC Television Network, and most of the 53 radio stations are affiliated with the ABC Radio Networks. The company's television stations reach 24 percent of the nation's television households, while the radio stations reach an audience of 15 million.

The company's cable and international broadcast operations owns the Disney Channel, Toon Disney, SoapNet, 80 percent of ESPN, Inc., 37.5 percent of the A&E Television, Networks, 50 percent of Lifetime Entertainment Services, 39.6 percent of E! Entertainment Television, and various other international investments.

The Walt Disney Company also develops, produces, and distributes television programming under the Buena Vista Television, Buena Vista Production, Touchstone Television, and Walt Disney Television names. The company produces original television movies, prime-time specials for network television, and live-action syndicated programming, which includes *Live! with Regis and Kelly*, *Ebert & Roeper and the Movies*, *Your Big Break*, and *Win Ben Stein's Money*.

Although the company maintains a presence on the Internet through its portals ABC.com, ABCNEWS.com, ABCSports.com, ESPN.com, Disney.com, Family.com, and Movies.com, it closed its major Internet push GO.com last year.

In its amusement park and resort business segment, the company operates the Walt Disney World Resort and Disney Cruise Line in Florida and the Disneyland Resort in California. The company licenses the operations of the Tokyo Disneyland

Resort in Japan and licenses and manages the Disneyland Resort Paris in France. The company also maintains a significant hospitality business at and around its amusement parks. The company owns and operates 13 resort hotels and a complex of villas and suites at the Walt Disney World Resort, with a total of approximately 20,000 rooms and 318,000 square feet of conference meeting space. In addition, Disney's Fort Wilderness camping and recreational area offers approximately 800 campsites and 400 wilderness homes.

The movie and television studios produce live-action and animated motion pictures, and television animation programs. The company produces and acquires live-action and animated motion pictures for distribution to the theatrical, television, and home video markets, and it produces original animated television programming for network, first-run syndication, pay, and international syndication markets. The company also is engaged directly in the home video and television distribution of its film and television library.

The consumer products division licenses the company's characters and other intellectual property to consumer manufacturers, retailers, show promoters, and publishers throughout the world. Character merchandising and publications licensing promotes the company's films and television programs, as well as its other operations. Subsidiaries also engage in direct retail distribution of products based on the company's characters and films through the Disney Stores, books, magazines, and comics worldwide.

In a recent development, the *Wall Street Journal* reported that Disney has taken preliminary steps toward the development of a major theme park in China. If concluded, the park would probably be opened in time for the 2008 Olympic Games being held in Beijing.

The company has experienced and should continue to experience revenue declines during the balance of 2002, principally as a result of the weak economy's declining advertising and reduced travel. (See Figure 16.7.) However, the company has chosen to avoid cost cutting to improve short-term results in anticipation of long-term performance. As a result, the company

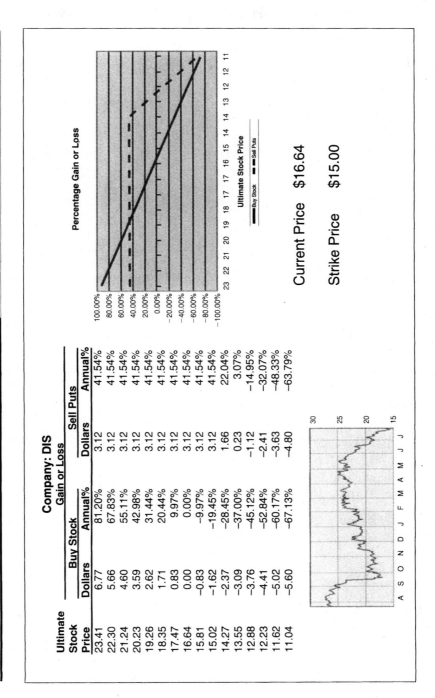

Company: DIS

Gain or Loss

Ultimate Stock Price	Buy Stock		Sell Puts	
	Dollars	Annual%	Dollars	Annual%
23.41	6.77	81.20%	3.12	41.54%
22.30	5.66	67.83%	3.12	41.54%
21.24	4.60	55.11%	3.12	41.54%
20.23	3.59	42.98%	3.12	41.54%
19.26	2.62	31.44%	3.12	41.54%
18.35	1.71	20.44%	3.12	41.54%
17.47	0.83	9.97%	3.12	41.54%
16.64	0.00	0.00%	3.12	41.54%
15.81	−0.83	−9.97%	3.12	41.54%
15.02	−1.62	−19.45%	3.12	41.54%
14.27	−2.37	−28.45%	1.66	22.04%
13.55	−3.09	−37.00%	0.23	3.07%
12.88	−3.76	−45.12%	−1.12	−14.95%
12.23	−4.41	−52.84%	−2.41	−32.07%
11.62	−5.02	−60.17%	−3.63	−48.33%
11.04	−5.60	−67.13%	−4.80	−63.79%

Percentage Gain or Loss

Ultimate Stock Price
Buy Stock — — Sell Puts

Current Price $16.64

Strike Price $15.00

will remain poised to rebound as the general economy improves and the fear of travel subsides.

Although the company currently trades at a healthy P/E ratio of 30, it is at a much lower price-earnings multiple than it has historically traded. Also, its projected P/E for 2003 is just 19.3. The company pays a 21 cents annual dividend, which yields a current stockholder 1.26 percent. Like most other stocks, the company currently trades well below its 52-week high. In the past year the stock price has fallen 38 percent. The stock, however, continues to retain strong institutional support with almost 60 percent of its shares owned by large institutions or mutual funds. The company also trades at a relatively low book value of 1.46. Morgan Stanley has a 1-year price target on the stock of $24, although it currently maintains an "underweight" rating on the company. Morningstar currently values the company at $22 a share.

By selling a put 10 percent below the stock's current price, the stock will not be put to us unless the stock falls and remains below $15. Based on the January 2003 put strike price of $15, we will receive a $1.45 premium. This reduces our breakeven price on the transaction to just $13.44, almost 20 percent below its current price. This trade produces an annualized yield of 41.54 percent, assuming the stock price ends up above the $15 strike price. Based on our diversification requirements we will sell 26 put contracts on Disney. This sale will add $3770 ($1.45 premium × 26 contracts × 100 shares per contract) to our portfolio.

JOHNSON & JOHNSON

The next stock we will add to our portfolio is Johnson & Johnson (JNJ). Johnson & Johnson, which was founded in 1887, engages in the manufacture and sale of various products in the health care field. The company conducts business in virtually every country. The company's business is divided into three divisions: consumer, pharmaceutical, and medical devices and diagnostics.

The company has been active in acquisitions over the past year. In June 2001, the company merged with ALZA Corporation.

Under the terms of the merger, ALZA Corporation will retain its name as a direct, wholly owned subsidiary of Johnson & Johnson. ALZA Corporation is a research-based pharmaceutical company that offers drug delivery technologies for its own portfolio and for many other pharmaceutical companies. ALZA's sales and marketing efforts are focused on urology, oncology, and central nervous system products.

In November 2001, the company acquired the diabetes care products business from Inverness Medical Technology, Inc. Inverness's principal products are advanced electrochemical blood glucose monitoring systems that are used by people with diabetes to determine their blood glucose levels in order to manage their disease.

In April 2002, the company acquired Tibotec-Virco NV, a privately held biopharmaceutical company focused on developing antiviral treatments.

The consumer division's principal products include personal care and hygienic products, including nonprescription drugs, adult skin and hair care products, baby care products, oral care products, first aid products, and sanitary protection products. Major brands include Aveeno skin care products, Band-Aid Brand Adhesive Bandages, Benecol food products, Carefree Panty Shields, Monistat, adult and children's Motrin IB ibuprofen products, Clean & Clear teen skin care products, Imodium A-D antidiarrheal, Johnson's Baby line of products, Johnson's pH 5.5 skin and hair care products, Lactaid lactose-intolerance products, , Mylanta gastrointestinal products and Pepcid AC Acid Controller, Neutrogena skin and hair care products, Natusan baby care products, Piz Buin and Sundown sun care products, Reach toothbrushes, RoC skin care products, Shower to Shower personal care products, Splenda (a noncaloric sugar substitute), Stayfree sanitary protection products, Tylenol acetaminophen products, and Viactiv calcium supplements.

The pharmaceutical division's principal franchises are in the antifungal, anti-infective, cardiovascular, dermatology, gastrointestinal, hematology, immunology, neurology, oncology, pain management, psychotropic, urology, and women's health fields. These products are distributed directly and through wholesalers for use by health care professionals and the general public.

The company's principal prescription drugs include Nizoral (ketoconazole), Sporanox (itraconazole), Terazol (terconazole), Daktarin (miconazole nitrate), Floxin (ofloxacin), Levaquin (levofloxacin), Retvase (reteplase), Reopro (abciximab), Retin-A Micro (tretinoin), Aciphex (rabeprazole sodium), GERD, Imodium (loperamide HCl), Motilium (domperidone), Remicade (infliximab), Procrit (epoetin alfa, sold outside the United States as Eprex), OrthocloneE OKT-3 (muromonab-CD3), Reminyl (galantamine), Topamax (topiramate), Stugeron (cinnarizine), Doxil, Ergamisol (levamisole hydrochloride), Leustatin (cladribine), Duragesic (fentanyl transdermal system, sold abroad as Durogesic), Ultracet, Ultram (tramadol hydrochloride), Risperdal (risperidone), Haldol (haloperidol), Ditropan XL, Ortho-Novum (norethindrone/ethinyl estradiol), and Tricilest (norgestimate/ethinyl estradiol, sold in the United States as Ortho Tri-Cyclen).

The medical devices and diagnostics division includes a broad range of products used by or under the direction of health care professionals, including suture and mechanical wound closure products, surgical equipment and devices, wound management and infection prevention products, interventional and diagnostic cardiology products, diagnostic equipment and supplies, joint replacements, and disposable contact lenses.

JNJ's stock price hit the skids this week as the *New York Times* reported that the government is conducting a criminal investigation into a Johnson & Johnson factory that makes an anemia drug, which has been linked to a spate of serious illnesses in Europe and Canada. (See Figure 16.8.) The factory, in Puerto Rico, manufactures Eprex, a drug that is used to increase the levels of red blood cells in people who are undergoing kidney dialysis or suffering from anemia caused by chemotherapy. According to the *New York Times*, health authorities in Europe and North America have become increasingly concerned over the last few months about a mysterious rise in the number of Eprex users who have developed pure red cell aplasia, a condition in which the body can lose its ability to produce red blood cells, leaving the patient dependent on blood

FIGURE 16.8

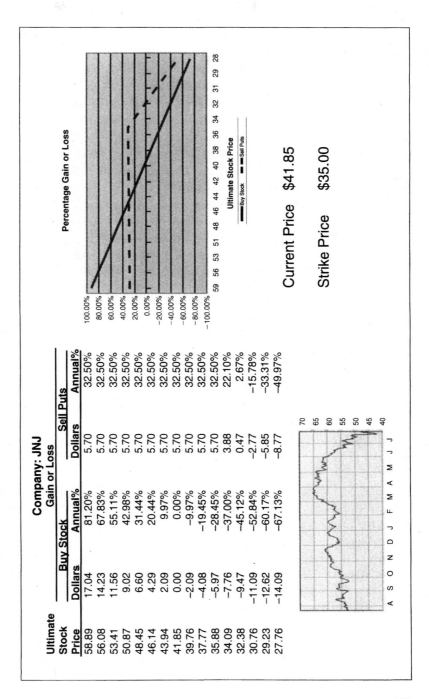

Company: JNJ
Gain or Loss

Ultimate Stock Price	Buy Stock		Sell Puts	
	Dollars	Annual%	Dollars	Annual%
58.89	17.04	81.20%	5.70	32.50%
56.08	14.23	67.83%	5.70	32.50%
53.41	11.56	55.11%	5.70	32.50%
50.87	9.02	42.98%	5.70	32.50%
48.45	6.60	31.44%	5.70	32.50%
46.14	4.29	20.44%	5.70	32.50%
43.94	2.09	9.97%	5.70	32.50%
41.85	0.00	0.00%	5.70	32.50%
39.76	−2.09	−9.97%	5.70	32.50%
37.77	−4.08	−19.45%	5.70	32.50%
35.88	−5.97	−28.45%	5.70	32.50%
34.09	−7.76	−37.00%	3.88	22.10%
32.38	−9.47	−45.12%	0.47	2.67%
30.76	−11.09	−52.84%	−2.77	−15.78%
29.23	−12.62	−60.17%	−5.85	−33.31%
27.76	−14.09	−67.13%	−8.77	−49.97%

Percentage Gain or Loss

Current Price $41.85

Strike Price $35.00

transfusions to survive. The investigation by the Food and Drug Administration and the Justice Department, is tied to a whistle-blower lawsuit filed against Johnson & Johnson by Hector Arce, a former employee at the factory. Arce, who was fired in March 1999, contends he was pressed to falsify data to cover up manufacturing lapses and then was suspended a few days before an expected interview with FDA inspectors.

In spite of the potential litigation, Johnson & Johnson remained tied for second on the *Hulbert Financial Digest* list of stocks recommended by investment newsletters. Of 160 newsletters monitored by the *Hulbert Financial Digest*, 12 newsletters recommend buying the stock. One letter even e-mailed its subscribers with a special buy recommendation based on the large price drop. Todd Lebor, Morningstar analyst, suggests that although "Eprex troubles are worrisome, they shouldn't topple this health-care giant. We have modeled a fairly pessimistic scenario for Eprex and are lowering our fair value estimate from $66 to $58, but still believe the shares are attractive. We assume the company takes a $500 million charge and Eprex's non-U.S. sales plummet 50 percent in 2003 while it resolves whatever manufacturing troubles it faces at the Puerto Rico plant. Beyond that, we expect J&J to resume its steady revenue growth and incremental margin improvement. Over the years, the company has shown resilience (the Propulsid recall) as well as integrity (the Tylenol cyanide scare), and we believe it will follow the same course in addressing this issue." He places a $58 current valuation on the stock, well above its current $41.85 price.

Obviously, the recent drop in price, down 29 percent year to date, makes the financial ratios look good, especially in historical comparison. (See Figure 16.8.) The stock is currently trading at a 21.13 price-earnings ratio, down from a high of 47.56. Based on its current price and its estimated 2003 earnings, it would be trading at a 16 P/E ratio. The company pays a healthy dividend of 82 cents a year, yielding current stockholders almost 2 percent yield. The company's PEG ratio is just 1.49, an excellent number for a mature company.

As a result of the company's recent price drop, volatility is high, presenting an unusual opportunity to sell high-yielding puts. Normally, the volatility is so low on JNJ that selling puts on the company is not worthwhile. However, today's January 2003 put with a $35 strike price will garner a $2.60 premium, which produces an annualized yield of 32.5 percent. In spite of this high yield, the breakeven price on the transaction is only $32.15, a full 23 percent below the stock's current price and almost half of many analysts' price targets. In fact, the stock can fall 16 percent more from its current levels and the put seller will still make the full 32.5 percent annualized gain. Based on our diversification requirements, we will sell 11 put contracts on Johnson & Johnson. This sale will add $2860 ($2.60 premium × 11 contracts × 100 shares per contract) to our portfolio.

OMNICOM GROUP

Our ninth stock for the portfolio will be Omnicom Group (OMC). Omnicom Group, Inc., is a marketing and corporate communications company. The company was formed in 1986 through the merger of three marketing and corporate communications networks: BBDO, Doyle Dane Bernbach, and Needham Harper. Since then, Omnicom has grown to over 1500 subsidiary agencies operating in more than 100 countries. The company's agencies provide a broad range of marketing and corporate communications services, including advertising, brand consultancy, crisis communications, custom publishing, database management, digital and interactive marketing, direct marketing, and directory and business-to-business advertising. Omnicom also provides field marketing, health-care communications, marketing research, media planning and buying, multicultural marketing, nonprofit marketing, promotional marketing, public affairs, public relations, recruitment communications, specialty communications, and sports and events marketing.

Omnicom has also been active in the acquisitions area (39 acquisitions) over the past year. Three of the larger acquisitions include the May 2001 acquisition of Wolff Olins, an international brand consultancy. In January 2002, the company acquired Allyn & Company, Inc., an independent public relations firm in

Texas, southwestern United States, and Mexico. In April 2002, the company acquired Aaron Walton Entertainment, a Los Angeles–based entertainment marketing agency.

Omnicom has over 5000 clients, many of which were served by more than one of its agency brands. The company's 10 largest and 200 largest clients in the aggregate accounted for 17 and 48 percent, respectively, of its 2001 consolidated revenue. Omnicom's largest client was served by 20 of its agency brands last year. This client accounted for 5.4 percent of the company's 2001 consolidated revenue. No other client accounted for more than 2.5 percent of its consolidated revenue.

Shares of Omnicom fell sharply when it was revealed that the SEC staff was investigating its accounting practices with regard to its acquisitions and the handling of some poor Internet investments. (See Figure 16.9.) In addition, Moody's put some of the company's debt on review for a downgrade—a move that added fuel to questions about the company's accounting practices. The company issued a statement that it has "ample liquidity to meet all foreseeable business and capital requirements." The company added that it has "a one-year $1.5 billion commercial paper program backed by a $1.6 billion credit facility that can be extended to April 2004, along with an undrawn $500 million revolving credit line committed through June 30, 2003," neither of which would suffer from a rating change. In spite of the company's statements, as a result of these concerns, Omnicom traded down to its lowest level in more than 3 years, less than half of its 52-week high of $97.35 on March 4. It fell as low as $36.50, but has rebounded over the past month to a current price of $49.98.

Merrill Lynch analyst Lauren Fine said in a note to investors that in addition to the negative watch from Moody's, "end-of-quarter window dressing could be pressuring the stock given its poor performance." Another factor, she continued, is that "news flow from most agencies globally is that they are not seeing a real pickup in client spending. In general we think investors are concerned about an ad pickup. However, from a fundamental perspective, things are going well at OMC. We expect organic revenue growth to be fairly modest but positive in the second quarter." As a result, Fine maintained her strong

FIGURE 16.9

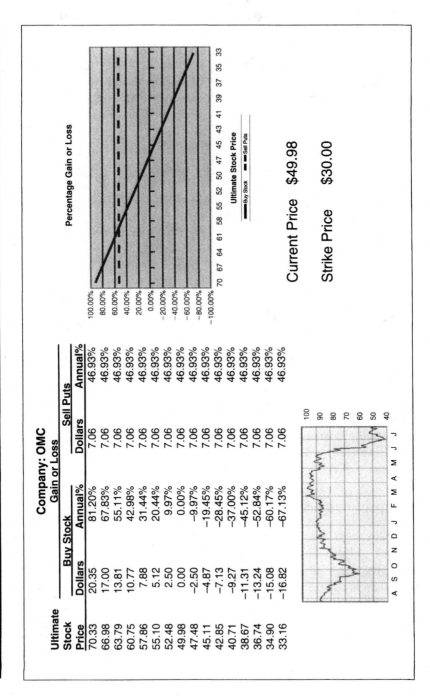

Company: OMC
Gain or Loss

Ultimate Stock Price	Buy Stock		Sell Puts	
	Dollars	Annual%	Dollars	Annual%
70.33	20.35	81.20%	7.06	46.93%
66.98	17.00	67.83%	7.06	46.93%
63.79	13.81	55.11%	7.06	46.93%
60.75	10.77	42.98%	7.06	46.93%
57.86	7.88	31.44%	7.06	46.93%
55.10	5.12	20.44%	7.06	46.93%
52.48	2.50	9.97%	7.06	46.93%
49.98	0.00	0.00%	7.06	46.93%
47.48	-2.50	-9.97%	7.06	46.93%
45.11	-4.87	-19.45%	7.06	46.93%
42.85	-7.13	-28.45%	7.06	46.93%
40.71	-9.27	-37.00%	7.06	46.93%
38.67	-11.31	-45.12%	7.06	46.93%
36.74	-13.24	-52.84%	7.06	46.93%
34.90	-15.08	-60.17%	7.06	46.93%
33.16	-16.82	-67.13%	7.06	46.93%

Percentage Gain or Loss

Buy Stock — Sell Puts

Ultimate Stock Price

Current Price $49.98

Strike Price $30.00

209

buy rating on the stock. Subsequent to Fine's report, the company reiterated its 2002 and guidance for both revenues and earnings.

Omnicom has also achieved some major victories over the past year by winning over major clients (Daimler/Chrysler and Pepsico) from its chief rival Interpublic Group. This bodes well for the company's future.

The company is currently trading at an attractive P/E ratio of 17.52 with a PEG ratio of just 1.16. As a result, at its current price, the company's 2003 P/E ratio would be around 12. The company currently pays an 80 cent annual dividend, yielding current stockholders 1.6 percent. A very high percentage (84 percent) of its shares are held by large institutions and mutual funds.

The recent volatility provides us an excellent opportunity to place a very conservative, low-risk trade on Omnicom. We will receive a $3.30 premium on the sale of a January 2003 put with a strike price of only $30, 40 percent below the stock's current price! The way out-of-the-money put sale will still yield us a 46.93 percent annualized profit if the stock stays above $30, well below Morningstar's current $53 valuation. For us to lose money on this trade, the stock would have to fall over 47 percent to $26.47. At that price the dividend yield alone would be over 3 percent. Based on our diversification requirements, we will sell 13 put contracts on OMC. This sale will add $4290 ($3.30 premium × 13 contracts × 100 shares per contract) to our portfolio.

THE HOME DEPOT

Our last stock for this abbreviated portfolio will be Home Depot (HD). The Home Depot, Inc., is a home improvement retailer. The company operates over 1400 Home Depot stores throughout the United States, Canada, Argentina, and Mexico, and 41 EXPO Design Center stores in the United States. Home Depot stores sell a wide variety of building materials and home improvement and lawn and garden care products, and they provide a number of services. EXPO Design Center stores sell products and services primarily for design and renovation projects, such as kitchen and bathroom cabinetry, tiles, flooring, and lighting fixtures as well as installation services. The company also operates smaller subsidiaries in related building supply and design areas.

Home Depot stores offer a broad assortment of merchandise and services, and they serve three primary customer groups: do-it-yourself customers, do-it-for-me customers, and professional customers. A typical Home Depot store stocks approximately 40,000 to 50,000 product items, including variations in color and size. Major product groups include building materials including lumber and millwork; plumbing, electrical, and kitchen equipment and fixtures; hardware and seasonal goods, and paint, floor, and wall coverings. To complement the national brand-name products it offers, the company has formed strategic alliances with vendor partners to market products under brand names that are only offered through the Home Depot. Currently, the company offers products under more than 30 proprietary and other exclusive brands, including Thomasville kitchen and bathroom cabinets; RIDGID power tools; Behr Premium Plus paint; Mill's Pride cabinets; GE SmartWater water heater; and Vigoro fertilizer.

EXPO Design Center stores offer complete interior design services and installation services to assist its customers in their home décor and remodeling projects. Typically, customers at EXPO Design Center stores are middle- to upper-income do-it-for-me customers, who purchase merchandise for installation by others. As a result, the company offers installation services for most of the products it sells at these stores. Additionally, its trade customers are custom builders, remodelers, designers, and architects. The stores offer interior design products and installation services in kitchens, baths, décor, lighting, flooring, appliances, patio, decorative fabrics, window treatments, and home storage and organization products and accessories.

The company also has a Web presence located at www.homedepot.com. The site offers information about projects and its products, calculators to estimate the amount and kinds of materials needed to complete a project, and information about Home Depot. Customers can purchase approximately 20,000 products available at stores in their local market on its

Web site, and the products are priced based on the market in which the customer lives. Orders are fulfilled from its stores and are shipped by the United Parcel Service.

In recent news, Merrill Lynch analyst Peter Caruso lowered his ratings on Home Depot citing slower sales and lower inventory levels. As a result, the company's stock continued its slide, off over 43 percent for the year. (See Figure 16.10.) In response, the company announced that its board of directors has approved a share repurchase program of up to $2 billion effective immediately. The company added that it is comfortable with the second-quarter consensus earnings estimate of $0.47 per share, according to Multex. The company also reaffirmed its 3-year guidance of 15 to 18 percent annual sales growth and 18 to 20 percent annual earnings growth through fiscal 2004.

Peter Benedict, who covers both Home Depot and Lowe's for CIBC World Markets, says, "I still have concerns about growth, but I think at the valuation the stock is trading at, you've got a pretty good risk-reward." He says Home Depot's current valuation of about 18 times this year's estimated earnings puts the stock at its lowest valuation in at least 10 years. We can increase the risk and reward by selling an out-of-the-money put on Home Depot.

The company is currently trading at a respectable 20.71 price-earnings ratio and has an excellent PEG ratio of 1.13. The company has significant institutional ownership of over 62 percent, and though modest in amount (20 cents), it pays an annual dividend. We can reduce our risk on this stock by selling a put at a $25 strike price. The January 2003 put is paying $2.25 per share. This works out to a 38.85 percent annualized return, even if the stock falls 13 percent to $25. The breakeven price for the transaction is $22.72, more than 20 percent below its current price. Based on our diversification requirements, we will sell 16 put contracts on Home Depot. This sale will add $3600 ($2.25 premium × 16 contracts × 100 shares per contract) to our portfolio.

Now that all of our equity puts have been sold, it is time to purchase the index puts as a hedge against a market collapse. To do that, we first need to analyze our put sales. As you can see in

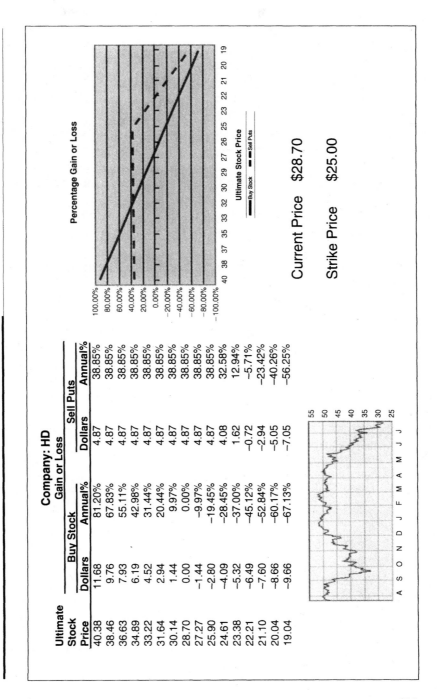

FIGURE 16.10

Company: HD

Gain or Loss

Ultimate Stock Price	Buy Stock		Sell Puts	
	Dollars	Annual%	Dollars	Annual%
40.38	11.68	81.20%	4.87	38.85%
38.46	9.76	67.83%	4.87	38.85%
36.63	7.93	55.11%	4.87	38.85%
34.89	6.19	42.98%	4.87	38.85%
33.22	4.52	31.44%	4.87	38.85%
31.64	2.94	20.44%	4.87	38.85%
30.14	1.44	9.97%	4.87	38.85%
28.70	0.00	0.00%	4.87	38.85%
27.27	-1.44	-9.97%	4.87	38.85%
25.90	-2.80	-19.45%	4.87	38.85%
24.61	-4.09	-28.45%	4.08	32.58%
23.38	-5.32	-37.00%	1.62	12.94%
22.21	-6.49	-45.12%	-0.72	-5.71%
21.10	-7.60	-52.84%	-2.94	-23.42%
20.04	-8.66	-60.17%	-5.05	-40.26%
19.04	-9.66	-67.13%	-7.05	-56.25%

Percentage Gain or Loss

Ultimate Stock Price
Buy Stock   Sell Puts

Current Price $28.70

Strike Price $25.00

Table 16.1, we took in a total of $36,155 of premium. Our average premium, relative to the current stock price, was a little over 9 percent. Our average put position was taken 18 percent out of the money, which means that our average stock position could fall 18 percent before the stocks would be put to us (see Table 16.1). According to our original assumptions we would purchase the index puts below their current price by an amount equal to the average out-of-the-money delta, which in this case is 18 percent, and 75 percent of the average premium received, which in this case is 6.9 percent (9.2 percent × 0.75). For purposes of this portfolio, we will purchase our index puts on the S&P 500 index, which was trading on July 19 at 847.75. We reduce the current price of the index by 24.9 percent (18 percent average out-of-money delta) and 6.9 percent (75 percent of average premium) to arrive at a tentative strike price for the index puts of $636. We then round up to the next highest available strike price and purchase the index puts on the S&P 500 index at a $650 strike price. The current cost for the index puts is $11.50 per index share or $1150 per contract.

Next we need to determine how many contracts to buy. We sold approximately $400,000 worth of equity puts, so we need to

TABLE 16.1

Sample Portfolio

Stock Symbol	Price at Open	Strike Price	Breakeven Price	Premium Received	Contracts Sold	Total Premium	Percent Premium Received	Percent Out-of-the Money
AMGN	$35.46	$25	$23.02	$1.80	16	$ 2,880	7.20%	29.50%
AOL	11.58	10	8.22	1.80	40	7,200	18.00	13.64
DIS	16.64	15	13.44	1.45	26	3,770	9.67	9.86
GE	26.52	25	22.26	2.55	16	4,080	10.20	5.73
HD	28.70	25	22.72	2.25	16	3,600	9.00	12.89
IBM	72.00	60	55.99	3.60	6	2,160	6.00	16.67
JNJ	41.85	35	32.15	2.60	11	2,860	7.43	16.37
MWD	38.65	30	27.74	2.05	13	2,665	6.83	22.38
OMC	49.98	30	26.47	3.30	13	4,290	11.00	39.98
WMT	46.50	40	37.07	2.65	10	2,650	6.63	13.98
Total/Average						$36,155	9.20	18.10

purchase $400,000 worth of index puts. By dividing $400,000 by the current index price (847.75), we arrive at the correct number of index share options to purchase. That equals 478 index shares ($400,000/847.75). Remember, we can buy options only in contracts of 100. As a result, we round up to 500 index shares, or 5 contracts. Those five contacts at $1150 per contract cost us $5750. That works out to a little less than 15 percent of the premium we received from selling the individual stock puts.

Our potential profit is now reduced by the cost of the index puts, but it is increased by the interest earnings. Here is what our potential profit picture looks like:

Total premium received	$36,155
Index put cost	−5,750
Interest earnings	+2,864
Total potential profit	$33,269

This profit is based on a $200,000 investment for about 6 months, which computes to an approximate 34 percent annualized return. Remember, this return will be realized even if the average stock falls 18 percent in price over the next 6 months and includes the cost of insuring the portfolio against a market collapse. One caveat: The current market volatility is very high, which produces higher-than-normal option premiums. Under more normal circumstances, your percentage of potential return may decrease as much as 20 to 30 percent, which in this example would calculate to about 25 percent.

CHAPTER

17

Back Testing the Dow

A 10-Year Back Test on Every Stock in the Dow Jones Industrial Average

Over the past several years as I have been presenting this strategy to investors all over the country, many have asked if I have back tested the strategy to prove its effectiveness. My normal response has always been, "That's not necessary because the results are empirical." In other words, it is possible to prove mathematically that by selling puts, you reduce risk while still gaining a reasonable upside potential.

This strategy was not designed to help you pick stocks (although it allows you to take positions in less volatile ones and still reach your financial goals). It was designed to help you reduce risk on the stocks you do pick and still make double-digit gains in years when the market is relatively flat.

Many people have still wanted to see the results of a back test, so I finally agreed to perform one. The first challenge was to select a group of stocks to use for the test. I didn't want to handpick a group of stocks and then have others suggest that I had picked only stocks that looked good. I didn't want to pick too many or too few. Since I recommend that investors use large-cap, industry leaders for their universe of potential stock

TABLE 17.1

Dow Jones Industrial Stocks
Percentage Gain or Loss If Puts Were Sold

Company	1992	1993	1994	1995	1996
GE	27.38	27.38	24.46	27.38	27.38
PG	17.05	19.21	19.21	19.21	19.21
UTX	24.55	27.17	27.17	27.17	27.17
MSFT	27.59	27.59	27.59	27.59	27.59
EK	34.29	34.29	34.29	34.29	34.29
CAT	25.49	25.49	25.49	25.49	25.49
DD	24.02	24.02	24.02	24.02	24.02
MO	22.56	−2.13	22.56	22.56	22.56
JPM	29.05	29.05	29.05	29.05	29.05
GM	26.33	26.33	−38.69	26.33	26.33
SBC	24.65	24.65	24.65	24.65	24.65
IP	15.74	26.75	26.68	26.75	26.75
MRK	−13.79	15.25	22.98	22.98	22.98
XOM	21.51	21.51	15.50	21.51	21.51
HON	32.82	32.82	24.05	32.82	32.82
MMM	23.19	23.19	23.19	23.19	23.19
AA	34.50	34.50	34.50	34.50	34.50
BA	−27.01	28.42	28.42	28.42	28.42
KO	17.95	17.95	17.95	17.95	17.95
HWP	38.69	38.69	38.69	38.69	38.69
C	22.35	22.35	3.50	22.35	22.35
JNJ	−9.98	17.32	17.32	17.32	17.32
DIS	33.87	33.87	33.87	33.87	33.87
AXP	25.91	25.91	25.91	25.91	25.91
T	17.32	17.32	−0.87	17.32	−58.86
MCD	23.40	23.40	23.40	23.40	12.71
IBM	−54.07	25.49	25.49	25.49	25.49
WMT	19.83	−10.68	−0.24	5.36	19.83
HD	28.42	−5.88	28.42	28.42	28.42
INTC	33.45	33.45	33.45	33.45	33.45
Total	18.90	22.82	21.40	25.58	23.17

TABLE 17.1

continued

1997	1998	1999	2000	2001	Total
27.38	27.38	27.38	27.38	4.30	24.78
19.21	19.21	19.21	−31.92	19.21	13.88
27.17	27.17	12.54	27.17	5.13	23.24
27.59	27.59	27.59	−41.65	27.59	20.66
−6.18	34.29	34.29	−14.06	−33.96	18.58
25.49	16.13	25.49	25.49	25.49	24.55
24.02	14.65	24.02	−17.43	22.31	18.77
22.56	22.56	−77.52	22.56	22.56	10.08
29.05	29.05	29.05	29.05	−29.72	23.17
26.33	26.33	26.33	−30.41	24.79	14.00
24.65	24.65	−7.40	24.65	−14.64	17.52
26.75	9.68	26.75	−0.51	26.75	21.21
22.98	22.98	22.98	22.98	−27.10	13.52
21.51	21.51	21.51	21.51	14.02	20.16
32.82	32.82	32.82	32.82	−34.37	25.23
23.19	20.01	23.19	23.19	23.19	22.87
34.50	34.50	34.50	34.50	26.17	33.67
12.24	−19.92	28.42	28.42	−29.86	10.06
17.95	17.95	1.67	17.95	−17.59	12.77
38.69	38.69	38.69	−18.56	−30.86	26.01
22.35	22.35	22.35	22.35	9.01	19.13
17.32	17.32	17.32	17.32	17.32	14.59
33.87	26.00	33.87	8.71	−19.41	25.24
25.91	25.91	25.91	4.47	−9.44	20.23
17.32	17.32	−2.30	−84.81	17.32	−4.29
23.40	23.40	19.09	−12.54	11.04	17.07
25.49	25.49	25.49	25.49	25.49	17.53
19.83	19.83	19.83	19.83	19.83	13.33
28.42	28.42	28.42	5.38	28.42	22.69
33.45	33.45	33.45	−38.36	−6.98	22.23
24.18	22.89	19.83	5.03	3.87	18.77

candidates, I decided to use the 30 stocks in the Dow Jones Industrial Average as a basis for the test.

In Table 17.1 you will see the result of that back test. One caveat: Since historical option quotes were not available to me I had to interpolate the actual option premiums. This could result in a small statistical error. Also, I used the 30 stocks in the Dow, as of July 2002, but as you know, several have been deleted or added over the past 10 years. I also assumed that there was an option available for sale 3 percent below the stock's then-current price, and I used 200 percent leverage. In addition, the study reflects only the sale of puts with no monitoring or management. In other words, puts (LEAPS) were sold at the beginning of each year on every stock and were held until expiration the following January. No attempt was made to move in and out of the put positions as the stocks went up and down. And every position was taken at the beginning of the year, even if a technical and fundamental analysis would have indicated that the stock was already highly valued at the time.

Referring to Table 17.1, you will note the following important conclusions: (1) The average return for all stocks over the entire 10-year period was 18.77 percent, (2) Only one stock, AT&T, produced a loss over the 10-year period. And most importantly, (3) there was never a losing year, including 2001 when the Dow Jones Industrial Average fell about 10 percent.

Another interesting point is that with 30 stocks over 10 years, there were only 25 losses out of 300 individual stock time periods analyzed with respect to selling puts. You will also note that there was significantly less overall volatility. The annual results were between a low of +3.87 percent to a high of +25.58 percent. As I mentioned earlier, achieving consistent gains is as important as limiting your risk.

So now we have a back test that proves once again what we knew all along: Selling puts reduces risk while providing investors the opportunity to accomplish their financial goals.

AFTERWORD

Throughout my life, I have found that conventional wisdom is not always so wise. History is full of such discoveries. Whether it's learning, hundreds of years ago, that the earth is not flat, or discovering the appropriate nutritional lifestyle in Diane Schwarzbein's book, that dispels traditional medical advice regarding proper nutrition,[*] we often find that some of the experts are not correct. To the extent possible, we need to research and evaluate most teachings for ourselves.

A BRIEF REVIEW

The following paragraphs summarize point by point what we discussed in this book. I want you to double-check, when possible, the correctness of those presumptions; and draw your own conclusions from there. I'm not asking you to believe in me. I only want to serve as your guide to information you can independently verify.

1. It is possible to sell out-of-the-money puts on stocks of quality companies and receive 10 to15 percent annualized premiums. As we did earlier, you can check the veracity of that statement by looking up option premiums at one of several option quote Web sites.

2. It is possible to purchase index puts to protect our equity put positions for approximately 20 to 25 percent of the put premium received. The cost of the "insurance" will depend on which index you need to purchase puts on and how close to the current index price you set the index strike price. Normally, you would set the strike price below the current price by an amount equal to the average out-of-the-money equity put sold plus 75 percent of the option premium

---

[*]*The Schwarzbein Principle, The Truth About Losing Weight, Health and Aging* (Deerfield, Florida: Health Communications, 1999).

received. You can take a look at index option premiums to confirm the price required to insure your portfolio.

3. That means it is possible to net 7 to 12 percent per year in option premiums. Merely subtracting the index put cost from the equity put premiums substantiates this claim.

4. You can sell two times your portfolio value in puts, so the annual net yield can be 14 to 24 percent from the sale of equity puts, after deducting the cost of purchasing index puts to protect against a market correction. Double check with different brokers to confirm that their margin requirements allow you to sell puts equal to at least twice the amount of your underlying marginable portfolio.

5. We can earn around 2 to 5 percent on the capital in money market funds or Treasury bills used as collateral for the put portfolio. This is easy to confirm, but this rate changes from time to time as interest rates go up and down.

6. You will achieve the aforementioned results as long as the stocks in which you take positions go up a lot, go up a little, stay level, or go down just a little. In other words, as long as the stocks on which you choose to sell puts on do not go below your strike price, you earn your full profit.

7. We will not lose money in a major market correction as long as we have purchased an adequate number of puts on the appropriate index and our stocks do not underperform the general market.

8. We can increase our profits by properly monitoring our portfolio, buying back puts on stocks that have risen sharply, and placing new positions on ones that are closer to their historical support level.

Therefore, the only way we lose money is if we continually pick stocks that go down (and don't come back in the short to mid term) when the market is not going down. Certainly, this scenario is possible, but, even here, I've shown you how we can minimize our loss probabilities.

As long as a stock is appropriately priced when we place our position, there are only two reasons that stock can go down dramatically:

1. The market goes down.
2. Unforeseen bad news about the company.

If the market goes down, we are covered because we purchased the index puts—so no problem there.

The second possible scenario, a drop because of unforeseen bad news, is the only scenario out of the five that could result in a loss. It is impossible to create an equity-based trading strategy that protects you against every possibility of loss. However, even in the bad news scenario, the use of out-of-the-money puts at least reduces your potential loss.

In other words, yes, you will lose money if a company you pick misses analysts' earnings expectations or gets sued by the federal government, or something equally adverse and unforeseeable happens. But the good news is, even on these trades, you will lose less money than you would have lost had you simply bought the stock outright instead. One important caveat: If you use leverage when you sell the puts **and** you wouldn't have used the same amount of leverage when buying the stock, it is possible to lose more if the stock drops dramatically. That is why it is paramount that you properly diversify your portfolio and purchase the index put hedge.

In most cases, even when using leverage, we lose less because when we sold the put, we picked a strike price that was lower than the stock's then-current purchase price. Had we bought the stock instead, we would have paid more for it than we did when it was put to us.

In addition, keep in mind that nobody was willing to pay you to buy the stock outright. They *were* willing to pay you for selling the put though. If you subtract from the strike price the premium you received when you sold the put, you arrive at our much lower "net cost."

Since it cost us less to purchase the stock using the SafetyNet Trading System than it would have had we simply purchased the stock outright, we lose less money when the stock goes down.

So, in four out of five possible scenarios, we make our full profit. In the fifth scenario, we (a) break even (market collapse), (b) wait for the stock to recover and then earn our full profit, or (c) worst case, lose less money than we would have lost had we simply bought the stock outright.

TAXATION

You also need to consider taxation when choosing an investment strategy. Unless you sell puts and hold the position for more than a year, the gains will be considered short-term capital gains, which are subject to ordinary-income tax rates. One advantage of selling puts, however, is that option income is not taxed until the option is exercised or expires. Consequently, you can defer the income for at least a year by selling LEAPS that expire in January. Of course, should it be necessary for you to close out positions early, the taxes would be computed at the ordinary-income tax rates.

There are couple of potential solutions to the tax problem: (1) Use the strategy of selling puts inside entities that do not get taxed such as pension plans, IRAs, or charitable remainder trusts, or (2) purchase a variable annuity or life insurance product that has a fund manager that uses this strategy.

As previously mentioned, Jim Huguet and I are currently negotiating with various life insurance companies to offer an investment subaccount that utilizes this strategy. Both annuities and life insurance products defer taxes on investment gains inside the policies, until the money is withdrawn. With some types of variable life policies the taxes can be deferred forever, even when you access the cash in the policy. This type of variable life policy is called a *nonmodified endowment policy*. With the nonmodified endowment policy, taxes are deferred on all the investment growth, and you can borrow against the cash value without incurring a tax. When the insured dies, the loans are repaid with the tax-free death benefit, thus completely avoiding the tax forever. Many wealthy, sophisticated investors have been utilizing this strategy for years.

SOME FINAL THOUGHTS

And last, nothing in this book is intended to suggest that by using this approach to investing you are eliminating risk. I can assure you from personal experience that even the best-laid plans can go astray. I am suggesting, however, that using this strategy will reduce the risk typically associated with buying stocks. I have found solace, in even my darkest market days, that had I bought the stocks I sold puts on, I would have lost even more.

Historical Examples

During some of the year 2001, we published "examples of the week" on our Web site at safetynettrading.com. In all we posted 22 examples of possible trades starting in the beginning of March. All of the examples used a January 18, 2002, expiration date.

Obviously, the expiration date has passed, so we can examine the results of our suggestions. During this period of time, the Nasdaq-100 index fell just over 14 percent, and the Dow Jones index dropped over 9 percent.

As you review the spreadsheet in Table A.1, you will note that when the positions are equally weighted, those particular stocks would have lost about 8 percent in value. In other words, we picked stocks that on average did a little bit better than the overall market. Not a lot, but a little better.

The good news is that, by selling puts instead of buying the stock, we made over 15 percent annualized gains at the same time the market went down an average of 11 to 12 percent. Now that's a track record to be proud of. And it's the type of record you can have if you use a strategy that is less risky than that of buying the stocks outright.

In addition, these results did not take into account monitoring the portfolio and adjusting it as needed. As I suggested earlier, it is important to monitor existing positions with the goal of exiting a position early to capitalize on positive price movements.

The two biggest losers from the year's examples (CIEN and JDSU) would have been closed out early for annualized gains of over 1000 percent within 6 days of taking the initial position. Adjusting the performance for just those two positions would have almost doubled the returns for the year.

You may not make 30 percent or more in a year, but you can achieve consistent double-digit gains in even flat or slightly down markets with the SafetyNet Trading System.

TABLE A.1

Web Site Suggested Put Options March 9, 2001 through January 18, 2002

Inception Date	Stock Symbol	Start Price	Strike Price	Ending Price	Premium and Interest Received	Gain/Loss Buy Stock	Gain/Loss Sell Put	Number of Shares	Weighted Gain/Loss Buy Stock	Weighted Gain/Loss Sell Put
24-Aug-01	EMLX	$19.12	$10.00	$42.82	$1.93	$23.70	1.93	5,230	$123,954	$10,111
17-Aug-01	LEH	63.99	55.00	64.09	9.05	0.10	9.05	1,563	156	14,143
10-Aug-01	MCD	28.09	27.50	26.43	4.85	-1.66	2.71	3,560	-5,910	9,655
20-Jul-01	AOL	44.31	40.00	29.58	7.98	-14.73	-12.86	2,257	-33,243	-29,027
13-Jul-01	KO	46.01	45.00	45.44	7.46	-0.57	7.46	2,173	-1,239	16,206
7-Jul-01	EMC	21.60	20.00	15.50	5.98	-6.10	-3.02	4,630	-28,241	-13,965
29-Jun-01	DELL	26.15	22.50	28.10	4.25	1.95	4.25	3,824	7,457	16,270
22-Jun-01	MU	38.38	30.00	31.79	7.25	-6.59	7.25	2,606	-17,170	18,888
15-Jun-01	PMCS	27.66	20.00	21.66	4.88	-6.00	4.88	3,615	-21,692	17,625
1-Jun-01	WMT	51.72	45.00	56.35	7.12	4.63	7.12	1,933	8,952	13,766
25-May-01	SCH	20.80	17.50	14.87	4.56	-5.93	-0.70	4,808	-28,510	-3,344
17-May-01	ORCL	16.28	15.00	16.48	6.17	0.20	6.17	6,143	1,229	37,880
11-May-01	C	49.26	45.00	49.96	9.32	0.70	9.32	2,030	1,421	18,921
4-May-01	CIEN	54.25	50.00	13.54	28.74	-40.71	-44.18	1,843	-75,041	-81,441
27-Apr-01	JDSU	19.26	15.00	8.18	7.54	-11.08	-6.10	5,192	-57,529	-31,658
20-Apr-01	AXP	42.00	40.00	37.02	11.97	-4.98	6.01	2,381	-11,857	14,303
13-Apr-01	IBM	96.20	95.00	114.25	29.15	18.05	29.15	1,040	18,763	30,302
6-Apr-01	T*	15.31	15.00	18.53	5.07	3.22	5.07	6,532	21,032	33,126
30-Mar-01	CSCO	15.81	15.00	18.85	7.13	3.04	7.13	6,325	19,228	45,089
23-Mar-01	GE	39.99	37.50	38.68	10.21	-1.31	10.21	2,501	-3,276	25,519
16-Mar-01	MER	54.80	52.50	56.46	19.94	1.66	19.94	1,825	3,029	36,379
9-Mar-01	SUNW	17.50	15.00	12.12	5.18	-5.38	-0.58	5,714	-30,743	-3,325
Total									-109,229	195,423
									-7.66%	15.37%

	Nasdaq Composite	Dow Jones
March 9, 2001	1,804	10,798
Jan. 18, 2002	1,544	9,782
Percent change	-14.43	-9.41

*Includes spinoff.

Short Option Symbols

NOTATION

Long equity option symbols are made up of four components: stock symbol, expiration month, strike price, and put or call indicator. An IBM call with a $100 strike price that expires in June would look like this:

IBM JUN100C

Short symbols also begin with the stock's symbol, but they use letters as codes to indicate the expiration month, strike price, and whether it is a call or a put. The same IBM June 100 call would look like this:

IBM FT

Following the stock symbol, the first letter tells you two things: 1) whether it is a put or a call, and 2) the expiration month. The first 12 letters of the alphabet (A through L) signify call options, and each letter stands for a different month (A is January, B is February, and so on). The next 12 letters (M through X) signify puts.

Thus, the letter F in IBM FT tells us it's a June call. The second letter after the stock symbol determines the option's strike price. The letter "A" can represent a strike price of $5, $105, $205, $305, and so on. Typically, it will represent the price closest to the stock's current trading range.

For example, the letter T in IBM FT might possibly signify a strike price of $100, $200, or $300. Since IBM was currently trading in the range of between $100 and $120 as of June 2000, the letter T stands for a strike price of $100.

TABLE B.1

Expiration Month Codes

	Jan.	Feb.	March	April	May	June	July	Aug.	Sep.	Oct.	Nov.	Dec.
Calls	A	B	C	D	E	F	G	H	I	J	K	L
Puts	M	N	O	P	Q	R	S	T	U	V	W	X

TABLE B.2

Strike Price Codes

A	B	C	D	E	F	G	H	I	J	K	L	M
5	10	15	20	25	30	35	40	45	50	55	60	65
105	110	115	120	125	130	135	140	145	150	155	160	165
205	210	215	220	225	230	235	240	245	250	255	260	265
305	310	315	320	325	330	335	340	345	350	355	360	365
405	410	415	420	425	430	435	440	445	450	455	460	465
505	510	515	520	525	530	535	540	545	550	555	560	565
605	610	615	620	625	630	635	640	645	650	655	660	665
705	710	715	720	725	730	735	740	745	750	755	760	765
N	**O**	**P**	**Q**	**R**	**S**	**T**	**U**	**V**	**W**	**X**	**Y**	**Z**
70	75	80	85	90	95	100	7½	12½	17½	22½	27½	32½
170	175	180	185	190	195	200	37½	42½	47½	52½	57½	62½
270	275	280	285	290	295	300	67½	72½	77½	82½	87½	92½
370	375	380	385	390	395	400	97½	102½	107½	112½	117½	122½
470	475	480	485	490	495	500	127½	132½	137½	142½	147½	152½
570	575	580	585	590	595	600	157½	162½	167½	172½	177½	182½
670	675	680	685	690	695	700	187½	192½	197½	202½	207½	212½
770	775	780	785	790	795	800	217½	222½	227½	232½	237½	242½

STOCK SYMBOLS

The first group of letters (up to three) in an option symbol indicates the underlying stock being represented. Many companies
use more than three letters in their stock symbols. Those that
do so are assigned a three-letter symbol for use in options' short
symbols. For example, Microsoft's stock symbol MSFT is
replaced with the three-letter option symbol MSQ for use in
option symbols.

STOCKS TRADING IN A WIDE RANGE

Some stocks trade within a very wide range or move up or down
from one price range to another very quickly, either due to high
volatility or a stock split. It would be impossible to determine
which specific strike price was being indicated in such cases.

Therefore, those options are given new three-letter symbols whenever they move from one price range to another.

At the time this was written, Microsoft, for example, was using the symbol MSQ for options with strike prices from $50 to $130. Microsoft options with strike prices above $130 were using the symbol MQV, and Microsoft options with strike prices below $50 were using MQF. LEAPS, which are very long term options that can expire in a year or more, use entirely different three-letter symbols.

AN OCCASIONAL VARIATION

When there is a hyphen followed by a letter at the end of the symbol, the letter indicates the exchange upon which that option is traded:

E = CBOE (Chicago Board Options Exchange)

A = AMEX (American Stock Exchange)

X = PHLX (Philadelphia Stock Exchange)

P = PCX or PSE (Pacific Stock Exchange)

So the symbol IBM FT-E signifies an IBM June *call* with a $100 *strike price* trading at the CBOE.

Nasdaq-100 Index Tracking Stock (QQQ)

The introduction of the Nasdaq-100 Index Tracking Stock (QQQ) allows investors to purchase a share of stock in order to invest in the largest and most actively traded companies on the Nasdaq stock market—the companies of the Nasdaq-100 index. Nasdaq-100 Index Tracking Stock trades under the ticker symbol QQQ. With the Nasdaq-100 Index Tracking Stock, you can buy or sell shares in the collective performance of the Nasdaq-100 index in a single transaction—just as you buy or sell shares of individual stocks. It's a one-investment portfolio that gives you ownership in the 100 stocks of the Nasdaq-100 index. And because Nasdaq-100 Index Tracking Stock trades like stock, you can buy them on margin, sell short, or hold your shares for the long term. When you purchase Nasdaq-100 Index Tracking Stock, you're investing in the Nasdaq-100 Trust, a unit investment trust that holds shares of the companies in the Nasdaq-100 index. The trust is designed to closely track the price and yield performance of the index—so you can expect your Nasdaq-100 Index Tracking Stock to move up or down in value when the index moves up or down.

The initial market value of QQQ generally approximates 1/40 the value of the underlying Nasdaq-100 (NDX) index. So, for example, if the NDX price level is 1400, the QQQs generally would be expected to be priced around $35. QQQs may be bought and sold at intraday prices throughout the trading day—something you can't do with conventional index mutual funds that are generally purchased or redeemed only at an end-of-day closing price related to net asset value. The pricing of Nasdaq-100 Index Tracking Stock is continuous, subject to any trading halts, during exchange trading hours.

Table C.1 lists the CBOE Mini-NDX, Nasdaq-100, and Nasdaq-100 Index Tracking Stock as of March 1, 2002.

TABLE C.1

Symbol	Company Name	Percent of Index
ABGX	Abgenix, Inc.	0.14
ADCT	ADC Telecommunications, Inc.	0.37
ADLAC	Adelphia Communications Corporation	0.54
ADBE	Adobe Systems, Incorporated	0.86
ALTR	Altera Corporation	1.08
AMZN	Amazon.com, Inc.	0.36
AMGN	Amgen, Inc.	2.75
ADRX	Andrx Group	0.27
APOL	Apollo Group, Inc.	0.55
AAPL	Apple Computer, Inc.	1.1
AMAT	Applied Materials, Inc.	1.95
AMCC	Applied Micro Circuits Corporation	0.29
ATML	Atmel Corporation	0.26
BEAS	BEA Systems, Inc.	0.49
BBBY	Bed Bath & Beyond, Inc.	1.28
BGEN	Biogen, Inc.	0.95
BMET	Biomet, Inc.	1.07
BRCM	Broadcom Corporation	0.57
BRCD	Brocade Communications Systems, Inc.	0.56
CDWC	CDW Computer Centers, Inc.	0.47
CEPH	Cephalon, Inc.	0.25
CHTR	Charter Communications, Inc.	0.33
CHKP	Check Point Software Technologies, Ltd.	0.69
CHIR	Chiron Corporation	1.13
CIEN	CIENA Corporation	0.3
CTAS	Cintas Corporation	0.91
CSCO	Cisco Systems, Inc.	3.8
CTXS	Citrix Systems, Inc.	0.32
CMCSK	Comcast Corporation	1.49
CPWR	Compuware Corporation	0.27
CMVT	Comverse Technology, Inc.	0.29
CEFT	Concord EFS, Inc.	1.75
CNXT	Conexant Systems, Inc.	0.29
COST	Costco Wholesale Corporation	0.94
CYTC	CYTYC Corporation	0.28
DELL	Dell Computer Corporation	2.45

TABLE C.1

(Continued)

Symbol	Company Name	Percent of Index
EBAY	eBay, Inc.	1.08
DISH	EchoStar Communications Corporation	0.64
ERTS	Electronic Arts, Inc.	0.74
ESRX	Express Scripts, Inc.	0.35
FISV	Fiserv, Inc.	0.99
FLEX	Flextronics International, Ltd.	0.8
GMST	Gemstar-TV Guide International, Inc.	0.85
GENZ	Genzyme General	1.14
GILD	Gilead Sciences, Inc.	0.67
HGSI	Human Genome Sciences, Inc.	0.25
ITWO	i2 Technologies, Inc.	0.25
ICOS	ICOS Corporation	0.22
IDPH	IDEC Pharmaceuticals Corporation	1.04
IMCL	ImClone Systems, Incorporated	0.19
IMNX	Immunex Corporation	2.09
IDTI	Integrated Device Technology, Inc.	0.27
INTC	Intel Corporation	7.04
INTU	Intuit, Inc.	1.01
IVGN	Invitrogen Corporation	0.16
JDSU	JDS Uniphase Corporation	0.67
JNPR	Juniper Networks, Inc.	0.2
KLAC	KLA-Tencor Corporation	1.39
LLTC	Linear Technology Corporation	1.67
ERICY	LM Ericsson Telephone Company	0.43
MXIM	Maxim Integrated Products, Inc.	2.21
MEDI	MedImmune, Inc.	1.07
MERQ	Mercury Interactive Corporation	0.29
MCHP	Microchip Technology, Incorporated	0.4
MSFT	Microsoft Corporation	10.99
MLNM	Millennium Pharmaceuticals, Inc.	0.56
MOLX	Molex, Incorporated	0.28
NTAP	Network Appliance, Inc.	0.62
NXTL	Nextel Communications, Inc.	0.46
NVLS	Novellus Systems, Inc.	0.68
NVDA	NVIDIA Corporation	0.84
ORCL	Oracle Corporation	3.58

TABLE C.1

(Continued)

Symbol	Company Name	Percent of Index
PCAR	PACCAR, Inc.	0.61
SPOT	PanAmSat Corporation	0.42
PAYX	Paychex, Inc.	1.31
PSFT	PeopleSoft, Inc.	1.34
PMCS	PMC - Sierra, Inc.	0.28
PDLI	Protein Design Labs, Inc.	0.12
QLGC	QLogic Corporation	0.39
QCOM	QUALCOMM, Incorporated	3.2
RATL	Rational Software Corporation	0.38
RFMD	RF Micro Devices, Inc.	0.3
SANM	Sanmina-SCI Corporation	0.55
SEPR	Sepracor, Inc.	0.33
SEBL	Siebel Systems, Inc.	1.59
SSC	Smurfit-Stone Container Corporation	0.37
SPLS	Staples, Inc.	0.6
SBUX	Starbucks Corporation	1.2
SUNW	Sun Microsystems, Inc.	1.21
SYMC	Symantec Corporation	0.52
SNPS	Synopsys, Inc.	0.26
TLAB	Tellabs, Inc.	0.24
TMPW	TMP Worldwide, Inc.	0.34
USAI	USA Networks, Inc.	1.13
VRSN	VeriSign, Inc.	0.57
VRTS	VERITAS Software Corporation	1.55
VTSS	Vitesse Semiconductor Corporation	0.16
WCOM	WorldCom, Inc.	0.82
XLNX	Xilinx, Inc.	1.69
YHOO	Yahoo! Inc.	0.43

Currently Available Options

This appendix lists all companies with currently available options, their symbol prefix, the exchange on which their options are traded, and their option cycle. The three option cycles are (1) January, April, July, October; (2) February, May, August, November; and (3) March, June, September, December.

Company Name	Option Symbol	Stock Symbol	Exchange(s)	Cycle
24/7 Media, Inc.	BMQ	TFSM	ACP	1
360networks Inc.	IXQ	TSIX	ACX	3
3Com Corp.	THQ	COMS	ACPX	1
3DFX Interactive, Inc.	FQ	TDFX	ACP	3
3DO Company (The)	TUD	THDO	C	1
4Front Technologies, Inc.	QFO	FFTI	A	1
4Kids Entertainment, Inc.	KDE	KDE	AC	2
724 Solutions, Inc.	QXY	SVNX	AC	3
8x8, Inc.	EDQ	NTRG	C	2
99 Cents Only Stores	NDN	NDN	AP	3
AAR Corp.	AIR	AIR	X	1
Abbott Laboratories	ABT	ABT	ACIPX	2
Abercrombie & Fitch Company	ANF	ANF	ACP	2
Abgenix, Inc.	AZU	ABGX	AC	1
ABIOMED, Inc.	IBU	ABMD	A	3
Abitibi-Price, Inc.	ABY	ABY	C	1
Able Telcom Holding Corp.	QZB	ABTE	P	3
About.com	AUB	BOUT	AC	2
Acacia Research Corp.	KRU	ACRI	A	2
Acclaim Entertainment, Inc.	KKQ	AKLM	C	1
Accredo Health, Incorporated	DZU	ACDO	C	1
Accure Software, Inc.	AUJ	ACRU	AC	1
ACE, Ltd.	ACL	ACL	P	2
Aclara Biosciences, Inc.	GQA	ACLA	AP	1
ACNielsen Corp.	ART	ART	A	2
ACT Manufacturing, Inc.	MMQ	ACTM	C	1
ACT Networks, Inc.	QTE	ANET	C	1
Actel Corp.	LQA	ACTL	PX	3
Acterna Corp.	UWC	ACTR	AC	1
Action Performance Companies, Inc.	QNC	ACTN	C	1
Active Power, Inc.	ACQ	ACPW	ACP	1
Active Software, Inc.	QAS	ASWX	AX	1
Activision, Inc.	AQV	ATVI	C	2
Actuate Corp.	UHQ	ACTU	A	2
ACTV, Inc.	AUC	IATV	CPX	2
Acuson Corp.	ACN	ACN	P	1
Acxiom Corp.	UQA	ACXM	AC	2
ADAC Laboratories	QAB	ADAC	A	2
Adaptec, Inc.	APQ	ADPT	ACPX	1
Adaptive Broadband Corp.	CQI	ADAP	AC	1
ADC Telecommunications, Inc.	TLQ	ADCT	ACIPX	2
Ade Corp.	QDE	ADEX	A	3

Company Name	Option Symbol	Stock Symbol	Exchange(s)	Cycle
Adelphia Business Solutions, Inc.	QPI	ABIZ	C	1
Adelphia Communications (Class A)	ADU	ADLAC	ACIPX	1
Adept Technology, Inc.	QN	ADTK	ACPX	3
Administaff, Inc.	ASF	ASF	C	1
Adobe Systems, Inc.	AEQ	ADBE	ACIPX	1
ADTRAN, Inc.	RQA	ADTN	APX	2
Advanced Digital Information Corp.	QXG	ADIC	ACIP	3
Advanced Energy Industries	OEQ	AEIS	CP	1
Advanced Fibre Communications	AQF	AFCI	ACIPX	3
Advanced Lighting Technologies, Inc.	LQY	ADLT	X	3
Advanced Micro Devices, Inc.	AMD	AMD	ACIPX	1
Advanced Polymer Systems, Inc.	QAP	APOS	P	3
Advanced Radio Telecom Corp.	AOQ	ARTT	AP	2
AdvancePCS	QVD	ADVP	AP	3
ADVANTA Corp. (Class A)	AVQ	ADVNA	AC	1
ADVANTA Corp. (Class B)	ABQ	ADVNB	A	1
Advantage Learning Systems, Inc.	AIU	ALSI	CP	1
Advent Software Inc.	UIV	ADVS	PX	2
ADVO Inc.	AD	AD	A	2
Aegon NV ADR	AEG	AEG	CX	1
Aerial Communications, Inc.	IQA	AERL	C	3
Aeroflex Incorporated	ARX	ARXX	CP	3
AES Corp.	AES	AES	ACPX	2
Aether Systems, Inc.	EHU	AETH	ACIPX	2
Aetna Inc.	AET	AET	ACIPX	1
Affiliated Computer Services, Inc.	ACS	ACS	CP	1
Affiliated Managers Group, Inc.	AMG	AMG	A	3
Affymetrix, Inc.	FIQ	AFFX	ACIPX	2
AFLAC Incorporated	AFL	AFL	ACX	2
Aftermarket Technology Corp.	AQK	ATAC	X	2
AGCO Corp.	AG	AG	P	2
AGENCY.COM, Ltd.	AUY	ACOM	A	2
Agile Software Corp.	AUG	AGIL	ACP	1
Agilent Technologies, Corp.	A	A	ACPX	2
AGL Resources, Inc.	ATG	ATG	P	3
Agnico-Eagle Mines Ltd.	AEM	AEM	CP	2
AgriBioTech, Inc.	QXQ	ABTXQ	C	1
Agrium, Inc.	AGU	AGU	C	1
Air Express International Corp.	XPQ	AEIC	P	2
Air Products & Chemicals, Inc.	APD	APD	PX	3
Airborne Freight Corp.	ABF	ABF	ACIX	2
Airgas Inc.	ARG	ARG	X	1
AirGate PCS, Inc.	CQO	PCSA	AP	1
Airnet Communications Corp.	UZE	ANCC	AC	2
AirTran Holdings, Inc.	AAI	AAI	AC	1
AK Steel Holding Corp.	AKS	AKS	C	3
Akamai Technologies, Inc.	UMU	AKAM	ACIPX	2

Key to Exchanges: A = AMEX (American Stock Exchange); C = CBOE (Chicago Board Options Exchange); I = International Securities Exchange; P = PCX or PSE (Pacific Stock Exchange); and X = PHLX (Philadelphia Stock Exchange).

Company Name	Option Symbol	Stock Symbol	Exchange(s)	Cycle
Aksys, Ltd.	KQK	AKSY	P	1
Akzo Nobel NV-ADR	OUQ	AKZOY	A	1
Alamosa Holdings, Inc.	CUT	APCS	P	1
Alaska Air Group, Inc.	ALK	ALK	A	1
Albany Molecular Research, Inc.	EUK	AMRI	ACP	2
Albemarle Corp.	ALB	ALB	P	3
Albertson's, Inc.	ABS	ABS	CX	3
Alcan Aluminum Limited	AL	AL	AC	3
Alcatel	ALA	ALA	ACIPX	3
Alcatel Optronics	UOV	ALAO	ACP	3
ALCOA Inc.	AA	AA	ACIPX	1
Alexander & Baldwin	XQD	ALEX	X	3
Alexion Pharmaceuticals, Inc.	XQN	ALXN	CX	2
Algos Pharmaceuticals Corp.	GQL	ALGO	A	1
Aliant Communications, Inc.	LSQ	ALNT	P	1
Align Technology, Inc.	UAF	ALGN	C	1
Alkermes, Inc.	QAL	ALKS	CP	2
Allaire Corp.	AUR	ALLR	CP	1
Allegheny Energy, Inc.	AYE	AYE	ACP	3
Allegheny Technologies Incorporated	ATI	ATI	C	1
Allegiance Telecom, Inc.	QGX	ALGX	CPX	3
Allen Group, Inc. (The)	ALN	ALN	A	3
Allergan, Inc.	AGN	AGN	ACX	1
Alliance Capital Management L.P.	AC	AC	C	1
Alliance Semiconductor Corp.	ASU	ALSC	ACPX	1
Allied Capital Corp.	CQL	ALLC	A	2
Allied Riser Communications Corp.	UKA	ARCC	AC	3
Allied Waste Industries, Inc.	AW	AW	AC	3
Allmerica Financial Corp.	AFC	AFC	A	2
Alloy Online, Inc.	YLQ	ALOY	CP	2
Allscripts Healthcare Solutions Inc.	HIQ	MDRX	A	1
Allstate Corp. (The)	ALL	ALL	ACIPX	1
ALLTEL Corp.	AT	AT	ACPX	1
Alpha Industries, Inc.	GAQ	AHAA	X	2
Alpharma, Inc. (Class A)	ALO	ALO	AX	3
Alteon Websystems, Inc.	UAO	ATON	AX	3
Altera Corp.	LTQ	ALTR	ACIPX	3
Alternative Living Services	ALI	ALI	AC	2
ALZA Corp.	AZA	AZA	ACIPX	1
Amazon.com Inc.	ZQN	AMZN	ACIPX	1
AMB Property Corp.	AMB	AMB	P	2
AMBAC, Inc.	ADE	ABK	P	2
AMC Entertainment Inc.	AEN	AEN	A	3
AMCOL International Corp.	ACO	ACO	X	3
AMCORE Financial, Inc.	FNQ	AMFI	X	2
Amdocs Ltd.	DOX	DOX	ACIP	1
Amerada Hess Corp.	AHC	AHC	ACX	2
Ameren Corp.	AEE	AEE	X	3
Amerian Water Works, Inc.	AWK	AWK	X	2
America Movil S.A. de C.V.	AMX	AMX	ACPX	2
America Online Latin America	AEU	AOLA	ACP	1
America West Holdings Corp. (Class B)	AWA	AWA	A	1

Company Name	Option Symbol	Stock Symbol	Exchange(s)	Cycle
American Business Information (Class A)	HAQ	IUSAA	X	1
American Capital Strategies, Ltd.	DQS	ACAS	C	2
American Disposal Services, Inc.	HIQ	ADSI	A	1
American Eagle Outfitters, Inc.	AQU	AEOS	CPX	2
American Electric Power Company, Inc.	AEP	AEP	C	2
American Express Company	AXP	AXP	ACIPX	1
American Financial Group, Inc.	AFG	AFG	X	3
American Freightways Corp.	FQD	AFWY	AX	1
American General Corp.	AGC	AGC	ACP	1
American Greetings Corp. (Class A)	AM	AM	P	1
American Home Products Corp.	AHP	AHP	ACIPX	1
American Homestar Corp.	HQF	HSTR	P	1
American International Group, Inc.	AIG	AIG	ACPX	2
American Italian Pasta Company	PLB	PLB	A	3
American Management Systems, Inc.	YAQ	AMSY	C	1
American Power Conversion Corp.	PWQ	APCC	ACPX	3
American Standard Companies Inc.	ASD	ASD	C	1
American Superconductor Corp.	QAY	AMSC	AX	1
American Tower Corp. (Class A)	AMT	AMT	CIPX	1
American Xtal Technology, Inc.	AQX	AXTI	C	1
AmeriCredit Corp.	ACF	ACF	ACP	2
Ameripath Inc.	AQE	PATH	A	3
AmeriSource Health Corp.	AAS	AAS	ACIPX	2
Ameritrade Holding Corp. (Class A)	TQA	AMTD	ACIP	2
Ames Department Stores, Inc.	QAF	AMES	AC	1
AMFM, Inc.	AFM	AFM	CI	1
Amgen, Inc.	AMQ	AMGN	ACIPX	1
Amkor Technology, Inc.	QEL	AMKR	ACPX	3
Amoco Corp. Adj.	AX	AX	P	2
Ampal-American Israel Corp. (Class A)	AIS	AMPL	A	3
Amphenol Corp.	APH	APH	CP	1
AMR Corp.	AMR	AMR	ACIPX	2
AmSouth Bancorporation	ASO	ASO	ACX	3
AmSurg Corp.	AUO	AMSGA	A	2
Amway Asia Pacific Ltd.	AAP	AAP	A	2
Amylin Pharmaceuticals, Inc.	UMQ	AMLN	ACP	1
Anadarko Petroleum Corp.	APC	APC	ACPX	2
Anadigics, Inc.	DQA	ANAD	ACPX	1
Analog Devices, Inc.	ADI	ADI	ACIPX	3
Analysts International Corp.	AQJ	ANLY	P	1
Anaren Microwave, Inc.	EUA	ANEN	ACP	1
Anchor Gaming	QLT	SLOT	C	1
Ancor Communications, Inc.	CUA	ANCR	ACP	2
Andrea Electronics Corp.	AND	AND	AC	2
Andrew Corp.	AQN	ANDW	CI	1
Andrx Corp.	QAX	ADRX	ACP	3
Anesta Corp.	NQB	NSTA	X	1

Key to Exchanges: A = AMEX (American Stock Exchange); C = CBOE (Chicago Board Options Exchange); I = International Securities Exchange; P = PCX or PSE (Pacific Stock Exchange); and X = PHLX (Philadelphia Stock Exchange).

Company Name	Option Symbol	Stock Symbol	Exchange(s)	Cycle
Anglogold Limited	AU	AU	ACP	1
Anheuser-Busch Companies, Inc.	BUD	BUD	ACPX	3
Anicom Inc.	NIQ	ANIC	X	3
Anika Therapeutics, Inc.	AKQ	ANIK	P	2
Anixter International, Inc.	AXE	AXE	A	2
Ann Taylor Stores, Inc.	ANN	ANN	CIP	3
AnswerThink Consulting Group	QRA	ANSR	AC	1
ANTEC Corp.	AQC	ANTC	CP	2
Anthracite Capital Inc.	AHR	AHR	X	2
AOL Time Warner, Inc.	AOL	AOL	ACIPX	1
AON Corp.	AOC	AOC	CP	1
Apache Corp.	APA	APA	ACIPX	1
Apartment Invt. & Mgmt. Co. (Class A)	AIV	AIV	A	3
Apex, Inc.	PXQ	APEX	ACP	3
Aphton Corp.	HQY	APHT	P	3
Apogee Enterprises, Inc.	EQG	APOG	P	2
Apollo Group, Inc.	OAQ	APOL	C	2
Apple Computer, Inc.	AAQ	AAPL	ACIPX	1
Apple South, Inc.	SQO	AVDO	A	3
Applebee's International, Inc.	AQB	APPB	C	2
Applera Corp.–Celera Genomics Group	CRA	CRA	ACPX	3
Applera Corp.–Applied Biosystems Group	ABI	ABI	ACIP	3
Applica	APN	APN	P	3
Applied Digital Solutions	DUU	ADSX	AC	2
Applied Graphics Technologies	GLJ	AGTX	A	3
Applied Industrial Technologies, Inc.	APZ	APZ	P	1
Applied Materials, Inc.	ANQ	AMAT	ACIPX	1
Applied Micro Circuits Corp.	QLL	AMCC	ACIPX	2
Applied Molecular Evolution, Inc.	AUM	AMEV	A	1
Applied Power, Inc.	APW	APW	AC	1
Applied Power, Inc.	ATU	ATU	AC	1
Applied Science & Technology, Inc.	AUT	ASTX	C	1
AppliedTheory Corp.	UZL	ATHY	A	2
Applix, Inc.	AUL	APLX	C	1
AppNet Systems, Inc.	UAP	APNT	AC	1
Apria Healthcare Group Incorporated	AHG	AHG	AC	3
AptarGroup Inc.	ATR	ATR	A	1
Aquila, Inc.	ILA	ILA	ACP	1
Aracruz Cellulose S.A. ADR	ARA	ARA	C	2
Aradigm Corp.	QRQ	ARDM	X	1
Arbitron Inc.	ARB	ARB	AC	2
Arcadia Financial Ltd.	AAC	AAC	A	1
Arch Coal, Inc.	ACI	ACI	C	1
Arch Wireless Inc.	UAZ	ARCH	C	2
Archer-Daniels-Midland Company	ADM	ADM	CPX	3
Archstone Communities Trust	ASN	ASN	P	1
Ardent Software Inc.	KQV	ARDT	A	2
AremisSoft Corp.	UKM	AREM	ACP	1
Argosy Gaming Company	AGY	AGY	ACX	2
ARIAD Pharmaceuticals, Inc.	UAQ	ARIA	AC	2
Ariba, Inc.	IRU	ARBA	ACPX	2

Company Name	Option Symbol	Stock Symbol	Exchange(s)	Cycle
Armor Holdings Inc.	AH	AH	PX	2
Armstrong World Industries, Inc.	ACK	ACK	X	3
ArQule, Inc.	ARQ	ARQL	A	3
Arrow Electronics, Inc.	ARW	ARW	AC	3
Arrow International Inc.	QRO	ARRO	X	2
Art Technology Group, Inc.	AYQ	ARTG	AC	2
Artesyn Technologies, Inc.	UAT	ATSN	ACP	2
ArthroCare Corp.	ARU	ARTC	A	3
Arthur J. Gallagher & Co	AJG	AJG	ACP	1
Artisoft, Inc.	AGQ	ASFT	AC	2
Arvin Industries, Inc.	ARV	ARV	A	2
ArvinMeritor, Inc.	ARM	ARM	AC	2
ASA Limited	ASA	ASA	ACPX	2
ASARCO Incorporated	AR	AR	A	3
Ascent Entertainment Group, Inc.	NDQ	GOAL	A	2
ASE Test Limited	QDQ	ASTSF	C	2
Ashanti Goldfields Company Limited	ASL	ASL	A	2
Ashford.com	AFU	ASFD	CA	2
Ashland, Inc.	ASH	ASH	X	1
Ashton Technology Group, Inc. (The)	TUS	ASTN	AC	3
Asia Pacific Fund, Inc. (The)	APB	APB	A	3
Asia Pulp & Paper Company Ltd. ADR	PAP	PAP	A	3
Asiainfo Holdings Inc.	EUJ	ASIA	AC	1
Ask Jeeves, Inc.	AUK	ASKJ	ACX	1
ASM International N.V.	IQB	ASMI	C	3
ASM Lithography Holding N.V.	MFQ	ASML	CP	1
Aspect Development Inc.	QDV	ASDV	ACP	3
Aspect Telecommunications Corp.	ATQ	ASPT	ACIP	3
Aspen Technology, Inc.	ZQP	AZPN	A	2
Associated Banc-Corp.	QVS	ASBC	CX	3
Associated Group, Inc. (Class B)	AQD	AGRPB	P	3
Associated Group, Inc.	JAQ	AGRPA	P	3
Associates First Capital Corp.	KVG	KVG	AC	3
Astec Industries Inc.	QYA	ASTE	A	3
Astoria Financial Corp.	AQR	ASFC	CX	1
AstraZeneca plc ADS	AZN	AZN	CX	1
AstroPower, Inc.	PUW	APWR	A	3
Asyst Technologies, Inc.	QQY	ASYT	APX	3
At Home Corp. Ser. A	AHQ	ATHM	ACIPX	1
AT&T Canada, Inc. (Class B)	MFU	ATTC	CX	1
AT&T Corp.–Liberty Media Group (Class A)	LMG	LMGA	ACIPX .	1
AT&T Corp.	T	T	ACIPX	1
AT&T Latin America	TUT	ATTL	ACP	1
AT&T Wireless Group	AWE	AWE	ACPX	1
Atlantic Coast Airlines Holdings	QKA	ACAI	AX	2
Atlantic Richfield Company	ARC	ARC	ACP	1
Atlas Air Worldwide Holdings, Inc.	CGO	CGO	C	1

Key to Exchanges: A = AMEX (American Stock Exchange); C = CBOE (Chicago Board Options Exchange); I = International Securities Exchange; P = PCX or PSE (Pacific Stock Exchange); and X = PHLX (Philadelphia Stock Exchange).

Company Name	Option Symbol	Stock Symbol	Exchange(s)	Cycle
Atmel Corp.	AQT	ATML	ACPX	2
ATMI Inc.	ASQ	ATMI	A	3
Atrix Laboratories Inc.	OQF	ATRX	X	2
Atwood Oceanics Inc.	ATW	ATW	PX	1
Audible, Inc.	OBQ	ADBL	ACX	3
AudioCodes Ltd.	UXR	AUDC	ACP	1
Audiovox Corp.	UXX	VOXX	AX	1
Aurora Biosciences Corp.	UDA	ABSC	AC	1
Aurora Foods Inc.	AOR	AOR	P	1
Auspex Systems, Inc.	XUM	ASPX	C	1
Authentic Fitness Corp.	ASM	ASM	P	1
Authentidate Holding Corp.	BUW	ADAT	A	3
Autobytel.com	UBL	ABTL	ACX	1
Autodesk, Inc.	ADQ	ADSK	P	1
Automatic Data Processing, Inc.	ADP	ADP	ACPX	2
AutoNation, Inc.	AN	AN	AC	1
Autoweb.com	UWB	AWEB	AC	2
Autozone, Inc.	AZO	AZO	C	3
Avalon Bay Communities, Inc.	AVB	AVB	P	2
Avanex Corp.	UYN	AVNX	ACIP	3
AVANT Immnotherapeutics, Inc.	AFQ	AVAN	AC	1
AVANT! Corp.	NVQ	AVNT	P	1
Avaya Inc.	AV	AV	ACPX	1
Aventis ADS	AVE	AVE	AC	1
Avery Dennison Corp.	AVY	AVY	X	1
Aviall, Inc.	AVL	AVL	X	3
Avici Systems, Inc.	QYV	AVCI	ACPX	3
Avid Technology, Inc.	AQI	AVID	AC	3
Avigen, Inc.	GKU	AVGN	AC	2
Aviron	QCV	AVIR	AC	2
Avis Rent A Car Inc.	AVI	AVI	ACX	3
Avista Corp.	AVA	AVA	C	1
Avnet, Inc.	AVT	AVT	ACP	2
Avocent Corp.	QVX	AVCT	ACP	2
Avon Products, Inc.	AVP	AVP	ACP	1
AVX Corp.	AVX	AVX	ACPX	2
Aware, Inc.	WUQ	AWRE	CPX	1
AXA Financial, Inc.	AXF	AXF	AC	1
Axa-Spons ADR	AXA	AXA	ACP	1
Axcelis Technologies, Inc.	ULS	ACLS	AC	1
Axent Technologies, Inc.	XQJ	AXNT	X	2
Axys Pharmaceuticals	QAR	AXPH	P	1
Aztar Corp.	AZR	AZR	C	2
B2B Internet HOLDRS	BHH	BHH	AC	2
BackWeb Technologies Ltd.	UBW	BWEB	ACPX	3
Baker (J.), Inc.	JBQ	JBAK	C	3
Baker Hughes Incorporated	BHI	BHI	ACIPX	1
Baldor Electric Company	BEZ	BEZ	P	2
Ball Corp.	BLL	BLL	A	2
Ballard Medical Products	BMP	BMP	A	1
Ballard Power Systems Inc.	DFQ	BLDP	ACIP	2
Bally Total Fitness Holding Corp.	BFT	BFT	A	2

Company Name	Option Symbol	Stock Symbol	Exchange(s)	Cycle
Banco Bilbao Vizcaya SA-ADR	BBV	BBV	A	1
Banco de Galicia y Buenos Aires S.A.	QYL	BGALY	APX	2
Banco Frances del Rio de la Plata S.A. ADR	BFR	BFR	C	1
Banco Rio de La Plata S.A. ADR	BRS	BRS	C	1
Banco Santander S.A.	STD	STD	A	3
Bancorp Hawaii, Inc.	BOH	BOH	A	2
BancTec, Inc.	BTC	BTC	C	2
Bank of America Corp.	BAC	BAC	ACPX	2
Bank of Boston Corp.	BKB	BKB	AX	2
Bank of Commerce	QMB	BCOM	C	1
Bank of New York Company, Inc. (The)	BK	BK	ACIPX	1
Bank of Tokyo Mitsubishi ADR	MBK	MBK	CP	2
Bank One Corp.	ONE	ONE	ACIPX	2
Bank Plus Corp.	QBP	BPLS	P	1
Bank United Corp.-(Class A)	BKQ	BNKU	X	2
BankAtlantic Bancorp, Inc.	BBX	BBX	A	3
Banknorth Group Inc.	EQP	BKNG	C	2
BankUnited Financial Corp.	QBF	BKUNA	P	1
BanPonce Corp.	BQW	BPOP	X	1
Banta Corp.	BN	BN	X	3
Bard (C.R.) Inc.	BCR	BCR	ACX	1
Barnes & Noble, Inc.	BKS	BKS	AC	1
Barnsandnoble.com	BEU	BNBN	ACX	2
Barr Laboratories, Inc.	BRL	BRL	AX	2
Barrett Resources Corp.	BRR	BRR	ACX	3
Barrick Gold Corp.	ABX	ABX	ACPX	1
Basic Industries SPDR	XLB	XLB	A	3
Basin Exploration, Inc.	QBS	BSNX	X	2
BAT Industries PLC ADR	BTI	BTI	A	1
Bausch & Lomb Incorporated	BOL	BOL	AC	1
Baxter International, Inc.	BAX	BAX	ACIP	2
BayView Capital Corp.	BVC	BVC	X	2
BB&T Corp.	BBT	BBT	CX	3
BCE, Inc.	BCE	BCE	ACPX	3
BE Aerospace, Inc.	BQV	BEAV	X	1
Be Free, Inc.	UFB	BFRE	AC	2
Be Incorporated	BUO	BEOS	CX	2
BEA Systems, Inc.	BRQ	BEAS	ACPX	3
Bear Stearns Companies, Inc. (The)	BSC	BSC	ACPX	1
Beckman Instruments	BEC	BEC	AX	2
Becton Dickinson & Company	BDX	BDX	CIPX	3
Bed Bath & Beyond, Inc.	BHQ	BBBY	ACX	2
Bedford Property Investors	BED	BED	P	2
Belco Oil & Gas Corp.	BOG	BOG	A	2
Belden Inc.	BWC	BWC	A	3
Bell & Howell Company	BHW	BHW	X	2
Bell Microproducts Inc.	QBL	BELM	P	3

Key to Exchanges: A = AMEX (American Stock Exchange); C = CBOE (Chicago Board Options Exchange); I = International Securities Exchange; P = PCX or PSE (Pacific Stock Exchange); and X = PHLX (Philadelphia Stock Exchange).

Company Name	Option Symbol	Stock Symbol	Exchange(s)	Cycle
BellSouth Corp.	BLS	BLS	ACPX	1
Bemis Company	BMS	BMS	A	1
Benchmark Electronics, Inc.	BHE	BHE	P	2
Bergen Brunswig Corp. (Class A)	BBC	BBC	C	3
Beringer Wine Estates(Class B)	QIB	BERW	A	1
Berry Petroleum-(Class A)	BRY	BRY	P	3
Best Buy Co., Inc.	BBY	BBY	ACIPX	3
BestFoods	BFO	BFO	AP	1
Bethlehem Steel Corp.	BS	BS	C	1
Beverly Enterprises, Inc.	BEV	BEV	P	3
Bid.Com International Inc.	BDU	BIDS	ACPX	2
Big Flower Press Holdings, Inc.	BGF	BGF	X	3
Billing Information Concepts Corp.	QBI	BILL	P	2
Bindley Western Industries	BDY	BDY	X	3
Bindview Development Corp.	BVU	BVEW	C	1
BioChem Pharma, Inc.	BQX	BCHE	ACIPX	1
Biogen, Inc.	BGQ	BGEN	ACIP	1
Biomatrix, Inc.	XMU	BXM	AX	2
Biomet, Inc.	BIQ	BMET	CP	1
Biomira, Inc.	BSU	BIOM	AC	2
Biopure Corp.	QPU	BPUR	A	1
Biosite Diagnostics, Inc.	BQS	BSTE	C	1
Biotech HOLDRS Trust	BBH	BBH	ACP	1
Bio-Technology General Corp.	QTG	BTGC	C	1
Biotime Inc.	BTX	BTX	AC	3
Biovail Corporation International	BVF	BVF	ACIPX	1
BISYS Group, Inc. (The)	BQY	BSYS	AX	3
BJ Services Company	BJS	BJS	ACIP	1
BJ's Wholesale Club, Inc.	BJ	BJ	C	3
Black & Decker Corp. (The)	BDK	BDK	C	2
Black Box Corp.	QBX	BBOX	P	3
Block (H & R), Inc.	HRB	HRB	AP	1
Blockbuster Inc-(Class A)	BBI	BBI	ACPX	1
Blue Martini Software, Inc.	UVB	BLUE	ACPX	3
Bluestone Software, Inc.	XAP	BLSW	CPX	1
Blyth Industries, Inc.	BTH	BTH	A	3
BMC Software, Inc.	BMC	BMC	ACIPX	2
Bob Evans Farms, Inc.	BFQ	BOBE	P	1
BOC Group PLC ADR	BOX	BOX	X	3
Boca Resorts, Inc.	RST	RST	C	1
Boeing Company (The)	BA	BA	ACIPX	2
Boise Cascade Corp.	BCC	BCC	AC	2
Bookham Technology plc	BUI	BKHM	ACPX	3
Books-A-Million Inc.	QMZ	BAMM	ACX	2
Borden Chemicals & Plastics, L.P.	BCU	BCU	C	2
Borders Group, Inc.	BGP	BGP	AC	2
Borland Software Corp.	BLQ	BORL	AC	1
Boston Beer Co. Inc. (The)	SAM	SAM	AX	3
Boston Communications Group, Inc.	QGB	BCGI	AC	3
Boston Properties, Inc.	BXP	BXP	X	1
Boston Scientific Corp.	BSX	BSX	ACIPX	2
Bowater Incorporated	BOW	BOW	P	3

Company Name	Option Symbol	Stock Symbol	Exchange(s)	Cycle
Bowne & Co., Inc.	BNE	BNE	A	1
Boyds Collection, Ltd. (The)	FOB	FOB	X	1
BP Amoco plc	BP	BP	ACIPX	1
Brady Corp.	BRC	BRC	P	1
Brandywine Realty Trust	BDN	BDN	PX	2
Brasil Telecom Participacoes	BRP	BRP	A	1
Breakaway Solutions, Inc.	BUA	BWAY	ACP	1
BreezeCom Ltd.	UEV	BRZE	AC	1
Briggs and Stratton Corp.	BGG	BGG	X	1
Bright Horizons Family Solutions, Inc.	BFU	BFAM	P	2
Brightpoint, Inc.	QEF	CELL	C	3
Brinker International, Inc.	EAT	EAT	PX	1
Brio Technology, Inc.	UBR	BRIO	AC	3
Bristol-Myers Squibb Company	BMY	BMY	ACIPX	3
Brite Voice Systems, Inc.	VQB	BVSI	A	3
British Airways PLC ADR	BAB	BAB	X	1
British Telecommunications PLC ADR	BTY	BTY	C	1
Broad Vision, Inc.	BDV	BVSN	ACPX	3
Broadband HOLDRS	BDH	BDH	AC	2
Broadbase Software, Inc.	UUO	BBSW	AC	3
Broadcom, Inc.	RCQ	BRCM	ACIPX	2
BroadWing, Inc.	BRW	BRW	AC	1
Brocade Communications	UBF	BRCD	ACIPX	1
Brooks Automation, Inc.	BQE	BRKS	A	1
Brooktrout Technology, Inc.	BUQ	BRKT	AP	1
Brown Shoe Company, Inc.	BWS	BWS	A	3
Brunswick Corp.	BC	BC	C	3
Brusch Wellman Inc.	BW	BW	X	2
BSQUARE Corp.	BQL	BSQR	C	1
Buckeye Technologies Inc.	BKI	BKI	A	3
Buckle, Inc. (The)	BKE	BKE	PX	2
Budget Group, Inc.	BD	BD	X	2
Building Material Holdin Corp.	BWQ	BMHC	P	2
Building One Services Corp.	QYB	BOSS	C	2
Burlington Coat Factory Warehouse Corp.	BCF	BCF	X	1
Burlington Industries, Inc.	BUR	BUR	A	1
Burlington Northern Santa Fe Corp.	BNI	BNI	ACP	1
Burlington Resources, Inc.	BR	BR	ACPX	2
Burnham Pacific Properties, Inc.	BPP	BPP	P	2
Burr-Brown Corp.	BQB	BBRC	P	1
Business Objects S.A. ADR	BBQ	BOBJ	C	1
C H Robinson Worldwide, Inc.	CJQ	CHRW	X	2
C&D Technologies, Inc.	CHP	CHP	AC	2
C.I.T. Group, Inc.	CIT	CIT	ACX	1
Cable & Wireless Comms ADR	CWZ	CWZ	CX	2
Cable & Wireless HKT Ltd. ADS	HKT	HKT	AC	1
Cable & Wireless PLC ADR	CWP	CWP	C	2

Key to Exchanges: A = AMEX (American Stock Exchange); C = CBOE (Chicago Board Options Exchange); I = International Securities Exchange; P = PCX or PSE (Pacific Stock Exchange); and X = PHLX (Philadelphia Stock Exchange).

Company Name	Option Symbol	Stock Symbol	Exchange(s)	Cycle
Cable Design Technologies Corp.	CDT	CDT	PX	1
Cabletron Systems, Inc.	CS	CS	ACIPX	1
Cablevision Systems Corp.	CVC	CVC	CPX	3
Cabot Corp.	CBT	CBT	AC	1
Cabot Microelectronics Corp.	UKR	CCMP	ACP	1
Cabot Oil & Gas Corp.	COG	COG	P	1
CacheFlow, Inc.	FUJ	CFLO	CPX	1
CACI International	KFQ	CACI	X	3
Cadbury Schwepps PLC ADR	CSG	CSG	A	3
Cadence Design Systems, Inc.	CDN	CDN	ACIPX	2
Cadiz, Inc.	QAZ	CLCI	A	1
Caere Corp.	KAQ	CAER	A	2
Cal Dive International Inc.	KPQ	CDIS	A	3
Calgon Carbon Corp.	CCC	CCC	X	2
Calico Commerce, Inc.	OUC	CLIC	AC	1
California Amplifier, Inc.	UMP	CAMP	C	1
California Pizza Kitchen, Inc.	CUH	CPKI	AP	1
Caliper Technologies Corp.	DQQ	CALP	ACP	1
Callaway Golf Company	ELY	ELY	C	2
Calpine Corp.	CPN	CPN	ACIPX	1
Cambrex Corp.	CBM	CBM	P	1
Cambridge Technology Partners, Inc.	TQP	CATP	CX	3
Campbell Soup Company	CPB	CPB	AC	2
Canadian National Railway Company	CNI	CNI	C	1
Canadian Pacific Limited	CP	CP	X	1
Candela Corp.	UKZ	CLZR	A	2
Capital Automotive REIT	CQC	CARS	X	1
Capital One Financial Corp.	COF	COF	ACP	3
Capital Senior Living Corp.	CSU	CSU	A	2
Caprock Communications	KQL	CPRK	X	3
Capstone Turbine Corp.	CZU	CPST	ACP	2
Captaris, Inc.	QAT	CAPA	A	2
Carbon Energy Corp.	CRB	CRB	A	2
Cardinal Health, Inc.	CAH	CAH	ACIPX	3
Caremark RX, Inc.	CMX	CMX	ACX	3
Caribiner Intl Inc.	CWC	CWC	X	3
Carmike Cinemas, Inc. (Class A)	CKE	CKE	X	2
Carnival Corp. (Class A)	CCL	CCL	ACPX	1
Carpenter Technology Corp.	CRS	CRS	X	3
Carreker Corp.	CDU	CANI	ACP	2
Carrier 1 Int'l. S.A.	UFO	CONE	CP	3
Carrier Access Corp.	UCN	CACS	ACPX	1
Carter-Wallace, Inc.	CAR	CAR	C	1
Cascade Corp.	CAE	CAE	P	2
Casella Waste Systems, Inc.	KWQ	CWST	AX	3
Cash America Intl. Inc.	PWN	PWN	X	1
Catalina Marketing Corp.	POS	POS	A	2
Catalytica, Inc.	CSN	CTAL	C	1
Catellus Development Corp.	CDX	CDX	C	3
Caterpillar, Inc.	CAT	CAT	ACIPX	2
Cavalier Homes, Inc.	CAV	CAV	P	2
CBRL Group, Inc.	CBQ	CBRL	P	3

Company Name	Option Symbol	Stock Symbol	Exchange(s)	Cycle
CBS Corp.	CBS	CBS	ACP	1
CCC Information Services Group, Inc.	KDQ	CCCG	X	2
C-COR Electronics, Inc.	LQE	CCBL	A	3
C-Cube Microsystems, Inc.	UQB	CUBE	AC	2
Cdnow, Inc.	NWQ	CDNW	ACPX	2
CDW Computer Centers, Inc.	DWQ	CDWC	CX	1
CEC Entertainment Inc.	CEC	CEC	P	3
Celeritek, Inc.	UCK	CLTK	A	3
Celestica Inc.	CLS	CLS	ACIPX	3
Celgene Corp.	LQH	CELG	ACX	1
Cell Genesys, Inc.	UCG	CEGE	ACX	3
Cell Pathways Inc.	QJC	CLPA	ACX	1
Cell Therapeutics, Inc.	CUC	CTIC	ACP	2
CellNet Data Systems, Inc.	KQN	CNDSQ	A	3
Cellstar Corp.	EQL	CLST	AC	2
Celsion Corp.	CLN	CLN	A	3
Cemex S.A. de C.V.	CX	CX	A	1
Cendant Corp.	CD	CD	ACIPX	2
CENTEX Corp.	CTX	CTX	C	1
Centillium Communications, Inc.	UUM	CTLM	AC	1
Central & South West Corp.	CSR	CSR	P	2
Central Garden & Pet Company	EQH	CENT	C	2
Central Parking Corp.	CPC	CPC	X	3
Centura Banks, Inc.	CBC	CBC	X	3
Century Business Services	SSQ	CBIZ	P	1
Century Communications Corp. (Class A)	CQA	CTYA	C	2
Centurytel Inc.	CTL	CTL	P	1
Cephalon, Inc.	CQE	CEPH	AC	2
Ceragon Networks Ltd.	UKE	CRNT	A	1
Ceridian Corp. New	CEN	CEN	CP	2
Cerner Corp.	CQN	CERN	AC	3
Cerus Corp.	CEQ	CERS	APX	1
Champion Enterprises, Inc.	CHB	CHB	A	1
Champion International Corp.	CHA	CHA	CP	3
Charles River Laboratories International, Inc.	CRL	CRL	A	2
Charter Communications, Inc.	CUJ	CHTR	ACIPX	1
Chartered Semiconductor Mfg. Ltd	UCT	CHRT	AP	3
Chattem, Inc.	HQT	CHTT	A	3
Cheap Tickets Inc.	UEY	CTIX	CPX	1
Check Point Software Technologies Ltd.	KGE	CHKP	ACIPX	1
Checkfree Corp.	FCQ	CKFR	ACX	2
Checkpoint Systems, Inc.	CKP	CKP	P	2
Cheesecake Factory Incorporated (The)	CFQ	CAKE	AP	1
ChemFirst, Inc.	CEM	CEM	P	1
Chesapeake Corp.	CSK	CSK	A	2
Chevron Corp.	CHV	CHV	ACPX	3
Chico's FAS, Inc.	CHS	CHS	C	2

Key to Exchanges: A = AMEX (American Stock Exchange); C = CBOE (Chicago Board Options Exchange); I = International Securities Exchange; P = PCX or PSE (Pacific Stock Exchange); and X = PHLX (Philadelphia Stock Exchange).

Company Name	Option Symbol	Stock Symbol	Exchange(s)	Cycle
Children's Place	TUY	PLCE	APX	3
China Telecom Limited ADR	CHL	CHL	ACX	3
China Unicom Limited	CHU	CHU	CP	1
Chinadotcom Corp.	UIH	CHINA	ACX	2
Chiquita Brands International, Inc.	CQB	CQB	X	3
ChiRex, Inc.	RHQ	CHRX	P	2
Chiron Corp.	CIQ	CHIR	ACIPX	1
Choice One Communications, Inc.	HQD	CWON	P	1
ChoicePoint, Inc.	CPS	CPS	P	1
Chris-Craft Industries, Inc.	CCN	CCN	A	1
Christopher & Banks Corp.	URH	CHBS	AC	3
Chronimed, Inc.	HQC	CHMD	C	2
CHS Electronics, Inc.	HS	HS	AC	1
Chubb Corp. (The)	CB	CB	C	1
CIBER, Inc.	CBR	CBR	AP	2
CIDCO, Inc.	CDU	CDCO	ACX	3
Ciena Corp.	EUQ	CIEN	ACIPX	1
CIGNA Corp.	CI	CI	CP	1
CIMA Labs Inc.	UVK	CIMA	A	3
Cinar Corp.	CUF	CINRE	AC	1
Cincinnati Financial Corp.	CDQ	CINF	A	1
Cintas Corp.	NQQ	CTAS	AP	2
Circle International Group, Inc.	HQA	CRCL	P	1
Circuit City Stores, Inc.	CC	CC	ACIP	1
Cirrus Logic, Inc.	CUQ	CRUS	ACIP	3
Cisco Systems, Inc.	CYQ	CSCO	ACIPX	1
Citadel Communications Corp.	JTQ	CITC	AC	1
Citigroup, Inc.	C	C	ACIPX	3
Citizens Utilities Co. (Class B)	CZN	CZN	C	2
Citrix Systems, Inc.	XSQ	CTXS	ACPX	3
City National Corp.	CYN	CYN	C	2
Claire's Stores, Inc.	CLE	CLE	C	2
Clarent Corp.	KGQ	CLRN	AC	2
Clarify, Inc.	QCY	CLFY	C	2
Clarus Corp.	RUR	CLRS	ACPX	2
Clayton Homes, Inc.	CMH	CMH	CX	2
Clear Channel Communications, Inc.	CCU	CCU	ACIPX	1
Clearnet Communications Inc. (Class A)	CKQ	CLNT	A	2
Cleco Corp.	CNL	CNL	P	3
Clorox Company (The)	CLX	CLX	CIPX	1
C-MAC Industries, Inc.	EMS	EMS	P	1
CMGI, Inc.	QGC	CMGI	ACIPX	3
CMS Energy Corp.	CMS	CMS	C	3
CNA Financial Corp.	CNA	CNA	A	2
CNET, Inc.	QKW	CNET	ACIP	1
CNF Transportation Inc.	CNF	CNF	C	3
CNH Global N.V.	CNH	CNH	A	3
Coach, Inc.	COH	COH	AC	2
Coachman Industries, Inc.	COA	COA	A	3
Coastal Corp. (The)	CGP	CGP	AC	3
Coastcast Corp.	PAR	PAR	A	2
Cobalt Networks, Inc.	CJT	COBT	ACP	3

Company Name	Option Symbol	Stock Symbol	Exchange(s)	Cycle
Coca-Cola Company (The)	KO	KO	ACIPX	2
Coca-Cola Enterprises, Inc.	CCE	CCE	ACIPX	2
Coca-Cola Femsa S.A. ADR	KOF	KOF	C	1
Coeur d'Alene Mines Corp.	CDE	CDE	C	2
Cognex Corp.	QCG	CGNX	X	2
Cognos Incorporated	CRQ	COGN	ACP	2
Coherent, Inc.	HRQ	COHR	AP	2
Cohu, Inc.	QCH	COHU	P	2
Coinstar, Inc.	QLR	CSTR	CX	1
Cole National Corp.	CNJ	CNJ	X	2
Colgate-Palmolive Company	CL	CL	ACIP	2
Colonial BancGroup, Inc.	CNB	CNB	X	3
Colorado Medtech Inc.	QCW	CMED	CP	2
COLT Telecom Group plc ADR	CQF	COLT	AC	1
Columbia Energy Group	CWA	CG	AC	2
Columbia Laboratories, Inc.	COB	COB	AC	3
Com21, Inc.	CQH	CMTO	ACPX	1
Comair Holdings, Inc.	KHQ	COMR	C	3
Comcast Corp. (Class A)	CCQ	CMCSA	X	1
Comcast Corp. (Special Class A)	CQK	CMCSK	ACIPX	1
Comdial Corp.	TQC	CMDL	P	1
Comdisco, Inc.	CDO	CDO	ACP	1
Comerica Incorporated	CMA	CMA	ACPX	1
Commerce Bancorp, Inc.	CBH	CBH	X	3
Commerce Bancshares Inc.	UBA	CBSH	P	2
Commerce One, Inc.	RUC	CMRC	ACIPX	1
Commercial Federal Corp.	CFB	CFB	X	3
Commercial Net Lease Realty	NNN	NNN	P	2
Commscope, Inc.	CTV	CTV	AP	1
Commtouch Software, Ltd.	CUY	CTCH	AC	2
Community First Bankshares	QSJ	CFBX	P	2
Community Health Care	CYH	CYH	AC	1
Compania Anonima Nacional Venezuela	VNT	VNT	AC	1
Compania de Telecomunicaciones de Chile S.A. ADR	CTC	CTC	C	2
Compaq Computer Corp.	CPQ	CPQ	ACIPX	1
Compass Bancshares, Inc.	JQK	CBSS	P	1
CompuCredit Corp.	CUE	CCRT	ACP	1
CompUSA, Inc.	CPU	CPU	AC	2
Computer Associates International, Inc.	CA	CA	ACIPX	2
Computer Horizons Corp.	ZQH	CHRZ	C	3
Computer Learning Centers, Inc.	QXT	CLCX	A	2
Computer Sciences Corp.	CSC	CSC	ACPX	3
Computer Task Group, Inc.	CTG	CTG	X	2
ComputerNetwork Technology Corp.	QDO	CMNT	ACPX	1
Compuware Corp.	CWQ	CPWR	ACIP	2
Comstat Corp.	CQ	CQ	CX	1
Comstock Resources, Inc.	CRK	CRK	C	2

Key to Exchanges: A = AMEX (American Stock Exchange); C = CBOE (Chicago Board Options Exchange); I = International Securities Exchange; P = PCX or PSE (Pacific Stock Exchange); and X = PHLX (Philadelphia Stock Exchange).

Company Name	Option Symbol	Stock Symbol	Exchange(s)	Cycle
Comverse Technology, Inc.	CQV	CMVT	ACIPX	1
ConAgra, Inc.	CAG	CAG	ACIP	3
Concentric Network Corp.	QXF	CNCX	ACPX	1
Concord Camera Corp.	DVU	LENS	AC	2
Concord Communications Inc.	UCD	CCRD	ACPX	1
Concord EFS, Inc.	EQF	CEFT	CPX	3
Concur Technologies	COQ	CNQR	ACX	2
Concurrent Computer Corporation	URC	CCUR	ACX	2
Conexant Systems, Inc.	QXN	CNXT	ACPX	1
CONMED Corp.	KQD	CNMD	A	2
Connectiv Inc.	CIV	CIV	X	1
Conoco Inc. (Class B)	CKO	COCB	ACPX	1
Conoco, Inc.	COC	COCA	ACPX	1
Conseco, Inc.	CNC	CNC	ACIPX	2
CONSOL Energy Inc.	CNX	CNX	C	2
Consolidated Edison, Inc.	ED	ED	AC	2
Consolidated Freightways Corp.	XQF	CFWY	C	1
Consolidated Papers, Inc.	CDP	CDP	P	1
Consolidated Stores Corp.	CNS	CNS	X	1
Constellation Brands, Inc.	STZ	STZ	A	1
Constellation Energy Corp.	CEG	CEG	X	1
Consumer Services SPDR	XLV	XLV	A	3
Consumer Staples SPDR	XLP	XLP	A	3
Continental Airlines, Inc. (Class B)	CAL	CAL	AC	3
Convergys Corp.	CVG	CVG	AC	1
Cooper Cameron Corp.	CAM	CAM	X	2
Cooper Companies, Inc. (The)	COO	COO	A	2
Cooper Industries, Inc.	CBE	CBE	A	1
Cooper Tire & Rubber Company	CTB	CTB	P	2
Coors (Adolph) Co. (Class B)	RKY	RKY	P	1
Copart Inc.	KQJ	CPRT	P	2
Copper Mountain Networks, Inc.	KUA	CMTN	ACIPX	3
COR Therapeutics, Inc.	CHQ	CORR	CPX	1
Cordant Technologies Inc.	CDD	CDD	X	1
Core Laboratories NV	CLB	CLB	PX	3
Corecomm Limited	MNU	COMM	AC	2
Corel Corp.	ORU	CORL	ACPX	1
Corinthian Colleges, Inc.	UCS	COCO	CP	2
Corixa Corp.	CVQ	CRXA	ACX	1
Corn Products International	CPO	CPO	P	1
Corning Incorporated	GLW	GLW	ACPX	2
Corporate ExecutiveBoard Company	EBU	EXBD	X	1
Corporate Express, Inc.	XQP	CEXP	C	1
Corsair Communications, Inc.	HHU	CAIR	ACP	1
Corus Group plc ADS	CGA	CGA	C	1
Corvis Corp.	UVF	CORV	ACPX	2
Cosine Communications, Inc.	KUK	COSN	ACP	2
Cost Plus, Inc.	CUP	CPWM	PX	3
Costco Wholesale Corp.	PRQ	COST	ACIPX	1
Cotelligent Group Inc.	CGZ	CGZ	P	1
Coulter Pharmaceutical, Inc.	CJL	CLTR	CX	1

Company Name	Option Symbol	Stock Symbol	Exchange(s)	Cycle
Countrywide Credit Industries, Inc.	CCR	CCR	ACP	1
Covad Communications Group, Inc.	COU	COVDE	ACPX	3
Covance	CVD	CVD	C	2
Covanta Energy Corp.	COV	COV	C	2
Covas International, Inc.	CUG	CVAS	CP	1
Coventry Health Care Inc.	OVQ	CVTY	C	1
Covergent Communications	UVC	CONV	C	3
Cox Communications, Inc. (Class A)	COX	COX	ACP	3
Crane Company	CR	CR	X	1
Cray Inc.	QIP	CRAY	C	3
Creative BioMolecules, Inc.	DBQ	CBMI	AC	1
Creative Technology Limited	RFQ	CREAF	C	1
Credence Systems Corp.	CQS	CMOS	ACPX	2
Credit Acceptance Corp.	DCQ	CACC	A	3
Credit Suisse First Boston (USA), Inc. – CSFBdirect	DIR	DIR	ACPX	1
Cree Inc.	CQR	CREE	ACIP	3
Creo Products, Inc.	CUA	CREO	AP	1
Crescent Operating Inc.	QAD	COPI	P	2
Crescent Real Estate Equities, Inc.	CEI	CEI	P	1
Crestline Capital Corp.	CLJ	CLJ	X	1
Critical Path, Inc.	UPA	CPTH	AC	2
Crompton Corp.	CK	CK	C	2
Cross Timbers Oil Company	XTG	XTO	ACX	2
Crossroads Systems, Inc.	URY	CRDS	A	3
Crown Castle International Corp.	CCI	CCI	AC	1
Crown Cork & Seal Company, Inc.	CCK	CCK	X	1
CSG Systems International, Inc.	QGA	CSGS	C	3
CSK Auto Corp.	CAO	CAO	X	2
CSX Corp.	CSX	CSX	P	2
CTC Communications Group, Inc.	CUU	CPTL	ACPX	2
CTS Corp.	CTS	CTS	P	3
Cubist Pharmaceuticals, Inc.	UTU	CBST	ACX	2
Cummins Inc.	CUM	CUM	C	3
Cumulus Media Inc - (Class A)	UUC	CMLS	AP	1
Cuno Incorporated	OQG	CUNO	P	2
CuraGen Corp.	CQX	CRGN	AC	1
Curative Health Services, Inc.	NQH	CURE	C	3
Curis, Inc.	IUH	CRIS	AC	2
CUseeMe Networks	PWU	CUSM	AC	2
Cutter & Buck Inc.	KUT	CBUK	X	3
CV Therapeutics, Inc.	UXC	CVTX	ACP	1
CVS Corp.	CVS	CVS	ACIPX	2
Cyber-Care, Inc.	RSU	CYBR	C	2
Cybercash, Inc.	KBQ	CYCHQ	ACPX	3
Cyberian Outpost Inc.	QOO	COOL	ACP	2
Cyberonics, Inc.	QAJ	CYBX	AC	1
CyberSource Corp.	CAQ	CYBS	ACX	1

Key to Exchanges: A = AMEX (American Stock Exchange); C = CBOE (Chicago Board Options Exchange); I = International Securities Exchange; P = PCX or PSE (Pacific Stock Exchange); and X = PHLX (Philadelphia Stock Exchange).

Company Name	Option Symbol	Stock Symbol	Exchange(s)	Cycle
Cyclical/Transportation SPDR	XLY	XLY	A	3
Cygnus, Inc.	YNQ	CYGN	CPI	3
Cylink Corp.	YQB	CYLK	C	2
Cymer Inc.	CQG	CYMI	ACX	2
Cypress Semiconductor Corp.	CY	CY	ACIPX	3
Cyprus Amax Minerals Company	CYM	CYM	C	1
Cyrk, Inc.	KQY	CYRK	X	3
CyroLife, Inc.	CRY	CRY	A	3
Cytec Industries, Inc.	CYT	CYT	A	2
CYTOGEN Corp.	UOR	CYTO	ACP	2
CYTYC Corp.	YQK	CYTC	AC	2
D.R. Horton, Inc.	DAF	DHI	P	2
DaimlerChrysler AG	DCX	DCX	ACPX	1
Dain Rauscher Corp.	DRC	DRC	P	2
Daisytek Intl. Corp.	QDZ	DZTK	A	3
Dallas Semiconductor Corp.	DS	DS	APX	1
Dana Corp.	DCN	DCN	C	1
Danaher Corp.	DHR	DHR	X	3
Danka Business Systems PLC ADR	DNQ	DANKY	P	2
DAOU Systems, Inc.	QQX	DAOU	C	1
Darden Restaurants, Inc.	DRI	DRI	CP	1
Data Broadcasting Corp.	BQD	DBCC	AC	3
Data Return Corp.	DRU	DRTN	A	3
Data Transmission Network	OGQ	DTLN	A	2
DataScope Corp.	DTQ	DSCP	X	3
Datastream Systems, Inc.	DQK	DSTM	X	2
Dave & Buster's Inc.	DAB	DAB	AC	2
DaVita, Inc.	DVA	DVA	ACPX	1
Davox Corp.	VQ	DAVX	A	3
Ddi Corp.	QDI	DDIC	A	1
Dean Foods Company	DF	DF	P	2
deCODE genetics, Inc.	DOU	DCGN	A	1
Deere & Company	DE	DE	ACX	3
Del Webb Corp.	WBB	WBB	X	2
Delano Techology	UDV	DTEC	A	1
Delhaize America (Class A)	DZA	DZA	A	1
Delhaize America (Class B)	FBQ	DZB	A	1
Dell Computer Corp.	DLQ	DELL	ACIPX	2
Delphi Automotive Systems	DPH	DPH	ACX	3
Delphi Financial Group (Class A)	DFG	DFG	A	1
Delta & Pine Land Co.	DLP	DLP	AC	2
Delta Air Lines, Inc.	DAL	DAL	ACIPX	1
Deltek Systems, Inc.	DSQ	DLTK	P	1
Deltic Timer Corp.	DEL	DEL	P	2
Deluxe Corp.	DLX	DLX	P	1
Dendreon Corp.	UKO	DNDN	A	2
Dendrite International, Inc.	DEQ	DRTE	A	2
Dense-Pac Microsystems, Inc.	DHU	DPAC	AC	3
Department 56, Inc.	DFS	DFS	A	3
Descartes Systems Group Inc. (The)	DQY	DSGX	CP	2
Destia Communications, Inc.	CUH	DEST	CX	3
Deutsche Telekom AG ADR	DT	DT	ACIPX	1

Company Name	Option Symbol	Stock Symbol	Exchange(s)	Cycle
Devon Energy Corp.	DVN	DVN	ACIP	1
DeVRY, Inc.	DV	DV	P	2
Dexter Corp. (The)	DEY	DEX	A	1
Diageo PLC	DEO	DEO	A	1
Diagnostic Products Corp.	DP	DP	P	3
Dial Corp. (The) (New)	DL	DL	AP	1
Dialogic Corp.	DQL	DLGC	A	3
Diamond Offshore Drilling, Inc.	DO	DO	ACIP	3
DiamondCluster International, Inc.	DUP	DTPI	ACX	1
Diebold, Incorporated	DBD	DBD	PX	2
Digene Corp.	QDG	DIGE	A	3
Digex, Inc.	UDX	DIGX	ACP	1
Digi International, Inc.	DGQ	DGII	X	1
Digimarc Corp.	DQT	DMRC	P	2
Digital Insight Corp.	UGU	DGIN	A	2
Digital Island	SUH	ISLD	ACIPX	2
Digital Lightwave, Inc.	DGU	DIGL	ACP	1
Digital River, Inc.	DQI	DRIV	ACP	3
DigitalThink, Inc.	DTU	DTHK	ACP	1
DII Group, Inc. (The)	QID	DIIG	A	3
Dillard's Inc.	DDS	DDS	AP	2
Dime Bancorp, Inc.	DME	DME	AC	3
DiMon Incorporated	DMN	DMN	X	1
Direct Focus, Inc.	DQF	DFXI	ACP	1
Disney (The Walt) Holding Co.	DIS	DIS	ACIPX	1
Ditech Communications Corp.	DUI	DITC	ACX	2
Diversa Corp.	UFV	DVSA	AC	1
DMC Stratex Networks, Inc.	DMQ	STXN	CP	3
Dobson Communications Corp.	DDU	DCEL	CP	2
Documentum, Inc.	QDC	DCTM	AX	1
Dole Food Company, Inc.	DOL	DOL	P	3
Dollar General Corp.	DG	DG	CP	2
Dollar Thrifty Automotive Group, Inc.	DTG	DTG	C	1
Dollar Tree Stores, Inc.	DQO	DLTR	CP	2
Dominion Resources, Inc.	D	D	AX	1
Donaldson, Lufkin & Jenrette, Inc.	DLJ	DLJ	ACX	1
Donna Karen International, Inc.	DK	DK	A	1
Donnelley (R.R.) & Sons Company	DNY	DNY	A	3
Doral Financial Corp.	QDL	DORL	ACP	2
Doubleclick Inc.	QTD	DCLK	ACIPX	1
Dover Corp.	DOV	DOV	A	3
Dover Downs Entertainment	DVD	DVD	X	2
Dow Chemical Company (The)	DOW	DOW	CP	3
Dow Jones & Company, Inc.	DJ	DJ	AX	3
DQE, Inc.	DQE	DQE	P	3
Drexler Technology Corp.	RXQ	DRXR	A	1
Dreyer's Grand Ice Cream, Inc.	DYQ	DRYR	P	3
drkoop.com	DKU	KOOP	AC	3

Key to Exchanges: A = AMEX (American Stock Exchange); C = CBOE (Chicago Board Options Exchange); I = International Securities Exchange; P = PCX or PSE (Pacific Stock Exchange); and X = PHLX (Philadelphia Stock Exchange).

Company Name	Option Symbol	Stock Symbol	Exchange(s)	Cycle
Drugstore.com	UDU	DSCM	AX	3
DSET Corp.	DQV	DSET	PX	3
DSL.net, Inc.	RQV	DSLN	A	3
DSP Communications, Inc.	DQC	DSP	C	2
DSP Group	DPQ	DSPG	C	1
DST Systems, Inc.	DST	DST	AX	2
DT Industries, Inc.	DQD	DTII	X	3
DTE Energy Company Holdings	DTE	DTE	AX	1
du Pont (E.I.) de Nemours & Company	DD	DD	ACIPX	1
Duane Reade, Inc.	DRD	DRD	AX	1
Duke Energy Company	DUK	DUK	ACIPX	1
Duke-Weeks Realty Investment Inc.	DRE	DRE	P	3
Dun & Bradstreet Corp.	DNB	DNB	A	2
DuPont Photomasks, Inc.	DUD	DPMI	PX	3
Dura Pharmaceuticals, Inc.	DQR	DURA	AC	1
Duramed Pharmaceuticals, Inc.	DUQ	DRMD	CX	3
DUSA Pharmaceuticals, Inc.	QDU	DUSA	PX	3
Dycom Industries, Inc.	DY	DY	X	3
Dynegy Inc.	DYN	DYN	ACPX	3
E*Trade Group Inc.	ET	ET	ACPX	1
E. Piphany, Inc.	UEP	EPNY	ACX	1
E.Spire Communications Inc.	AQ	ESPI	ACX	3
E.W. Scripps Company (The)	SSP	SSP	A	2
E4L, Inc.	ETV	ETV	AC	1
Earthgrains Company	EGR	EGR	X	3
EarthLink Network, Inc.	MQD	ELNK	ACX	1
Earthshell Container Corp.	QER	ERTH	C	1
Eastern Enterprises	EFU	EFU	X	1
Eastern Utilities Associates	EUA	EUA	X	2
Eastman Chemical Company	EMN	EMN	C	3
Eastman Kodak Company	EK	EK	ACIPX	1
EasyLink Services Corp.	UMA	EASY	ACX	2
Eaton Corp.	ETN	ETN	C	1
eBay, Inc.	QXB	EBAY	ACIPX	1
Echelon Corp.	EUL	ELON	ACIPX	2
EchoStar Communications Corp.	QHS	DISH	ACPX	3
ECI Telecommunications Ltd.	ECQ	ECIL	CPX	2
Eclipse Surgical Technologies	ELQ	ESTI	P	1
Eclipsys Corp.	IQV	ECLP	AC	3
Eden Bioscience Corp.	EUD	EDEN	AC	1
Edgewater Technology, Inc.	FVQ	EDGW	PX	1
Edison International	EIX	EIX	ACP	1
Edison Schools, Inc.	USD	EDSN	AC	3
Education Management Corp.	UKN	EDMC	A	3
Edward Lifesciences Corp.	EW	EW	C	2
Edwards (A.G.) & Sons, Inc.	AGE	AGE	ACX	2
eFax.com	FUW	EFAX	ACX	2
Efficient Networks Inc.	QET	EFNT	ACPX	3
eFunds Corp.	EFU	EFDS	A	3
eGain Communications	EQZ	EGAN	AP	3
Egghead.com, Inc.	QOL	EGGS	ACPX	3
El Paso Corp.	EPG	EPG	ACP	1

Company Name	Option Symbol	Stock Symbol	Exchange(s)	Cycle
El Paso Electric Company	EE	EE	AP	3
El Sitio	ELU	LCTO	AC	2
Elan Corp. PLC ADR	ELN	ELN	CIPX	1
Elantec Semiconductor Inc.	ETQ	ELNT	APX	2
Elbit Systems	EQX	ESLT	P	1
Elcom International, Inc.	CEU	ELCO	AC	2
Electric Fuel Corp.	FUS	EFCX	AC	2
Electric Lightwave, Inc.	XQQ	ELIX	C	3
Electro Scientific Industries, Inc.	EQO	ESIO	C	3
Electroglas, Inc.	EIQ	EGLS	CP	1
Electronic Arts, Inc.	EZQ	ERTS	ACPX	3
Electronic Data Systems, Inc.	EDS	EDS	ACIPX	3
Electronics for Imaging, Inc.	EFQ	EFII	ACX	1
E-LOAN	ONQ	EELN	C	2
eLoyalty Corp.	UEO	ELOY	C	3
Embracadero Technologies, Inc.	MBQ	EMBT	AC	2
Embratel Participacoes S.A.	EMT	EMT	CP	1
Embratel Participacoes S.A.	EMT	EMT	P	1
EMC Corp.	EMC	EMC	ACIPX	1
EMCORE Corp.	EUH	EMKR	ACP	2
e-MedSoft.com	MED	MED	A	2
eMerge Interactive, Inc.	EUB	EMRG	AC	2
Emerging Vision Inc.	USH	ISEE	C	2
Emerson Electric Company	EMR	EMR	ACIPX	3
Emisphere Technologies, Inc.	MTQ	EMIS	AC	3
Emmis Communications Corp. (Class A)	QMJ	EMMS	A	3
Empresas ICA Sociedad Controladora S.A. de C.V. ADR	ICA	ICA	C	1
EMS Technologies, Inc.	EMQ	ELMG	P	1
Emulex Corp.	UML	EMLX	ACPX	1
EMusic.com Inc.	EMU	EMUS	AP	2
Enamelon, Inc.	QIL	ENML	A	2
Encompass Services Corp.	ESR	ESR	P	2
Encore Wire Corp.	QWR	WIRE	X	2
Endesa SA ADS	ELE	ELE	A	3
Energizer Holdings, Inc.	ENR	ENR	C	2
Energy Conversion Devices, Inc.	EQI	ENER	AX	3
Energy East Corp.	EAS	EAS	AC	1
Energy SPDR	XLE	XLE	A	3
Enersis S.A. ADR	ENI	ENI	P	1
Engage, Inc.	GQE	ENGA	AP	3
Engelhard Corp.	EC	EC	C	1
Engineering Animation Inc.	QNE	EAII	A	3
Enhance Financial Svcs. Group	EFS	EFS	A	3
ENI SPA	E	E	A	3
ENSCO International Incorporated	ESV	ESV	ACP	3
Enseco Group Inc.	ENC	ENC	A	2

Key to Exchanges: A = AMEX (American Stock Exchange); C = CBOE (Chicago Board Options Exchange); I = International Securities Exchange; P = PCX or PSE (Pacific Stock Exchange); and X = PHLX (Philadelphia Stock Exchange).

Company Name	Option Symbol	Stock Symbol	Exchange(s)	Cycle
Entercom Communications Corp.	ETM	ETM	AC	3
Entergy Corp.	ETR	ETR	C	3
Entrade Inc.	ETA	ETA	X	3
Entravision Communications Corp.	EVC	EVC	ACP	2
EntreMed Inc.	QMA	ENMD	ACP	2
Entrust Technologies, Inc.	QYE	ENTU	ACPX	1
Enzo Biochem, Inc.	ENZ	ENZ	ACIP	1
Enzon, Inc.	QYZ	ENZN	ACP	2
EOG Resources, Inc.	EOG	EOG	ACPX	1
Epicor Software Corp.	PQS	EPIC	C	1
Epitope, Inc.	QTP	EPTO	AC	1
ePresence Inc.	QYN	EPRE	AC	1
Equant NV	ENT	ENT	AC	2
Equifax, Inc.	EFX	EFX	P	1
Equitable Resources, Inc.	EQT	EQT	A	3
Equity Inns, Inc.	ENN	ENN	P	1
Equity Office Properties Trust	EOP	EOP	X	1
Equity Residential Properties Trust	EQR	EQR	P	1
Ericsson (L.M.) Telephone Co. ADR	RQC	ERICY	ACIPX	1
ESC Medical Systems, Limited	QFC	ESCM	CP	1
eSPEED, Inc.	ENU	ESPD	AP	2
Espirito Santo Financial Holding S.A.	ESF	ESF	A	3
ESS Technology, Inc.	SEQ	ESST	C	1
Estee Lauder Companies, Inc. (The) (Class A)	EL	EL	ACIX	1
Etec Systems, Inc.	EBQ	ETEC	AX	3
E-Tek Dynamics, Inc.	EVU	ETEK	ACPX	1
Ethan Allen Interiors, Inc.	ETH	ETH	X	2
Ethyl Corp.	EY	EY	P	1
eToys Inc.	ETU	ETYS	ACPX	2
Europe 2001 HOLDRs	EKH	EKH	A	3
Evans & Sutherland Computer Corp.	EQA	ESCC	P	3
Everest Reinsurance Holdings, Inc.	RE	RE	A	1
Evergreen Resources, Inc.	EKQ	EVER	X	2
Exar Corp.	EQC	EXAR	CP	1
Excalibur Technologies Corp.	XQA	EXCA	C	3
Excel Technology, Inc.	XNQ	XLTC	C	1
eXcelon Corp.	ODU	EXLN	AC	1
Exchange Applications, Inc.	QXW	EXAP	ACP	1
Exelixis, Inc.	XQT	EXEL	ACP	2
Exelon Corp.	EXC	EXC	CP	1
Exfo Electro-Optical Engineering, Inc.	FQO	EXFO	ACP	2
Exide Corp.	EX	EX	PX	2
Exodus Communication, Inc.	QED	EXDS	ACIPX	3
Expedia, Inc.	UED	EXPE	AC	1
Expeditors International of Washington, Inc.	URP	EXPD	ACP	2
Express Scripts Inc. (Class A)	XTQ	ESRX	ACP	2
Extended Stay America, Inc.	ESA	ESA	C	3
Extreme Networks, Inc.	EUT	EXTR	ACPX	3
Exxon Mobil Corp.	XOM	XOM	ACIPX	1
F5 Networks, Inc.	FQL	FFIV	ACP	1

Company Name	Option Symbol	Stock Symbol	Exchange(s)	Cycle
Factory 2-U Stores, Inc.	FEQ	FTUS	C	2
Fairchild Corp. (The)	FA	FA	X	3
Fairchild Semiconductor Int'l., Inc.	FCS	FCS	CPX	2
Fairfield Communities, Inc.	FFD	FFD	A	3
Family Dollar Stores, Inc.	FDO	FDO	X	1
Fastenal Company	FQA	FAST	ACP	2
Federal Home Loan Mortgage Corp. (Freddie Mac)	FRE	FRE	ACIPX	1
Federal Nat'l. Mortgage Ass'n. (Fannie Mae)	FNM	FNM	ACIPX	3
Federal Signal Corp.	FSS	FSS	A	2
Federal-Mogul Corp.	FMO	FMO	P	1
Federated Department Stores, Inc.	FD	FD	CX	2
Federated Investors Inc. (Class B)	FII	FII	A	1
FedEx Corp.	FDX	FDX	ACIPX	1
FEI Company	FQE	FEIC	P	3
Felcor Lodging Trust, Inc.	FCH	FCH	X	3
Fidelity Holdings, Inc.	FDU	FDHG	A	3
Fidelity National Financial, Inc.	FNF	FNF	CP	1
Fifth Third Bancorp.	FTQ	FITB	CIPX	2
Fila Holding S.p.A. ADR	FLH	FLH	CX	1
FileNet Corp.	ILQ	FILE	AC	1
Financial SPDR	XLF	XLF	A	3
Finisar Corp.	FQY	FNSR	ACIPX	3
Finish Line Inc.	FQN	FINL	C	3
FINOVA Group, Inc. (The)	FNV	FNV	A	1
FirePond, Inc.	FIU	FIRE	A	1
First American Corp. of Tennessee	FAM	FAM	P	3
First American Financial Corp. (The)	FAF	FAF	P	1
First Consulting Group Inc.	FSQ	FCGI	X	3
First Data Corp.	FDC	FDC	ACIP	2
First Health Group Corp.	FHQ	FHCC	CP	1
First Industrial Reality Trust Inc.	FR	FR	P	3
First Security Corp.	FQB	FSCO	AC	3
First Sentinel Bancorp, Inc.	SQB	FSLA	CP	3
First Sierra Financial, Inc.	TUM	BTOB	CPX	2
First Tennessee National Corp.	FTN	FTN	X	2
First Union Corp.	FTU	FTU	ACPX	1
First Union Real Estate Investments	FUR	FUR	C	1
First Virginia Banks, Inc.	FVB	FVB	X	3
First Virtual Communications, Inc.	FXQ	FVCX	ACX	2
First Years Inc. (The)	FYQ	KIDD	A	2
FirstEnergy Corp.	FE	FE	C	1
FirstMerit Corp.	FGQ	FMER	P	3
FIserv, Inc.	FQV	FISV	CX	3
FLAG Telecom Holdings Limited	FHU	FTHL	ACP	1
FlashNet Communications	UFL	FLAS	A	2
FleetBoston Financial Corp.	FBF	FBF	ACPX	1

Key to Exchanges: A = AMEX (American Stock Exchange); C = CBOE (Chicago Board Options Exchange); I = International Securities Exchange; P = PCX or PSE (Pacific Stock Exchange); and X = PHLX (Philadelphia Stock Exchange).

Option Company Name	Stock Symbol	Symbol	Exchange(s)	Cycle
Fleetwood Enterprises, Inc.	FLE	FLE	A	2
Fleming Companies, Inc.	FLM	FLM	P	2
Flextronics International Ltd.	QFL	FLEX	ACIPX	1
Flooring America, Inc.	FRA	FRA	X	3
Florida Progress Corp.	FPC	FPC	A	3
Flowers Industries, Inc.	FLO	FLO	CX	1
Flowserve Corp.	FLS	FLS	C	2
Fluor Corp. (New)	FLR	FLR	C	1
Foamex International, Inc.	FQX	FMXI	C	3
Focal Communications Corp.	FCU	FCOM	AC	2
Fomento Economico Mexicano S.A. ADR	FMX	FMX	X	1
Footstar, Inc.	FTS	FTS	P	2
Ford Motor Company	F	F	ACIPX	3
Forest Laboratories, Inc.	FRX	FRX	ACX	2
Forest Oil Corp.	FTV	FST	C	2
Forrester Research, Inc.	UER	FORR	A	1
Fort James Corp.	FJ	FJ	CX	3
Fortune Brands, Inc.	FO	FO	A	3
Fossil, Inc.	QFS	FOSL	A	3
Foster Wheeler Corp.	FWC	FWC	ACP	1
Foundry Networks, Inc.	OQ	FDRY	ACPX	3
Fox Entertainment Group, Inc.	FOX	FOX	ACP	1
FPL Group, Inc.	FPL	FPL	X	3
France Telecom, ADR	FTE	FTE	A	3
Franklin Convey Company	FC	FC	A	2
Franklin Resources, Inc.	BEN	BEN	P	1
FreeMarkets, Inc.	FAQ	FMKT	ACP	1
Freeport-McMoRan Copper & Gold Co., Inc. (Class A)	FXA	FCX/A	X	3
Freeport-McMoRan Copper & Gold Co., Inc. (Class B)	FCX	FCX	CX	2
Fremont General Corp.	FMT	FMT	X	2
French Fragrances, Inc.	GQG	FRAG	C	2
Fresenius Medical Care AG ADR	FMS	FMS	A	2
Fresh Del Monte Products Inc.	FDP	FDP	A	3
Friede Goldman Halter, Inc.	FGH	FGH	ACX	2
Friedman, Billings, Ramsey Group, Inc.	FBR	FBR	AX	3
Friedman's Inc.	FKQ	FRDM	X	2
Fritz Companies, Inc.	TQZ	FRTZ	A	2
Frontier Airlines Inc.	FUO	FRNT	ACPX	2
Frontier Insurance Group, Inc.	FTR	FTR	X	1
Frontline Capital Group	RUE	FLCG	A	3
Fruit of the Loom, Ltd. (Class A)	FTL	FTLAQ	C	2
FSI International, Inc.	FQH	FSII	C	3
FuelCell Energy, Inc.	FQG	FCEL	ACPX	1
Fuller (H.B.) Company	FUQ	FULL	X	2
Fundtech Ltd.	FNU	FNDT	CP	1
Furniture Brands International, Inc.	FBN	FBN	C	1
Furon Company	FCY	FCY	P	3
Gadzooks, Inc.	EQK	GADZ	CX	3
Gadzoox Networks, Inc.	OUO	ZOOX	ACX	1
Galileo International, Inc.	GLC	GLC	AC	1

Company Name	Option Symbol	Stock Symbol	Exchange(s)	Cycle
Galileo Technology Ltd.	FKS	GALT	ACX	1
Gallaher Group Plc	GLH	GLH	A	3
Gannett Company, Inc.	GCI	GCI	P	1
Gap, Inc. (The)	GPS	GPS	ACIPX	3
Garmin Ltd.	GQR	GRMN	CP	1
Gartner Group Inc., (Class B)	UIT	IT/B	AC	1
Gartner Group, Inc.	IT	IT	C	1
GaSonics International Corp.	GQS	GSNX	P	1
Gateway, Inc.	GTW	GTW	ACIPX	3
GATX Corp.	GMT	GMT	X	3
Gaylord Container Corp. (Class A)	GCR	GCR	C	3
Gaylord Entertainment Company (Class A)	GET	GET	C	3
Geltex Pharmaceuticals, Inc.	GQY	GELX	X	1
Gemstar-TV Guide Int'l., Inc.	QLF	GMST	ACIPX	2
Genaissance Pharmaceuticals, Inc.	UDG	GNSC	AC	1
Gene Logic Inc.	CGU	GLGC	ACPX	2
Genencor International, Inc.	UGO	GCOR	AP	2
Genentech, Inc.	DNA	DNA	ACIPX	3
General Cable Corp.	BGC	BGC	AC	2
General Dynamics Corp.	GD	GD	ACIX	2
General Electric Company	GE	GE	ACPX	3
General Magic, Inc.	GGQ	GMGC	ACP	2
General Mills, Inc.	GIS	GIS	CP	1
General Motors Corp.(Hughes Electronics) Class H	GMH	GMH	ACPX	3
General Motors Corp.	GM	GM	ACIPX	3
General Semiconductor, Inc.	SEM	SEM	X	3
Genesco, Inc.	GCO	GCO	A	3
Genesis Health Ventures, Inc.	GHV	GHV	A	3
Genesis Microchip, Inc.	QFE	GNSS	AC	3
Genome Therapeutics Corp.	GUG	GENE	ACX	1
Genomic Solutions, Inc.	UNU	GNSL	AC	1
GenRad, Inc.	GEN	GEN	X	2
Genta Incorporated	GJU	GNTA	ACP	2
Gentex Corp.	GXQ	GNTX	P	3
Genuine Parts Company	GPC	GPC	P	2
Genuity, Inc.	GQH	GENU	ACP	1
Genus, Inc.	GQG	GGNS	C	1
Genzyme Corp.-Biosurgery Division	TQG	GZBX	ACP	1
Genzyme Corp.	GZQ	GENZ	ACIP	1
Genzyme Transgenics Corp.	GEQ	GZTC	A	3
Genzyme-MolecularOncology	QGG	GZMO	A	2
Georgia Gulf Corp.	GGC	GGC	X	2
Georgia Pacific Timber Group	TGP	TGP	X	1
Geotel Communication Corp.	QEG	GEOC	CX	1
Geoworks Corp.	GWU	GWRX	ACX	2
Gerald Stevens, Inc.	GFU	GIFT	C	1

Key to Exchanges: A = AMEX (American Stock Exchange); C = CBOE (Chicago Board Options Exchange); I = International Securities Exchange; P = PCX or PSE (Pacific Stock Exchange); and X = PHLX (Philadelphia Stock Exchange).

Company Name	Option Symbol	Stock Symbol	Exchange(s)	Cycle
Gerber Scientific, Inc.	GRB	GRB	X	3
Geron Corp.	GQD	GERN	ACPX	3
Getty Images Inc.	QGT	GETY	CP	1
Gilat Satellite Networks, Ltd.	FQI	GILTF	AC	2
Gilead Sciences, Inc.	GDQ	GILD	CPX	2
Gillette Company (The)	G	G	ACIPX	3
Glatfelter Company	GLT	GLT	PX	2
GlaxoSmithKline plc ADR	GSK	GSK	ACPX	2
Glenayre Technologies, Inc.	GQM	GEMS	C	3
Glenborough Realty Trust Inc.	GLB	GLB	P	3
Gliatech Inc	QGL	GLIA	AC	3
Global Crossing Ltd.	GX	GX	ACIPX	1
Global Imaging Systems Inc.	GQC	GISX	C	2
Global Industries Ltd.	GQO	GLBL	CX	3
Global Marine, Inc.	GLM	GLM	ACIPX	1
Global Telesystems Group, Inc.	GTS	GTS	ACX	1
Globalstar Telecommunications Ltd.	YVQ	GSTRF	ACIPX	3
GlobeSpan, Inc.	GLQ	GSPN	ACPX	2
Globix Corp.	GUI	GBIX	C	1
Globo Cabo S.A.	GYU	GLCBY	ACIPX	2
Go2Net, Inc.	GQI	GNET	AC	1
GoAmerica, Inc.	GUA	GOAM	AC	2
Golden State Bancorp, Inc.	GSB	GSB	AC	1
Golden West Financial Corp.	GDW	GDW	X	2
Goldman Sachs Group, Inc. (The)	GS	GS	ACIPX	1
Goodrich (B.F.) Co.	GR	GR	CX	2
Goodyear Tire & Rubber Company (The)	GT	GT	ACIPX	1
Goody's Family Clothing	GQJ	GDYS	A	2
GP Strategies Corp.	GPX	GPX	P	3
Grace (W.R.) & Company	GRA	GRA	A	2
Graco Inc.	GGG	GGG	P	2
Grainger (W.W.), Inc.	GWW	GWW	A	1
Granite Broadcasting Corp.	GBQ	GBTVK	X	3
Granite Construction, Inc.	GVA	GVA	X	3
Grant Prideco, Inc.	GRP	GRP	ACX	1
Graphic Packaging International Corp.	GPK	GPK	A	2
Great Atlantic & Pacific Tea Company, Inc. (The)	GAP	GAP	A	1
Great Lakes Chemical Corp.	GLK	GLK	C	3
Great Plains Software Inc.	QGP	GPSI	A	1
Greater Bay Bancorp	BBU	GBBK	ACP	1
Greenpoint Financial Corp.	GPT	GPT	C	1
GRIC Communications	DQC	GRIC	AP	1
Groupe Danone ADR	DA	DA	A	1
Grupo Financiero Galicia S.A.	GKQ	GGAL	C	2
Grupo Televisa S.A. ADR	TV	TV	AC	1
GSI Lumonics, Inc.	HQJ	GSLI	ACP	1
GTE Corp.	GTE	GTE	ACP	3
GTECH Holdings Corp.	GTK	GTK	C	3
Gucci Group, N.V.	GUC	GUC	CX	1
Guidant Corp.	GDT	GDT	ACPX	1
Guilford Mills, Inc.	GFD	GFD	P	2

Company Name	Option Symbol	Stock Symbol	Exchange(s)	Cycle
Guilford Pharmaceuticals, Inc.	GQF	GLFD	C	3
Guitar Center Inc.	GUR	GTRC	C	1
Gymboree Corp. (The)	GMQ	GYMB	CP	1
H Power Corp.	HQF	HPOW	ACPX	1
Hadco Corp.	HDC	HDC	C	1
Hain Food Group, Inc.	QQH	HAIN	AC	2
Halliburton Company	HAL	HAL	ACIPX	1
HA-LO Industries Inc.	HMK	HMK	A	3
Hambrecht & Quist Group	HQ	HQ	ACP	2
Handspring, Inc.	HQA	HAND	ACPX	2
Hanger Orthopedic Group, Inc.	HGR	HGR	A	2
Hanna (M.A.) Company	MAH	MAH	C	3
Hannaford Brothers Company	HRD	HRD	P	1
Hanover Compressor Company	HC	HC	X	3
Hanson PLC ADR	HAN	HAN	C	3
Harbinger Corp.	BQ	HRBC	A	3
Harland (John H.) Company	JH	JH	C	3
Harley-Davidson, Inc.	HDI	HDI	ACIPX	2
Harmonic, Inc.	LOQ	HLIT	AC	1
Harrah's Entertainment, Inc.	HET	HET	AC	2
Harris Corp.	HRS	HRS	C	2
Harsco Corp.	HSC	HSC	P	1
Hartford Financial Services Group, Inc.	HIG	HIG	C	3
Hartford Life, Inc.	HLI	HLI	A	3
Hasbro, Inc.	HAS	HAS	P	1
Hawaiian Electric Industries, Inc.	HE	HE	P	2
HCC Insurance Holdings, Inc.	HCC	HCC	X	1
Health Axis Corp.	QMC	HAXS	PX	2
Health Care Reit Inc.	HCN	HCN	P	2
Health Mgmt. Associates, Inc. (Class A)	HMA	HMA	AC	2
Health Management Systems, Inc.	HQN	HMSY	X	3
Health Net, Inc.	HNT	HNT	C	1
Healthcare Company (The)	HCA	HCA	ACIP	2
HEALTHSOUTH Corp.	HRC	HRC	ACPX	3
HearMe	HEU	HEAR	AC	3
Hearst-Argyle Television Inc.	HTV	HTV	P	1
Heilig-Meyers Company	HMY	HMY	C	2
Heinz (H.J.) Company	HNZ	HNZ	ACP	3
Helen of Troy Ltd.	EHQ	HELE	P	2
Helix Technology Corp.	HHQ	HELX	A	1
Heller Financial Inc.	HF	HF	A	1
Helmerich & Payne, Inc.	HP	HP	C	3
Hemispherx Biopharma, Inc.	HEB	HEB	AC	2
Herbalife International, Inc. (Class A)	HQR	HERBA	C	1
Herbalife International, Inc. (Class B)	QTB	HERBB	C	1
Hercules Incorporated	HPC	HPC	ACP	3
Hershey Foods Corp.	HSY	HSY	A	2
Hertz Corp.	HRZ	HRZ	P	3

Key to Exchanges: A = AMEX (American Stock Exchange); C = CBOE (Chicago Board Options
    Exchange); I = International Securities Exchange; P = PCX or PSE (Pacific Stock
    Exchange); and X = PHLX (Philadelphia Stock Exchange).

Company Name	Option Symbol	Stock Symbol	Exchange(s)	Cycle
Hewlett-Packard Company	HWP	HWP	ACIPX	2
Hexcel Corp.	HXL	HXL	P	1
Hi/fn, Inc.	HXQ	HIFN	ACIP	1
Hibernia Corp. (Class A)	HIB	HIB	C	1
High Speed Access Corp.	HSU	HSAC	ACPX	1
Highwoods Properties, Inc.	HIW	HIW	C	2
Hillenbrand Industries, Inc.	HB	HB	A	3
Hilton Hotels Corp.	HLT	HLT	ACPX	1
Hispanic Broadcasting Corp.	HSP	HSP	C	1
Hitachi Ltd. ADR	HIT	HIT	C	1
HNC Software, Inc.	NSQ	HNCS	AX	1
Hoechst AG	HOE	HOE	AC	2
Hollinger International, Inc.	HLR	HLR	C	1
Hollis-Eden Pharmaceuticals, Inc.	HUP	HEPH	C	1
Hollywood Entertainment Corp.	HWQ	HLYW	AC	1
Hollywood Media Corp.	BGU	HOLL	A	2
Hologic, Inc.	XHQ	HOLX	A	3
Home Depot, Inc. (The)	HD	HD	ACIPX	2
HomeBase Inc.	HBI	HBI	C	3
Homestake Mining Company	HM	HM	CPX	1
Homestore.com	HMU	HOMS	CPX	1
HON Industries, Inc.	HNI	HNI	P	2
Honda Motor Company, Ltd. ADR	HMC	HMC	X	1
Honeywell International Inc.	HON	HON	ACPX	3
Hooper Holmes, Inc.	HH	HH	A	2
Horace Mann Educator Corp.	HMN	HMN	PX	2
Hormel Foods Corp.	HRL	HRL	X	2
Hospitality Properties Trust	HPT	HPT	C	3
Host Marriott Corp.	HMT	HMT	X	1
Hot Topic, Inc.	UHO	HOTT	AC	2
HotJobs.com, Ltd.	HQQ	HOTJ	C	1
Houghton Mifflin Company	HTN	HTN	P	1
Household International, Inc.	HI	HI	ACIP	1
Houston Exploration Company	THX	THX	A	3
Howmet International Inc.	HWM	HWM	A	1
HRPT Properties Trust	HRP	HRP	C	3
HS Resources, Inc.	HSE	HSE	P	3
HSB Group, Inc.	HSB	HSB	P	3
HSBC Holdings plc	HBC	HBC	ACX	3
Hubbell Incorporated	HFU	HUB/B	P	2
Hudson River Bancorp Inc.	HQW	HRBT	P	3
Hudson United Bancorp	HU	HU	C	1
Human Genome Sciences, Inc.	HQI	HGSI	ACIPX	1
Humana, Inc.	HUM	HUM	ACIX	2
Hummingbird Ltd.	UQH	HUMC	C	1
Hunt (J.B.) Transport Services, Inc.	JHQ	JBHT	P	2
Huntington Bancshares, Inc.	HQB	HBAN	CX	1
Hussman International, Inc.	HSM	HSM	C	3
Hutchinson Technology, Inc.	UTQ	HTCH	AC	2
Hypercom Corp.	HYC	HYC	X	1
HyperFeed Technologies, Inc.	PQT	HYPR	AC	2
Hyperion Solutions Corp.	WQE	HYSL	CP	2

Company Name	Option Symbol	Stock Symbol	Exchange(s)	Cycle
Hyseq Inc.	HUH	HYSQ	CP	3
I2 Technologies, Inc.	JQ	ITWO	ACIPX	2
iBEAM Corp.	UID	IBEM	A	1
Ibis Technology Corp.	UIB	IBIS	ACP	1
IBP, Inc.	IBP	IBP	ACPX	2
ICG Communications, Inc.	QIG	ICGXQ	AC	3
ICN Pharmaceuticals, Inc.	ICN	ICN	ACIP	3
ICOS Corp.	IIQ	ICOS	AC	1
IDACORP Inc. (Holding)	IDA	IDA	X	2
IDEC Pharmaceuticals Corp.	IDQ	IDPH	ACIPX	1
Identix Incorporated	IDX	IDX	ACPX	3
IDEXX Laboratories, Inc.	IQX	IDXX	AC	3
IDT Corp.	IDT	IDT	ACPX	3
IDX Systems Corp.	XQW	IDXC	AX	2
iGate Capital Corp.	QAC	IGTE	A	3
IGEN International, Inc.	GQ	IGEN	AX	3
IHOP Corp.	IHP	IHP	X	3
Ikon Office Solutions, Inc.	IKN	IKN	C	3
ILEX Oncology, Inc.	IUE	ILXO	ACP	2
Illinois Tool Works, Inc.	ITW	ITW	ACX	3
Illinova Corp.	ILN	ILN	A	3
Illuminet Holdings, Inc.	ILU	ILUM	P	1
Image Entertainment, Inc.	DIU	DISK	CP	3
ImageX.com, Inc.	UFE	IMGX	C	2
I-many, Inc.	MQN	IMNY	ACP	1
Imation Corp.	IMN	IMN	AC	1
Imax Corp.	IZQ	IMAX	X	2
IMC Global, Inc.	IGL	IGL	CP	1
ImClone Systems Incorporated	QCI	IMCL	ACPX	2
Immersion Corp.	FRQ	IMMR	AP	1
Immune Response Corp.	IMQ	IMNR	C	2
Immunex Corp.	IUQ	IMNX	ACIPX	3
ImmunoGen, Inc.	GMU	IMGN	ACX	1
Immunomedics, Inc.	QUI	IMMU	C	2
Impath Inc.	QPH	IMPH	C	1
Imperial Bancorp	IMP	IMP	X	3
Imperial Chemical Industries PLC ADR	ICI	ICI	C	1
Imperial Credit Commercial	UIQ	ICMI	P	1
Imperial Credit Industries, Inc.	BQJ	ICII	P	3
Imperial Oil Ltd.	IMO	IMO	A	2
IMPSAT Fiber Networks, Inc.	MXQ	IMPT	P	1
IMRglobal Corp.	QIQ	IMRS	CP	2
IMS Health Inc.	RX	RX	ACPX	2
In Focus Corp.	IQL	INFS	C	1
Inacom Corp.	ICO	ICO	AX	1
INAMED Corp.	UZI	IMDC	AC	1
Inco Limited	N	N	A	1

Key to Exchanges: A = AMEX (American Stock Exchange); C = CBOE (Chicago Board Options Exchange); I = International Securities Exchange; P = PCX or PSE (Pacific Stock Exchange); and X = PHLX (Philadelphia Stock Exchange).

Company Name	Option Symbol	Stock Symbol	Exchange(s)	Cycle
Incyte Pharmaceuticals, Inc.	IPQ	INCY	CIPX	3
Independence Community Bank Corp.	QYC	ICBC	A	3
Industrial SPDR	XLI	XLI	A	3
Indymac Mortgage Holdings	NDE	NDE	A	1
Inet Technologies, Inc.	JTU	INTI	C	1
Infineon Technologies AG	IFX	IFX	A	3
Infinity Broadcasting Corp.	INF	INF	ACX	1
Infinium Software, Inc.	FWQ	INFM	A	2
Infocure Corp.	UNC	VWKS	ACPX	2
Infonet Services Corp.	IN	IN	ACP	2
Informatica Corp.	UYF	INFA	AP	3
Informix Corp.	IFQ	IFMX	AC	2
InfoSpace.com, Inc.	IOU	INSP	ACIPX	1
Infousa Inc.	BQU	IUSA	X	1
ING Groep NV	ING	ING	C	1
Ingersoll-Rand Company	IR	IR	ACX	3
Ingram Micro, Inc.	IM	IM	ACX	3
Inhale Theraeutic Systems	QNH	INHL	ACP	2
Inktomi Corp.	QYK	INKT	ACPX	1
Innovex, Inc.	IVQ	INVX	AC	2
Input/Output, Inc.	IO	IO	C	2
Inrange Technologies Corp. (Class B)	UME	INRG	ACP	2
Insight Communications, Inc.	SCU	ICCI	C	2
Insight Enterprises, Inc.	NZS	NSIT	AX	2
Insignia Financial Group	IFS	IFS	A	3
Insituform Technologies, Inc. (Class A)	ISQ	INSUA	P	3
INSO Corp.	IJQ	INSO	X	3
Inspire Insurance Solutions	QNS	NSPR	A	3
Integrated Circuit Systems, Inc.	IUY	ICST	ACP	1
Integrated Device Technology, Inc.	ITQ	IDTI	ACIPX	2
Integrated Silicon Solutions, Inc.	XUS	ISSI	CPX	1
Integrated Systems, Inc.	QIN	INTS	P	3
Intel Corp.	INQ	INTC	ACIPX	1
InteliData Technologies Corp.	IUB	INTD	AC	2
Intelligroup, Inc.	ITU	ITIG	AC	1
InterDigital Communications Corp.	DAQ	IDCC	ACPX	3
Interface, Inc.	IQG	IFSIA	A	2
Intergraph Corp.	IGQ	INGR	A	1
Interleaf, Inc.	EEU	LEAF	AC	2
Interliant Inc.	IUT	INIT	C	3
Intermagnetics General Corp.	IMG	IMG	AP	1
Intermedia Communications, Inc.	QIX	ICIX	ACPX	3
Intermet Corp.	IQR	INMT	A	2
Intermune Pharmaceuticals, Inc.	IQY	ITMN	AP	1
Internap Network Services Corp.	IQE	INAP	ACX	2
International Business Machines Corp.	IBM	IBM	ACIPX	1
International FiberCom, Inc.	IQD	IFCI	ACIP	2
International Flavors & Fragrances, Inc.	IFF	IFF	C	2
International Game Technology	IGT	IGT	AC	1
International Home Foods	IHF	IHF	AX	3
International Network Services	XQS	INSS	A	3
International Paper Company	IP	IP	ACIPX	1

Company Name	Option Symbol	Stock Symbol	Exchange(s)	Cycle
International Rectifier Corp.	IRF	IRF	ACIPX	3
International Speedway Corp.	QWY	ISCA	A	3
Internet Architecture HOLDRS	IAH	IAH	A	2
Internet Capital Group, Inc.	EUG	ICGE	ACPX	3
Internet HOLDRS Trust (The)	HHV	HHH	ACP	2
Internet Infrastructure HOLDRS	IIH	IIH	AC	2
Internet Initiative Japan Inc.	IUJ	IIJI	AC	2
Internet Pictures Corp.	UPZ	IPIX	C	1
Interpublic Group of Companies, Inc. (The)	IPG	IPG	CX	1
Intersil Holding Corp.	UFH	ISIL	ACP	1
Interstate Bakeries Corp.	IBC	IBC	CX	1
InterTAN, Inc.	ITN	ITN	CX	1
Inter-Tel, Inc.	TPQ	INTL	P	1
Intertrust Technologies Corp.	QIU	ITRU	AX	3
InterVoice-Brite, Inc.	VQN	INTV	AC	1
InterVu, Inc.	QYU	ITVU	AC	3
InterWAVE Communications Int'l.	ICU	IWAV	A	3
InterWorld Corp.	IUD	INTW	A	3
Interwoven, Inc.	IUW	IWOV	ACPX	3
Intimate Brands, Inc. (Class A)	IBI	IBI	ACX	1
Intl. Specialty Products Inc.	ISP	ISP	X	3
IntraNet Solutions, Inc.	URU	INRS	CP	2
Intraware, Inc.	NIU	ITRA	AP	1
Intuit Corp.	IQU	INTU	ACIPX	1
Inverness Medical Tehnology, Inc.	IMA	IMA	A	2
Investment Technology Group (New)	ITG	ITG	CP	3
Investors Financial Services Corp.	FLQ	IFIN	C	1
Invitrogen Corp.	IUV	IVGN	ACPX	1
IONA Technologies	YWQ	IONA	AC	3
Ionics, Incorporated	ION	ION	AP	1
IPALCO Enterprises, Inc.	IPL	IPL	P	1
Iron Mountain Inc.	IRM	IRM	A	1
Isis Pharmaceuticals, Inc.	QIS	ISIP	AC	1
Ispat Intl. NV	IST	IST	A	3
ISS Group Inc.	ISU	ISSX	CX	1
i-STAT Corp.	TAQ	STAT	AC	1
IT Group Inc.	ITX	ITX	A	1
ITC Deltacom Inc.	QIJ	ITCD	AP	2
Itron, Inc.	IQQ	ITRI	X	1
ITT Industries Inc.	IIN	IIN	C	3
ITT Industries, Inc.	ITT	ITT	CP	1
ITXC Corp.	UXI	ITXC	AX	1
IVAX Corp.	IVX	IVX	ACPX	3
iVillage Inc.	IIU	IVIL	ACPX	2
Ixia	UJC	XXIA	AC	2
iXL Enterprises, Inc.	UIX	IIXL	ACX	1

Key to Exchanges: A = AMEX (American Stock Exchange); C = CBOE (Chicago Board Options Exchange); I = International Securities Exchange; P = PCX or PSE (Pacific Stock Exchange); and X = PHLX (Philadelphia Stock Exchange).

Company Name	Option Symbol	Stock Symbol	Exchange(s)	Cycle
Ixnet, Inc.	ULE	EXNT	A	1
IXYS Corp.	USX	SYXI	AC	1
J Net Enterprises, Inc.	J	J	C	3
J. Jill Group, Inc.	JUI	JILL	AC	3
J.D. Edwards & Company	QJD	JDEC	ACP	2
J.P. Morgan Chase & Co.	JPM	JPM	ACIPX	3
Jabil Circuit, Inc.	JBL	JBL	ACIPX	3
Jack Henry & Associates Inc.	JKQ	JKHY	A	3
Jack in the Box, Inc.	JBX	JBX	CP	3
Jacobs Engineering Group, Inc.	JEC	JEC	X	1
JAKKS Pacific, Inc.	UFF	JAKK	PX	3
Jazztel p.l.c.	JQJ	JAZZ	AC	2
JDA Software Group, Inc.	QAH	JDAS	AC	1
JDS Uniphase Corp.	UQD	JDSU	ACIPX	3
Jefferies Group Inc. (New)	JEF	JEF	P	1
Jefferson-Pilot Corp.	JP	JP	A	1
JLG Industries, Inc.	JLG	JLG	C	1
JNI Corp.	JOQ	JNIC	AC	3
John Hancock Financial Services, Inc.	JHF	JHF	ACPX	3
John Nuveen & Company (Class A)	JNC	JNC	A	1
Johns-Manville Corp.	JM	JM	C	1
Johnson & Johnson	JNJ	JNJ	ACIPX	1
Johnson Controls, Inc.	JCI	JCI	X	1
Jones Apparel Group, Inc.	JNY	JNY	C	2
Jones Intercable Inc. (Class A)	JOQ	JOINA	A	3
Jones Pharma Inc.	JQM	JMED	AC	3
Jostens, Inc.	JOS	JOS	C	3
Journal Register Company	JRC	JRC	A	2
Juniper Networks, Inc.	JUP	JNPR	ACIPX	1
Juno Lighting Inc.	JQA	JUNO	P	2
Juno Online Services, Inc.	UQL	JWEB	AC	1
Jupiter Media Metrix, Inc.	JMU	JMXI	C	1
Just For Feet, Inc.	JQF	FEETQ	AC	3
Justin Industries	JQV	JSTN	P	3
K Mart Corp.	KM	KM	ACIPX	3
Kafus Industries, Ltd.	KS	KS	A	3
Kaiser Aluminum Corp.	KLU	KLU	X	1
Kana Communications, Inc.	AQW	KANA	ACP	3
Kansas City Power & Light Company	KLT	KLT	P	1
Kansas City Southern Industries, Inc.	KSU	KSU	CP	3
Kaydon Corp.	KDN	KDN	X	3
KB HOME	KBH	KBH	X	1
Keane, Inc.	KEA	KEA	AX	2
Keebler Foods Co	KBL	KBL	ACPX	2
Keithley Instruments, Inc.	KEI	KEI	AC	1
Kellogg Company	K	K	AC	3
Kellstrom Industries, Inc.	KQC	KELL	C	3
KEMET Corp.	KEM	KEM	AC	1
Kendle International, Inc.	KQR	KNDL	A	2
Kennametal, Inc.	KMT	KMT	X	3
Kent Electronics Corp.	KNT	KNT	C	1

Company Name	Option Symbol	Stock Symbol	Exchange(s)	Cycle
KeraVision, Inc.	KVQ	KERA	CP	2
Kerr-McGee Corp.	KMG	KMG	ACX	1
Key Energy Group, Inc.	KEG	KEG	CPX	1
Key Production Company, Inc.	KP	KP	P	3
KeyCorp	KEY	KEY	APX	3
Keynote Systems, Inc.	NKU	KEYN	ACP	1
Keyspan Corp.	KSE	KSE	CX	2
Kilroy Realty Corp.	KRC	KRC	P	3
Kimberly-Clark Corp.	KMB	KMB	ACIP	1
Kimco Realty Corp.	KIM	KIM	A	3
Kinder Morgan Energy Partners	KMP	KMP	A	3
King Pharmaceuticals Inc.	KG	KG	ACPX	1
Kirby Corp.	KEX	KEX	C	2
KLA Instruments Corp.	KCQ	KLAC	ACPX	3
KLM Royal Dutch Airlines	KLM	KLM	C	3
KN Energy, Inc.	KMI	KMI	P	2
Knight/Trimark Group, Inc.	QTN	NITE	ACIPX	1
Knight-Ridder, Inc.	KRI	KRI	X	1
Kohl's Corp.	KSS	KSS	ACPX	1
Koninklijke Ahold NV-SP ADR	AHO	AHO	A	3
Koninklijke Philips Electronics N.V.	PHG	PHG	ACP	1
Kopin Corp.	KQO	KOPN	CX	3
Korn/Ferry Int'l.	KFY	KFY	P	2
Kos Pharmaceuticals, Inc.	KQW	KOSP	A	2
KPNQUEST N.V.	UKB	KQIP	AC	3
Krispy Kreme Doughnuts, Inc.	KK	KK	ACP	1
Kroger Company (The)	KR	KR	ACP	1
Kroll-O'Gara Company	KRQ	KROG	A	3
K-Swiss Inc.	SWU	KSWS	C	1
KTI, Inc.	QQJ	KTIE	X	2
Kulicke and Soffa Industries, Inc.	KQS	KLIC	CAP	1
Kushner Locke Co.	KCU	KLOC	C	1
L-3 Communications Holdings, Inc.	LLL	LLL	ACP	1
Labor Ready, Inc.	LRW	LRW	PX	2
Laboratory Corp. of America Holdings	LH	LH	ACP	2
LaBranche & Co., Inc.	LAB	LAB	ACX	2
Lafarge Corp.	LAF	LAF	PX	2
Laidlaw, Inc.	LDW	LDW	A	3
Lam Research Corp.	LMQ	LRCX	ACPX	3
Lamar Advertising Company	LJQ	LAMR	CX	1
Land America Financial Group	LFG	LFG	P	3
Landry's Seafood Restaurants, Inc.	LNY	LNY	C	1
Lands' End, Inc.	LE	LE	ACX	3
Large Scale Biology Corp.	UFR	LSBC	AC	1
LaSalle Hotel Properties	LHO	LHO	P	2
Laser Vision Centers Inc.	QVL	LVCI	CP	3
Lasersight Inc.	SUE	LASE	AC	2

Key to Exchanges: A = AMEX (American Stock Exchange); C = CBOE (Chicago Board Options
Exchange); I = International Securities Exchange; P = PCX or PSE (Pacific Stock
Exchange); and X = PHLX (Philadelphia Stock Exchange).

Company Name	Option Symbol	Stock Symbol	Exchange(s)	Cycle
Lason, Inc.	QLN	LSON	P	1
Lattice Semiconductor	LQT	LSCC	ACIPX	3
Launch Media, Inc.	NQL	LAUN	A	3
La-Z-Boy, Inc.	LZB	LZB	X	2
LCA-Vision, Inc.	URH	LCAV	AC	1
LCC International Inc. (Class A)	QXC	LCCI	A	3
Leap Wireless Intl., Inc.	UIN	LWIN	ACX	1
Lear Corp.	LEA	LEA	A	3
Learning Tree International, Inc.	UEU	LTRE	A	1
Legato Systems, Inc.	EQN	LGTO	ACPI	3
Legg Mason, Inc.	LM	LM	C	2
Leggett & Platt, Incorporated	LEG	LEG	A	3
Lehman Brothers Holdings, Inc.	LEH	LEH	ACIPX	1
Lennar Corp.	LEN	LEN	A	2
Lennox International	LII	LII	X	3
Lernout & Hauspie Speech Products	XQL	LHSPQ	ACPX	3
Leucadia National Corp.	LUK	LUK	A	3
Level 3 Communications, Inc.	QHN	LVLT	ACPX	3
Level One Communications, Inc.	LVQ	LEVL	AC	2
Lexicon Genetics Incorporated	EIU	LEXG	ACP	1
Lexmark International Group, Inc. (Class A)	LXK	LXK	ACIPX	1
LG&E Energy Corp.	LGE	LGE	X	3
Liberate Technologies	QIE	LBRT	ACPX	3
Liberty Digital, Inc.	DUL	LDIG	CP	2
Liberty Property Trust	LRY	LRY	P	2
Lifecore Biomedics Inc.	OLQ	LCBM	PX	2
Lifeminders.com, Inc.	MKQ	LFMN	P	1
LifePoint Hospitals, Inc.	PUN	LPNT	AC	2
Ligand Pharmaceuticals Incorporated (Class B)	LQP	LGND	A	2
Lightbridge, Inc.	LKQ	LTBG	X	1
LightPath Technologies, Inc.	HDU	LPTH	ACPX	2
Lilly (Eli) and Company	LLY	LLY	ACPX	1
Limited, Inc. (The)	LTD	LTD	ACPX	2
Lincare Holdings, Inc.	LQN	LNCR	ACX	2
Lincoln National Corp.	LNC	LNC	A	1
Linear Technology Corp.	LLQ	LLTC	ACIPX	2
Linens 'n Things, Inc.	LIN	LIN	A	1
Liposome Company	LPQ	LIPO	C	2
Liquid Audio	QLD	LQID	AC	1
Litton Industries, Inc.	LIT	LIT	C	3
Liz Claiborne, Inc.	LIZ	LIZ	CP	1
LNR Property Corp.	LNR	LNR	A	2
Lockheed Martin Corp.	LMT	LMT	ACPX	3
Lodgian, Inc.	LOD	LOD	AP	2
Loews Cineplex Entertainment	LCP	LCP	A	1
Loews Corp.	LTR	LTR	AC	3
LoJack Corp.	LQJ	LOJN	C	3
Lone Star Steakhouse & Saloon, Inc.	LQS	STAR	C	3
Lone Star Technologies, Inc.	LSS	LSS	X	2

Company Name	Option Symbol	Stock Symbol	Exchange(s)	Cycle
Long Beach Financial Corp.	QBB	LBFC	C	2
Longview Fibre Company	LFB	LFB	C	3
Looksmart Ltd.	UOO	LOOK	ACX	1
Loral Space & Communications Ltd.	LOR	LOR	ACPX	1
Louis Dreyfus Natural Gas	LD	LD	A	2
Louisiana-Pacific Corp.	LPX	LPX	A	2
Lowe's Companies, Inc.	LOW	LOW	ACIPX	1
LSI Logic Corp.	LSI	LSI	ACIPX	1
LTV Corp. (The)	LTV	LTV	AC	2
LTX Corp.	UXT	LTXX	ACX	2
Lubrizol Corp. (The)	LZ	LZ	X	2
Lucent Technologies, Inc.	LU	LU	ACPX	1
Luminent, Inc.	ULN	LMNE	ACP	1
Luminex Corp.	UEN	LMNX	A	3
Luxottica Group SPA	LUX	LUX	X	1
Lycos, Inc.	QWL	LCOS	ACP	1
Lynx Therapeutics Inc.	ULX	LYNX	AX	2
Lyondell Chemical Company	LYO	LYO	C	3
M&T Bank Corp.	MTB	MTB	P	1
Macdermid Inc.	MRD	MRD	P	2
Mack Cali Realty Corp.	CLI	CLI	P	1
Macrochem Corp.	QQ	MCHM	AC	3
Macromedia, Inc.	MRQ	MACR	ACIPX	2
Macrovision Corp.	MVU	MVSN	APX	1
Madge Networks N.V.	MQE	MADGF	AC	2
Magellan Health Services Inc.	MGL	MGL	AX	2
Magic Software Enterprises Ltd.	UMI	MGIC	A	2
Magna International, Inc. (Class A)	MGA	MGA	C	2
MagneTek, Inc.	MAG	MAG	P	3
Mail-Well, Inc	MWL	MWL	P	1
Mallinckrodt, Inc.	MKG	MKG	C	1
Mandalay Resort Group	MBG	MBG	ACPX	3
Manhattan Associates, Inc.	MQR	MANH	P	1
Manor Care Inc.	HCR	HCR	CPX	2
Manpower, Inc.	MAN	MAN	C	3
Manufacturers Services Limited	MSV	MSV	C	1
Manugistics Group, Inc.	ZUQ	MANU	ACPX	1
Manulife Financial Corp.	MFC	MFC	A	3
Mapics, Inc.	RQQ	MAPX	A	2
MapInfo Corp.	NDU	MAPS	ACP	1
MapQuest.com, Inc.	MYQ	MQST	A	3
marchFirst Inc.	WMQ	MRCHQ	ACP	2
Marconi plc	UIM	MONI	AC	1
Marimba, Inc.	MRU	MRBA	APX	3
Marine Drilling Companies, Inc.	MRL	MRL	CP	2
Market 2000+HOLDRS Trust	MKH	MKH	A	1
Marketing Services Group Inc.	UMS	MSGI	CP	2

Key to Exchanges: A = AMEX (American Stock Exchange); C = CBOE (Chicago Board Options Exchange); I = International Securities Exchange; P = PCX or PSE (Pacific Stock Exchange); and X = PHLX (Philadelphia Stock Exchange).

Company Name	Option Symbol	Stock Symbol	Exchange(s)	Cycle
Marriott International, Inc.	MAR	MAR	ACPX	1
Marsh & McLennan Companies, Inc.	MMC	MMC	CIP	1
Marshall & Ilsley Corp.	MI	MI	AX	3
Martek Biosciences Corp.	KQT	MATK	X	3
Martha Stewart Living (Class A)	MSO	MSO	AX	3
Marvell Technology Group Ltd.	UVM	MRVL	ACPX	2
Masco Corp.	MAS	MAS	AP	1
Massey Energy Company	MEE	MEE	C	1
Mastec, Inc.	MTZ	MTZ	AX	1
Material Sciences Corp.	MSC	MSC	X	2
MatrixOne, Inc.	MOU	MONE	AC	2
Mattel, Inc.	MAT	MAT	ACIPX	1
Mattson Technology, Inc.	QQM	MTSN	P	1
Maverick Tube Corp.	MVK	MVK	X	1
Maxicare Health Plans, Inc.	MQH	MAXI	A	3
Maxim Integrated Products, Inc.	XIQ	MXIM	ACIPX	2
Maxm Pharmaceuticals, Inc.	MMP	MAXM	AC	3
Maxtor Corp.	MXO	MXO	ACPX	1
Maxwell Technologies Inc.	QMW	MXWL	P	3
Maxygen, Inc.	MQQ	MAXY	P	2
May Department Stores Company (The)	MAY	MAY	CP	3
Maytag Corp.	MYG	MYG	CPX	1
MBIA, Inc.	MBI	MBI	AX	2
MBNA Corp.	KRB	KRB	ACPX	3
McAfee.com	CFU	MCAF	ACP	3
McCormick and Company, Inc.	MKC	MKC	X	3
McData Corp. (Class A)	MQG	MCDTA	AC	1
McData Corp.	DMU	MCDT	ACPX	1
McDermott International, Inc.	MDR	MDR	CX	2
McDonald's Corp.	MCD	MCD	ACIPX	3
McGraw-Hill Companies, Inc. (The)	MHP	MHP	X	2
MCK Communications, Inc.	QIK	MCKC	C	2
McKesson Corp.	MCK	MCK	ACPX	2
McLeodusa, Inc.	QMD	MCLD	CP	1
MCN Energy Corp.	MCN	MCN	AP	2
MDU Resources Group, Inc.	MDU	MDU	CP	1
MDU Resources Group, Inc.	MDU	MDU	X	3
Mead Corp. (The)	MEA	MEA	CX	1
Mechanical Technology Incorporated	UKY	MKTY	A	2
Medallion Financial Corp.	TQX	TAXI	A	2
Medarex, Inc.	MZU	MEDX	AC	2
Medco Research, Inc.	MRE	MRE	A	1
Mediacom Communications Corp.	MUD	MCCC	C	1
Mediaone Group Inc.	UMG	UMG	A	1
Mediaplex Inc.	LQZ	MPLX	AP	2
Medical Manager Corp.	YSS	MMGR	AX	3
Medicis Pharmaceutical Corp.	MRX	MRX	AC	1
MedImmune, Inc.	MEQ	MEDI	ACIPX	3
Meditrust Corp. (New)	MT	MT	AX	1
MedQuist	QQU	MEDQ	AP	2
Medscape, Inc.	QMM	MSCP	AX	3
Medtronic, Inc.	MDT	MDT	ACIPX	2

Company Name	Option Symbol	Stock Symbol	Exchange(s)	Cycle
Mellon Financial Corp.	MEL	MEL	CPX	3
MEMC Electronic Materials, Inc.	WFR	WFR	A	1
Men's Wearhouse, Inc. (The)	MW	MW	X	2
Mentor Corp.	MNQ	MNTR	AP	1
Mentor Graphics Corp.	MGQ	MENT	ACP	1
MERANT plc ADR	QGM	MRNT	A	1
Mercantile Bancorporation	MTL	MTL	A	3
Mercator Software	SUW	MCTR	ACX	1
Merck & Co., Inc.	MRK	MRK	ACIPX	1
Mercury Computer Systems, Inc.	QYR	MRCY	AP	2
Mercury General Corp.	MCY	MCY	X	3
Mercury Interactive Corp.	RQB	MERQ	ACIPX	1
Meredith Corp.	MDP	MDP	A	3
Meristar Hospitality, Corp.	MHX	MHX	PX	2
Meritor Automotive Inc.	MRA	MRA	C	2
Merix Corp.	KXQ	MERX	AC	3
Merrill Lynch & Co., Inc.	MER	MER	ACIPX	1
Mesa Air Group, Inc.	EAQ	MESA	C	2
Mesaba Holdings, Inc.	MLQ	MAIR	P	2
MessageMedia Inc.	MUG	MESG	CP	1
Metalink Ltd.	MUM	MTLK	C	1
Metamor Worldwide, Inc.	EQB	MMWW	C	3
MetaSolv, Inc.	QE	MSLV	CP	1
Metawave Communications Corp.	UWM	MTWV	A	1
Methode Electronics, Inc. (Class A)	QME	METHA	PC	1
MetLife, Inc.	MET	MET	ACP	3
Metricom, Inc.	MQM	MCOM	ACPX	1
Metris Companies, Inc.	MXT	MXT	AC	1
Metro One Telecommunications, Inc.	KQM	MTON	X	3
Metro-Goldwyn Mayer Inc.	MGM	MGM	AC	2
Metromedia Fiber Network, Inc.	QFN	MFNX	ACIPX	2
Metromedia International Group, Inc.	MMG	MMG	C	3
Mexico Fund, Inc. (The)	MXF	MXF	A	2
MGC Communications Inc.	MGU	MPWR	ACX	1
MGI PHARMA, Inc.	QOG	MOGN	AC	1
MGIC Investment Corp.	MTG	MTG	A	3
MGM Grand, Inc.	MGG	MGG	AC	3
Michael Foods Inc.	DQM	MIKL	P	2
Michaels Stores, Inc.	IKQ	MIKE	P	3
Micrel, Inc.	MIQ	MCRL	ACPX	2
Micro Warehouse, Inc.	MQR	MWHS	AX	2
MicroAge, Inc.	MQI	MICAQ	C	2
Microchip Technology, Inc.	UTM	MCHP	ACIX	1
Micromuse, Inc.	QUM	MUSE	ACIPX	1
Micron Electronics, Inc.	MQU	MUEI	ACP	1
Micron Technology, Inc.	MU	MU	ACIPX	1
MICROS Systems, Inc.	QXM	MCRS	A	3
Microsemi Corp	QMS	MSCC	A	3

Key to Exchanges: A = AMEX (American Stock Exchange); C = CBOE (Chicago Board Options
    Exchange); I = International Securities Exchange; P = PCX or PSE (Pacific Stock
    Exchange); and X = PHLX (Philadelphia Stock Exchange).

Company Name	Option Symbol	Stock Symbol	Exchange(s)	Cycle
Microsoft Corp.	MSQ	MSFT	ACPX	1
MicroStrategy Incorp.	EOU	MSTR	ACPX	1
Microtune, Inc.	TUF	TUNE	AC	1
Microvision, Inc.	QMV	MVIS	A	2
Mid Atlantic Medical Services, Inc.	MME	MME	A	3
MidAmerican Energy Holdings	MEC	MEC	P	3
MidCap SPDR	MDY	MDY	A	3
Midway Games Inc.	MWY	MWY	CX	2
Milacron, Inc.	MZ	MZ	X	2
Millennium Cell, Inc.	MUK	MCEL	A	1
Millennium Chemicals, Inc.	MCH	MCH	C	3
Millennium Pharmaceuticals, Inc.	QMN	MLNM	ACIPX	2
Miller (Herman), Inc.	MHQ	MLHR	C	2
Millicom International Cellular S.A.	MQS	MICC	C	1
Millipore Corp.	MIL	MIL	AC	1
MiniMed, Inc.	MAQ	MNMD	ACP	2
Minnesota Mining & Manufacturing Company	MMM	MMM	ACIPX	1
MIPS Technologies, Inc.	MUP	MIPS	ACX	1
MIPS Technologies, Inc. (Class B)	QOS	MIPSB	ACP	3
Mirant Corp.	MIR	MIR	AC	2
Miravant Medical Technologies	SQD	MRVT	APX	3
Mission Critical Software	UFJ	MCSW	AC	1
Mitchell Energy & Development Corp. (Class B)	MND	MND	ACP	3
Mitel Corp.	MLT	MLT	P	1
MKS Instruments, Inc.	QQB	MKSI	C	1
MMC Networks Inc.	CMQ	MMCN	AC	1
Modine Manufacturing Company	QMO	MODI	P	1
Modis Professional Services Inc.	MPS	MPS	C	1
Mohawk Industries Inc.	MHK	MHK	CP	2
Molecular Devices Corp.	MCQ	MDCC	ACP	1
Molex Incorporated	OXQ	MOLX	ACX	2
Monaco Coach Corp.	MNC	MNC	PX	1
Monsanto Company (New)	MON	MON	ACP	1
Montana Power Company	MTP	MTP	CPX	1
MONY Group, Inc. (The)	MNY	MNY	AX	2
Moody's Corp.	DNZ	MCO	A	2
Morgan Stanley Dean Witter & Co.	MWD	MWD	ACIPX	1
Morrison Knudsen Corp.	MK	MK	X	2
Mortgage.com, Inc.	DUM	MDCM	C	2
Motient Corp.	KQF	MTNT	P	3
Motorola, Inc.	MOT	MOT	ACIPX	1
MP3.com, Inc.	PUM	MPPP	CX	2
MRO Software Inc.	UPJ	MROI	A	3
MRV Communications Inc.	VQX	MRVC	ACIPX	1
MSC Industrial Direct Co., Inc.	MSM	MSM	C	1
M-Systems Flash Disk Pioneers Ltd.	FFU	FLSH	ACP	1
MTI Technology Corp.	QTX	MTIC	AC	1
MTS Systems Corp.	YEQ	MTSC	P	2
Mueller Industries, Inc.	MLI	MLI	X	1
Multex.com Inc.	UXM	MLTX	APX	2

Company Name	Option Symbol	Stock Symbol	Exchange(s)	Cycle
Murphy Oil Corp.	MUR	MUR	ACP	2
Musicland Stores Corp.	MLG	MLG	A	1
Mutual Risk Management Ltd.	MM	MM	X	2
Mylan Laboratories, Inc.	MYL	MYL	ACP	1
Mynd Corp.	YND	YND	A	2
MyPoints.com	MYU	MYPT	A	3
Myriad Genetics, Inc.	GSQ	MYGN	CX	2
Nabisco Group Holdings	NGH	NGH	ACX	3
Nabisco Holdings Corp. (Class A)	NA	NA	ACX	3
Nabors Industries, Inc.	NBR	NBR	ACIPX	3
NAC Re Corp.	NRC	NRC	X	3
Nalco Chemical Company	NLC	NLC	X	3
Nam Tai Electronics, Inc.	QNA	NTAI	A	3
Nanogen, Inc.	GUN	NGEN	X	3
Nanophase Technologies Corp.	NNU	NANX	A	3
Nasdaq-100 Shares	QQQ	QQQ	ACIPX	3
Nashua Corp.	NSH	NSH	A	1
National City Corp.	NCC	NCC	ACX	1
National Commerce Bancorp	QTQ	NCBC	C	1
National Computer Systems, Inc.	QEZ	NLCS	AC	1
National Data Corp.	NDC	NDC	X	2
National Discount Brokers	NDB	NDB	ACPX	1
National Information Consortium, Inc.	EGU	EGOV	CP	3
National Instruments Corp.	SJQ	NATI	P	3
National Oilwell, Inc.	NOI	NOI	ACP	2
National Semiconductor Corp.	NSM	NSM	ACIPX	2
National Service Industries, Inc.	NSI	NSI	X	3
National TechTeam, Inc.	QEA	TEAM	C	2
Nationwide Financial Services, Inc.	NFS	NFS	A	1
Natural Microsystems Corp.	YYQ	NMSS	PX	2
Nature's Sunshine Products, Inc.	UQP	NATR	A	3
Nautica Enterprises, Inc.	NQT	NAUT	C	1
Navarre Corp.	QHQ	NAVR	AC	1
Navigant Consulting, Inc.	NCI	NCI	ACP	2
NaviSite, Inc.	UAV	NAVI	AC	3
Navistar International Corp.	NAV	NAV	ACIP	1
NBC Internet Inc.	XQM	NBCI	ACPX	3
NBTY, Inc.	NBQ	NBTY	P	3
NCO Group, Inc.	GCQ	NCOG	PX	3
NCR Corp.	NCR	NCR	AC	1
Neff Corp.	NFF	NFF	CPX	1
Neoforma.com	NUB	NEOF	ACP	3
NeoMagic Corp.	GJQ	NMGC	CP	1
NeoRx Corp.	XUO	NERX	AC	3
Net Perceptions, Inc.	PEU	NETP	ACX	2
Net.B@nk, Inc.	NQA	NTBK	ACX	1
Net2Phone, Inc.	UPT	NTOP	AC	1
Netcentives, Inc.	ULY	NCNT	AP	2

Key to Exchanges: A = AMEX (American Stock Exchange); C = CBOE (Chicago Board Options
     Exchange); I = International Securities Exchange; P = PCX or PSE (Pacific Stock
     Exchange); and X = PHLX (Philadelphia Stock Exchange).

Company Name	Option Symbol	Stock Symbol	Exchange(s)	Cycle
Netegrity, Inc.	SAO	NETE	ACP	3
NetIQ Corp.	FSJ	NTIQ	ACPX	1
Netopia, Inc.	NQD	NTPA	CP	1
Netro Corp.	SRU	NTRO	ACX	3
NetSpeak Corp.	NNQ	NSPK	ACX	2
Network Access Solutions Corp.	UNW	NASC	AC	1
Network Appliance Corp.	NJQ	NTAP	ACIPX	3
Network Associates Inc.	CQM	NETA	ACPX	3
Network Commerce	NUH	NWKC	AC	1
Network Equipment Technologies, Inc.	NWK	NWK	P	3
Network Peripherals Inc.	XMQ	NPIX	ACPX	2
Network Plus Corp.	UTN	NPLS	CX	3
Network Solutions Inc. (Class A)	JNQ	NSOL	AC	1
NetZero, Inc.	NUR	NZRO	AC	1
Neuberger Berman Inc.	NEU	NEU	AP	1
Neurocrine Biosciences, Inc.	UOT	NBIX	AP	2
Neurogen Corp.	NQO	NRGN	AX	1
New Century Energies Inc.	NCE	NCE	X	3
New England Electric System	NES	NES	X	3
New Era of Networks Inc.	QNO	NEON	ACP	1
New Focus, Inc.	DUO	NUFO	ACP	1
New Plan Excel Realty Trust, Inc.	NXL	NXL	A	2
New York Community Bancorp, Inc.	NQK	NYCB	CP	1
New York Times Co. (Class A)	NYT	NYT	AP	1
Newbridge Networks Corp.	NN	NN	ACP	3
Newcourt Credit Group Inc.	NCT	NCT	AX	2
Newell Rubbermaid Inc.	NWL	NWL	CP	3
Newfield Exploration Company	NFX	NFX	A	3
Newmont Mining Corp.	NEM	NEM	ACIPX	3
Newpark Resources, Inc.	NR	NR	X	1
Newport Corp.	QNW	NEWP	ACIPX	2
Newport News Shipbuilding Inc.	NNS	NNS	A	2
NewPower Holdings, Inc.	NPW	NPW	A	1
News Corp. Ltd. ADR Preferred	NSW	NWS/A	A	1
News Corp. Ltd. (The) ADR	NWS	NWS	ACIPX	1
NewsEdge Corp.	QBE	NEWZ	C	1
NeXstar Pharmaceuticals, Inc.	NQX	NXTR	P	1
Next Level Communications, Inc.	NUX	NXTV	ACX	3
NextCard, Inc.	DQX	NXCD	ACP	1
NEXTEL Communications, Inc. (Class A)	FQC	NXTL	ACIPX	2
Nextel Partners, Inc.	KTU	NXTP	ACPX	2
NFO Worldwide, Inc.	NFO	NFO	X	3
Niagara Mohawk Power Corp.	NMK	NMK	A	3
Nice Systems Ltd.	QIC	NICE	C	1
NICOR, Inc.	GAS	GAS	P	1
NIKE, Inc. (Class B)	NKE	NKE	ACIPX	1
Niku Corp.	NFU	NIKU	AC	1
Nine West Group, Inc.	NIN	NIN	P	3
NISource Inc.	NI	NI	CP	1
Noble Affiliates, Inc.	NBL	NBL	ACI	2
Noble Drilling Corp.	NE	NE	CPX	3
Nokia Corp. ADR	NOK	NOK	ACIPX	1

Company Name	Option Symbol	Stock Symbol	Exchange(s)	Cycle
Nordstrom, Inc.	JWN	JWN	AP	1
Norfolk Southern Corp.	NSC	NSC	C	3
Norrell Corp.	NRL	NRL	X	3
Nortel Networks Corp.	NT	NT	ACPX	3
North American Palladium Ltd.	PAL	PAL	A	3
North American Scientific, Inc.	MUN	NASI	A	3
North American Vaccine, Inc.	NVX	NVX	A	3
North Face, Inc. (The)	QFI	TNFI	P	3
North Fork Bancorporation	NFB	NFB	PX	2
Northeast Utilities	NU	NU	C	1
Northern States Power Company	NSP	NSP	A	3
Northern Trust Corp.	NRQ	NTRS	CIX	1
Northfield Laboratories, Inc.	DHQ	NFLD	CX	2
Northpoint Communications Group Inc.	NUP	NPNTQ	ACPX	2
Northrop Grumman Corp.	NOC	NOC	ACP	2
Northwest Airlines Corp. (Class A)	NAQ	NWAC	ACX	3
Northwest Natural Gas Company	NWN	NWN	X	3
NOVA Chemicals Corp.	NCX	NCX	C	1
NOVA Corp/Georgia	NIS	NIS	AC	2
Novartis AG	NVS	NVS	ACP	1
Novatel Wireless, Inc.	NVU	NVTL	ACP	1
Novell, Inc.	NKQ	NOVL	ACPX	2
Novellus Systems, Inc.	NLQ	NVLS	ACPX	3
Noven Pharmaceuticals, Inc.	NPQ	NOVN	P	1
Novoste Corp.	QOH	NOVT	AC	1
NPC International Inc.	QQL	NPCI	P	3
NPS Pharmaceuticals, Inc.	QKK	NPSP	AC	2
NRG Energy, Inc.	NRG	NRG	AC	3
NS Group, Inc.	NSS	NSS	X	1
NSTAR	NST	NST	X	2
NTL Incorporated	NLI	NLI	CIP	3
Nu Horizons Electronics Corp.	NTQ	NUHC	CX	1
Nu Skin Enterprises, Inc.	NUS	NUS	A	3
Nuance Communications, Inc.	NUD	NUAN	CP	2
Nucor Corp.	NUE	NUE	C	1
Nuevo Energy Company	NEV	NEV	X	1
Numerical Technologies, Inc.	QEK	NMTC	AC	1
NVIDIA Corp.	UVA	NVDA	ACIPX	3
NX Networks, Inc.	UNX	NXWX	ACX	3
NYFIX, Inc.	NYF	NYFX	A	3
Oak Industries, Inc.	OAK	OAK	A	3
Oak Technology, Inc.	KAU	OAKT	ACP	3
Oakley, Inc.	OO	OO	C	2
Oakwood Homes Corp.	OH	OH	X	3
Occidental Petroleum Corp.	OXY	OXY	ACIPX	2
Ocean Energy, Inc. (New)	OEI	OEI	ACIPX	3
Oceaneering International, Inc.	OII	OII	P	1

Key to Exchanges: A = AMEX (American Stock Exchange); C = CBOE (Chicago Board Options Exchange); I = International Securities Exchange; P = PCX or PSE (Pacific Stock Exchange); and X = PHLX (Philadelphia Stock Exchange).

Company Name	Option Symbol	Stock Symbol	Exchange(s)	Cycle
Ocular Sciences, Inc.	QLO	OCLR	A	1
OEA, Inc.	OEA	OEA	A	1
Office Depot, Inc.	ODP	ODP	ACIPX	1
OfficeMax, Inc.	OMX	OMX	AC	3
Offshore Logistics, Inc.	OOQ	OLOG	A	2
Ohio Casualty Corp.	OHQ	OCAS	X	2
Oil Service Holdrs Trust	OIH	OIH	AP	1
Old Kent Financial Corp.	OK	OK	X	1
Old Republic International Corp.	ORI	ORI	PX	1
Olin Corp.	OLN	OLN	A	2
Olsten Corp. (The)	OLS	OLS	A	2
Olympic Steel, Inc.	ZQU	ZEUS	C	2
Omnicare, Inc.	OCR	OCR	PX	3
Omnicom Group, Inc.	OMC	OMC	CP	1
OmniSky Corp.	YQB	OMNY	ACP	2
On Assignment, Inc.	ODQ	ASGN	X	2
One Valley Bancorp, Inc.	OV	OV	X	3
OneMain.com, Inc.	ONW	ONEM	ACP	1
ONEOK, Inc.	OKE	OKE	X	2
OnHealth Network Company	OUN	ONHN	AC	1
ONI Systems Corp.	EUI	ONIS	ACPX	1
Onyx Pharmaceuticals, Inc.	OIQ	ONXX	AC	2
ONYX Software Corp.	ODQ	ONXS	ACP	1
Open Market Inc.	OQM	OMKT	AC	2
Open Text Corp.	QFT	OTEX	AC	2
Open TV Corp.	UOP	OPTV	AC	3
Openwave Systems, Inc.	UMN	OPWV	ACPX	2
Oplink Communications, Inc.	OKU	OPLK	ACP	1
Optical Coating Laboratory, Inc.	LNQ	OCLI	P	2
Optical Communications Products, Inc.	UHY	OCPI	ACP	1
Optical Robotics Corp.	OQG	OPMR	ACP	1
Oracle Corp.	ORQ	ORCL	ACIPX	3
Orasure Technologies	QTP	OSUR	C	1
Orbital Sciences Corp.	ORB	ORB	AC	3
Orbotech Ltd.	OKA	ORBK	APX	1
Orchid Biosciences, Inc.	UOH	ORCH	AC	1
Orckit Communications Ltd.	QFY	ORCT	ACP	1
Oregon Steel Mills, Inc.	OS	OS	X	2
O'Reilly Automotive, Inc.	OQR	ORLY	X	2
Organogenesis, Inc.	ORG	ORG	CP	1
Orion Capital Corp.	OC	OC	ACX	2
Orion Power Holdings, Inc.	ORN	ORN	AP	1
Ortel Corp.	OQE	ORTL	C	2
Orthodontic Centers of America, Inc.	OCA	OCA	A	3
Osteotech, Inc.	OQQ	OSTE	X	2
O'Sullivan Industries Holdings, Inc.	OSU	OSU	A	3
OTG Software, Inc.	UOG	OTGS	A	2
Outback Steakhouse, Inc.	OSI	OSI	ACP	2
Overture.com	GUO	OVER	ACX	2
Owens & Minor, Inc.	OMI	OMI	P	1
Owens Corning	OWC	OWC	X	3
Owens-Illinois, Inc.	OI	OI	C	2

Company Name	Option Symbol	Stock Symbol	Exchange(s)	Cycle
Oxford Health Plans, Inc.	OHP	OHP	CIPX	2
Oxigene, Inc.	QYO	OXGN	AC	1
P.F. Chang's China Bistro	HUO	PFCB	AX	1
PACCAR, Inc.	PAQ	PCAR	C	2
Pacific Gateway Exchange, Inc.	QAE	PGEX	AC	1
Pacific Sunwear of California, Inc.	PVQ	PSUN	X	3
PacifiCare Health Systems, Inc.	HYQ	PHSY	ACP	2
Packard Bioscience Company	PQC	PBSC	AP	1
Packeteer, Inc.	XOU	PKTR	P	2
Pactiv Corp.	PTV	PTV	AX	2
Pac-West Telecomm, Inc.	PFQ	PACW	APX	1
Paine Webber Group, Inc.	PWJ	PWJ	AC	1
PairGain Technologies, Inc.	PQG	PAIR	AC	1
Pall Corp.	PLL	PLL	C	3
Palm, Inc.	UPY	PALM	ACIPX	2
Pan American Silver Corp.	PZQ	PAAS	A	3
Panamerican Beverages, Inc. (Class A)	PB	PB	AC	1
PanAmSat Corp.	OQO	SPOT	CX	2
Papa John's International, Inc.	ZZQ	PZZA	C	1
Paradyne Networks, Inc.	UPD	PDYN	CPX	1
Parametric Technology Corp.	PMQ	PMTC	ACIPX	2
PAREXEL International Corp.	VBQ	PRXL	AX	3
Park Electrochemical Corp.	PKE	PKE	PX	3
Park Place Entertainment Corp.	PPE	PPE	ACP	1
Parker Drilling Company	PKD	PKD	CPX	1
Parker-Hannifin Corp.	PH	PH	X	2
Partner Communications Company	QPA	PTNR	A	1
PathoGenesis Corp.	PHQ	PGNS	AC	3
Patterson Dental Company	DOU	PDCO	C	1
Patterson Energy, Inc.	NZQ	PTEN	ACX	2
Paul Harris Stores, Inc.	PUQ	PAUH	P	1
Paxson Communications Corp.	PAX	PAX	C	3
Paychex, Inc.	PQX	PAYX	CPX	3
Payless ShoeSource, Inc.	PSS	PSS	C	3
PC Connection, Inc.	PQB	PCCC	C	1
P-COM, Inc.	PQP	PCOM	CPX	2
PC-Tel, Inc.	UKC	PCTI	AP	3
Peapod, Inc.	QPP	PPOD	AC	3
Pediatrix Medical Group, Inc.	PDX	PDX	ACP	2
Peerless Systems Corp.	QLS	PRLS	C	2
Pegasus Communications Corp.	GUQ	PGTV	ACX	3
Pegasus Systems, Inc.	PUG	PEGS	AC	1
Pemstar, Inc.	MQI	PMTR	C	1
Penn National Gaming, Inc.	UQN	PENN	P	1
Pennaco Energy Inc.	PN	PN	A	1
Penney (J.C.) Company, Inc.	JCP	JCP	ACIP	2
Pennzol-Quaker State Company	PZL	PZL	AC	1

Key to Exchanges: A = AMEX (American Stock Exchange); C = CBOE (Chicago Board Options Exchange); I = International Securities Exchange; P = PCX or PSE (Pacific Stock Exchange); and X = PHLX (Philadelphia Stock Exchange).

Company Name	Option Symbol	Stock Symbol	Exchange(s)	Cycle
Pentair, Inc.	PNR	PNR	X	2
Peoples Energy Corp.	PGL	PGL	P	3
PeopleSoft Inc.	PQO	PSFT	ACIPX	1
Pep Boys—Manny, Moe, & Jack (The)	PBY	PBY	C	1
Pepsi Bottling Group Inc.	PBG	PBG	ACPX	3
PepsiAmericas, Inc.	PAS	PAS	CP	1
PepsiCo, Inc.	PEP	PEP	ACIPX	1
Peregrine Systems Inc.	GQP	PRGN	ACIPX	1
Performance Food Group Company	PGU	PFGC	A	3
Pericom Semiconductor Corp.	PSQ	PSEM	ACP	
Perkin-Elmer, Inc.	PKI	PKI	ACX	3
Perot Systems Corp.	PER	PER	ACX	3
Perrigo Company	IQP	PRGO	C	2
Perrigo Company	POQ	PRGO	C	3
Per-Se Technologies, Inc.	MQA	PSTI	A	3
Persero P.T. Indonesian Satelite Corp.	IIT	IIT	A	3
Personnel Group of America, Inc.	PGA	PGA	P	3
Petco Animal Supplies, Inc.	QPT	PETC	P	3
PetroChina Company Limited	PTR	PTR	AC	3
Petroleo Brasileiro S.A. ADR	PBR	PBR	AC	1
Petroleum Geo-Services A/S ADR	PGO	PGO	AC	2
PETsMART, Inc.	PQM	PETM	X	2
PFF Bancorp Inc.	PQC	PFFB	P	2
Pfizer, Inc.	PFE	PFE	ACIPX	3
PG&E Corp.	PCG	PCG	ACIP	3
Pharmaceutical HOLDRS	PPH	PPH	AC	2
Pharmaceutical Product Development	PJQ	PPDI	X	1
Pharmacia & Upjohn, Inc.	PNU	PNU	CP	1
Pharmacia Corp.	PHA	PHA	ACIPX	1
Pharmacopeia, Inc.	PQA	PCOP	X	2
Pharmacyclics, Inc.	QPY	PCYC	X	3
PharmaPrint Inc.	QPN	PPRT	P	3
Phelps Dodge Corp.	PD	PD	ACP	1
Philip Morris Companies, Inc.	MO	MO	ACIPX	3
Philippine Long Distance Telephone Company ADR	PHI	PHI	C	1
Phillips Petroleum Company	P	P	ACIPX	2
Phillips Van Heusen Corp.	PVH	PVH	C	3
Phoenix Technologies Ltd..	PKQ	PTEC	A	3
Phosphate Resources Partners	PLP	PLP	A	3
Photon Dynamics, Inc.	PDU	PHTN	P	1
Photronics, Inc.	PQF	PLAB	AP	3
Physician Reliance Network, Inc.	PQE	PHYN	A	2
Picturetel Corp.	PTQ	PCTL	X	1
Pier 1 Imports, Inc.	PIR	PIR	C	3
Pilgrim's Pride Corporation	CHX	CHX	X	2
Pillowtek Corp.	PTX	PTX	C	2
Pilot Network Services, Inc.	PTU	PILT	ACX	1
Pinnacle Entertainment Inc.	PNK	PNK	C	3
Pinnacle Holdings Inc.	IUG	BIGT	A	1
Pinnacle Systems, Inc.	PUC	PCLE	C	1
Pinnacle West Capital Corp.	PNW	PNW	P	1

Company Name	Option Symbol	Stock Symbol	Exchange(s)	Cycle
Pioneer Group Inc.	QPR	PIOG	P	3
Pioneer Hi-Bred International, Inc.	PHB	PHB	A	3
Pioneer Natural Resources Company	PXD	PXD	A	3
Pioneer Standard Electronics, Inc.	OQJ	PIOS	P	1
Pitney Bowes, Inc.	PBI	PBI	AP	1
Pittston Brink's Group	PZB	PZB	X	2
Pittston Burlington Group	PZX	PZX	X	2
Pivotal Corp.	QFK	PVTL	ACP	1
Pixar, Inc.	PQJ	PIXR	AX	1
Pixelworks, Inc.	PUO	PXLW	AC	1
Placer Dome, Inc.	PDG	PDG	ACPX	3
Plains Resources, Inc.	PLX	PLX	A	1
Planar Systems, Inc.	PNQ	PLNR	A	3
Plantronics Inc.	PLT	PLT	A	2
Plasma-Therm, Inc.	YQP	PTIS	PX	1
Playboy Enterprises, Inc.	PLA	PLA	X	3
Playtex Products, Inc.	PYX	PYX	A	1
Plexus Corp. Inc.	QUA	PLXS	ACX	3
Plug Power, Inc.	PQL	PLUG	ACP	3
Plum Creek Timber Company, LP	PCL	PCL	AX	2
PLX Technology, I Inc.	PIU	PLXT	ACP	1
PMC-Sierra Inc.	SQL	PMCS	ACIPX	2
PNC Bank Corp.	PNC	PNC	CPX	2
Pogo Producing Company	PPP	PPP	CP	2
Pohang Iron & Steel Company Ltd.	PKX	PKX	ACX	2
Polaris Industries, Inc.	PII	PII	A	3
Polaroid Corp.	PRD	PRD	C	1
Polo Ralph Lauren Corp.	RL	RL	ACX	1
Polycom, Inc.	QHD	PLCM	CX	1
Polymedica Corp.	PM	PLMD	ACIP	3
Pomeroy Computer Resources	PBQ	PMRY	A	1
Portal Software, Inc.	PUS	PRSF	CIPX	1
Possis Medical, Inc.	UPQ	POSS	P	1
Potash Corp. of Saskatchewan Inc.	POT	POT	C	3
Potlatch Corp.	PCH	PCH	C	3
Potomac Electric Power Company	POM	POM	X	2
Power Integrations Inc.	QPW	POWI	AP	1
Power-One, Inc.	OGU	PWER	ACPX	1
Powertel, Inc.	IQF	PTEL	P	3
Powerwave Technologies, Inc.	VFQ	PWAV	ACPX	2
PP & L Resources, Inc.	PPL	PPL	PX	2
PPG Industries, Inc.	PPG	PPG	X	2
PRAECIS Pharmaceuticals Incorporated	FGU	PRCS	ACP	2
Praxair, Inc.	PX	PX	A	1
Precise Software Solutions Ltd.	PUI	PRSE	A	2
Precision Castparts Corp.	PCP	PCP	AC	2
Precision Drilling Corp.	PDS	PDS	X	3
Precision Response Corp.	MQX	PRRC	C	1

Key to Exchanges: A = AMEX (American Stock Exchange); C = CBOE (Chicago Board Options Exchange); I = International Securities Exchange; P = PCX or PSE (Pacific Stock Exchange); and X = PHLX (Philadelphia Stock Exchange).

Company Name	Option Symbol	Stock Symbol	Exchange(s)	Cycle
Premisys Communications, Inc.	RQS	PRMS	C	1
Prentiss Properties Trust	PP	PP	P	2
Pre-Paid Legal Services, Inc.	PPD	PPD	ACX	2
Presidential Life Corp.	QPL	PLFE	X	3
Presstek, Inc.	PQK	PRST	AC	1
PRI Automation Inc.	UXQ	PRIA	ACPX	2
Price Communications Corp.	PR	PR	ACPX	2
Priceline.com Inc.	PUZ	PCLN	ACPX	1
Pride International	PDE	PDE	APX	1
Primark Corp.	PMK	PMK	C	1
Prime Hospitality Corp.	PDQ	PDQ	X	1
Prime Medical Services, Inc.	QSI	PMSI	C	1
Prime Retail, Inc.	PRT	PRT	P	3
Primedia Inc.	PRM	PRM	CPX	3
Primus Telecommunications Group, Inc.	PQW	PRTL	X	3
Priority Healthcare Corp.	UHP	PHCC	ACX	1
Prison Realty Trust	PZN	PZN	P	2
ProBusiness Services, Inc.	PQU	PRBZ	A	3
Procter & Gamble Company (The)	PG	PG	ACPX	1
Prodigy Communications Corp.	PUY	PRGY	ACPX	3
Professional Detailing, Inc.	PKU	PDII	ACP	1
Profit Recovery Group Intl	FPQ	PRGX	A	1
Progenics Pharmaceuticals, Inc.	GUB	PGNX	C	2
Progress Energy, Inc.	PGN	PGN	APX	1
Progress Software Corp.	RGQ	PRGS	A	3
Progressive Corp. (The)	PGR	PGR	CPX	2
Promus Hotel Corp.	PRH	PRH	P	1
Protective Life Corp.	PL	PL	C	1
Protein Design Labs, Inc.	PQI	PDLI	CX	2
Proton Energy Systems, Inc.	PAU	PRTN	CP	1
Provell, Inc.	DQN	PRVL	C	2
Provident Bankshares Corp.	QEB	PBKS	C	1
Provident Companies, Inc.	PVT	PVT	X	3
Provident Financial Group	GQV	PFGI	C	1
Providian Financial Corp. (New)	PVN	PVN	ACIP	3
Proxicom, Inc.	PUX	PXCM	AP	3
Proxim, Inc.	WQG	PROX	CP	3
ProxyMed, Inc.	PQQ	PILL	AC	1
PSC, Inc.	QPS	PSCX	P	1
PsiNet Inc.	SQP	PSIX	ACIPX	1
PSS World Medical	PYQ	PSSI	X	2
PT Telekomunikasi Indonesia ADR	TLK	TLK	AP	1
PTEK Holdings, Inc.	TQO	PTEK	AC	2
Public Service Enterprise Group Incorporated	PEG	PEG	A	3
Public Storage, Inc.	PSA	PSA	X	3
Puma Technology, Inc.	PUP	PUMA	CPX	2
Purchase Pro.com Inc.	PPU	PPRO	ACPX	1
Qiagen N.V.	QXE	QGENF	A	2
QLogic Corp.	QLC	QLGC	ACPX	1
QLT Phototherapeutics, Inc.	QTL	QLTI	ACPX	3
QuadraMed Corp.	QCD	QMDC	CPX	2

Company Name	Option Symbol	Stock Symbol	Exchange(s)	Cycle
Quaker Oats Company (The)	OAT	OAT	APX	1
Quaker State Corp.	KSF	KSF	A	3
QUALCOMM, Inc.	QAQ	QCOM	ACIPX	1
Quanta Services, Inc.	PWR	PWR	ACPX	2
Quantum Corp.-DLT & Storage Systems Group	DSS	DSS	ACP	2
Quantum Corp.-Hard Disk Drive Group	HDD	HDD	C	2
Quentra Networks, Inc.	QTO	QTRAQ	AC	1
quepasa.com	AUP	PASA	AC	3
Quest Diagnostics Incorporated	DGX	DGX	CX	2
Quest Software, Inc.	QUD	QSFT	ACP	1
Questar Corp.	STR	STR	CP	1
Questar Corp.	STR	STR	X	2
QuickLogic Corp.	GIL	QUIK	AX	3
Quiksilver Inc.	ZQK	ZQK	X	2
Quintiles Transnational Corp.	QRT	QTRN	AC	1
Quintus Corp.	QUJ	QNTS	A	2
Quorum Health Group, Inc.	HQG	QHGI	A	1
Qwest Communications Int'l.	Q	Q	ACIPX	1
R&B Falcon Corp.	FLC	FLC	ACPI	3
R.H. Donnelley Co.	RHD	RHD	A	2
R.J. Reynolds Tobacco Company	RJR	RJR	ACPX	2
Racing Champions Corp.	MCQ	RACN	P	3
Radian Group	RDN	RDN	P	2
Radica Games, Ltd.	QDR	RADA	C	1
Radio One, Inc.	UDO	ROIA	A	2
RadioShack	RSH	RSH	ACIP	1
RadiSys Corp.	MKU	RSYS	AP	1
RADVision Ltd.	RJU	RVSN	CP	1
Rainbow Media Group	RMG	RMG	ACPX	3
Rainbow Technologies Inc.	BQO	RNBO	P	1
Rainforest Cafe, Inc.	QRI	RAIN	C	2
Ralston Purina Company	RAL	RAL	C	3
Rambus, Inc.	BNQ	RMBS	ACIPX	2
Ramp Networks, Inc.	MUB	RAMP	C	2
Rare Hospitality International, Inc.	QRW	RARE	PX	2
Rare Medium Group Inc.	RRU	RRRR	ACP	2
Rational Software Corp.	RAQ	RATL	ACIX	1
Raychem Corp.	RYC	RYC	P	1
Raymond James Financial, Inc.	RJF	RJF	A	2
Rayovac Corp.	ROV	ROV	A	3
Raytheon Co (Class A)	RYA	RTN/A	C	2
Raytheon Company	RTN	RTNB	ACIP	2
Razorfish Inc.	RUF	RAZF	ACX	1
RCM Technologies, Inc.	RIQ	RCMT	PX	3
RCN Corp.	RBQ	RCNC	P	3

Key to Exchanges: A = AMEX (American Stock Exchange); C = CBOE (Chicago Board Options Exchange); I = International Securities Exchange; P = PCX or PSE (Pacific Stock Exchange); and X = PHLX (Philadelphia Stock Exchange).

Option Company Name	Stock Symbol	Symbol	Exchange(s)	Cycle
Reader's Digest Association, Inc. (Class A)	RDA	RDA	AC	1
Read-Rite Corp.	RDQ	RDRT	CP	1
RealNetworks Inc.	QRN	RNWK	ACIPX	2
Reckson Associates Realty Corp.	RA	RA	X	3
Recoton Corp.	ROQ	RCOT	A	2
Red Hat, Inc.	RQD	RHAT	ACPX	3
Redback Networks	BUK	RBAK	ACPX	1
Redwood Trust Inc.	RWT	RWT	P	1
Reebok International Ltd.	RBK	RBK	ACX	1
Regeneration Technologies, Inc.	RQK	RTIX	AC	2
Regeneron Pharmaceuticals, Inc.	RQP	REGN	X	2
Regional Bank HOLDRS	RKH	RKH	AC	2
Regions Financial Corp.	GVQ	RGBK	X	1
Regis Corp.	RJQ	RGIS	X	3
Register.com	RAU	RCOM	AC	2
Reliance Group Holdings, Inc.	REL	REL	AX	1
Reliant Energy, Inc.	REI	REI	ACP	2
ReliaStar Financial Corp.	RLR	RLR	A	1
REMEC, Inc.	RYQ	REMC	A	2
Remedy Corp.	LRQ	RMDY	CPX	3
Remington Oil & Gas Corp.	RQF	ROIL	C	2
Renaissance Worldwide, Inc.	QRG	REGI	C	2
Renal Care Group, Inc.	NUQ	RCGI	A	3
Renters Choice, Inc.	RQG	RCII	X	3
Repligen Corp.	RGU	RGEN	A	3
Repsol, S.A. ADR	REP	REP	AC	1
Republic Group, Inc.	RGC	RGC	P	1
Republic New York Corp.	RNB	RNB	ACPX	3
Republic Securities Financial Corp.	QRF	RSFC	CPX	3
Republic Services Inc. (Class A)	RSG	RSG	AC	1
Research in Motion	RUL	RIMM	ACIPX	3
Resmed, Inc.	RMD	RMD	A	2
Resource America Inc. (Class A)	QRE	REXI	A	3
Resource Bancshares Mtg. Group	RQH	RBMG	A	2
Resources Connection, Inc.	ORG	RECN	C	3
Respironics, Inc.	SBU	RESP	ACP	1
Restoration Hardware, Inc.	QYH	RSTO	ACX	3
Retek Inc.	QRD	RETK	ACP	2
Reuters Holdings PLC ADR	RTQ	RTRSY	A	2
Revlon, Inc. (Class A)	REV	REV	ACX	1
Rexall Sundown, Inc.	RKQ	RXSD	AC	2
Reynolds Metals Company	RLM	RLM	CP	2
RF Micro Devices, Inc.	RQZ	RFMD	ACIPX	2
Rhodia Inc.-Spons ADR	RHA	RHA	A	1
Rhythms NetConnections, Inc.	RYU	RTHM	ACPX	3
Ribozyme Pharmaceuticals, Inc.	URB	RZYM	A	3
Richfood Holdings, Inc.	RFH	RFH	P	2
Riggs National Corp.	RNQ	RIGS	P	2
Rite Aid Corp.	RAD	RAD	CPX	1
Riverstone Networks, Inc.	RQJ	RSTN	ACP	1
RMI Titanium Company	RTI	RTI	A	3

Company Name	Option Symbol	Stock Symbol	Exchange(s)	Cycle
RMI.Net	RMU	RMII	ACX	2
Roadway Express, Inc.	EJQ	ROAD	X	3
Robert Half International Inc.	RHI	RHI	X	3
Robert Mondavi Corp. (The) (Class A)	UQR	MOND	P	2
Rockwell International Corp.	ROK	ROK	C	1
Rogue Wave Software	RQR	RWAV	P	1
Rohm and Haas Company	ROH	ROH	A	1
Rollins Inc.	ROL	ROL	X	2
Rollins Truck Leasing Corp.	RLC	RLC	P	1
Romac International, Inc.	RPQ	KFRC	P	3
Rosetta Inpharmatics, Inc.	RRQ	RSTA	AP	1
Roslyn Bancorp, Inc.	OQU	RSLN	ACP	1
Ross Stores, Inc.	REQ	ROST	P	2
Rostelecom-ADR	ROS	ROS	CP	1
Rouge Industries Inc.	ROU	ROU	P	3
Rowan Companies, Inc.	RDC	RDC	ACP	1
Royal Caribbean Cruises Ltd.	RCL	RCL	AP	3
Royal Dutch Petroleum Company	RD	RD	ACP	1
RPM, Inc.	RPM	RPM	C	2
RSA Security, Inc.	QSD	RSAS	CPX	1
RSL Communications	QRL	RSLC	C	1
Ruby Tuesday, Inc.	RI	RI	C	1
Rudolph Technologies, Inc.	UXH	RTEC	AC	2
Rural/Metro Corp.	QWM	RURL	A	3
Russ Berrie and Company, Inc.	RUS	RUS	C	3
Russell Corp.	RML	RML	A	1
Ryanair Holdings Plc	ZQ	RYAAY	A	3
Ryan's Family Steak Houses	URA	RYAN	C	1
Ryder System, Inc.	R	R	ACIP	2
Ryerson Tull, Inc.	RT	RT	X	3
Ryland Group, Inc. (The)	RYL	RYL	X	3
S1 Corp.	QFB	SONE	AC	1
Saba Software, Inc.	BOQ	SABA	AC	3
Sabre Holdings Corp.	TSG	TSG	AC	2
SAFECO Corp.	SAQ	SAFC	C	2
Safeguard Scientifics, Inc.	SFE	SFE	AC	2
Safeskin Corp.	FQK	SFSK	A	1
Safeway, Inc.	SWY	SWY	ACIP	3
Saga Software, Inc.	AGS	AGS	CX	1
Sage, Inc.	UEJ	SAGI	AC	1
Sagent Technology, Inc.	GUS	SGNT	AP	3
Salton, Inc.	SFP	SFP	A	2
Sanchez Computer Associates	SUU	SCAI	ACPX	1
SanDisk Corp.	SWQ	SNDK	ACIPX	1
Sangamo BioSciences, Inc.	USJ	SGMO	A	3
Sangstat Medial Corp.	QDY	SANG	X	1
Sanmina Corp.	SQN	SANM	ACIPX	1
Santa Cruz Operation, Inc.	UQS	SCOC	CP	1

Key to Exchanges: A = AMEX (American Stock Exchange); C = CBOE (Chicago Board Options Exchange); I = International Securities Exchange; P = PCX or PSE (Pacific Stock Exchange); and X = PHLX (Philadelphia Stock Exchange).

Company Name	Option Symbol	Stock Symbol	Exchange(s)	Cycle
Santa Fe International Corp.	SDC	SDC	ACX	1
Santa Fe Snyder Corp.	SFS	SFS	A	1
SAP AG	SAP	SAP	ACPX	3
Sapiens International Corp. N.V.	QHH	SPNS	CP	1
Sapient Corp.	QPE	SAPE	CPX	1
Sara Lee Corp.	SLE	SLE	ACP	1
Satyam Infoway Limited	SUY	SIFY	C	2
Sawtek Inc.	QWS	SAWS	ACPX	3
SBA Communications	SJU	SBAC	ACP	2
SBC Communications, Inc.	SBC	SBC	ACIPX	1
SBS Technologies, Inc.	BQK	SBSE	AC	3
Scana Corp.	SCG	SCG	X	1
SCB Computer Technology, Inc.	TQL	SCBI	P	1
SCG Holding Corp.	NMQ	ONNN	ACP	3
Schein (Henry), Inc.	HQE	HSIC	CP	1
Schering-Plough Corp.	SGP	SGP	ACIPX	2
Schlumberger Limited	SLB	SLB	ACPX	2
Scholastic Corp.	USC	SCHL	A	3
School Specialty, Inc.	HCQ	SCHS	C	2
Schulman (A.), Inc.	SQC	SHLM	P	3
Schwab Corp. (The Charles)	SCH	SCH	ACIPX	3
Schweitzer-Mauduit Intl. Inc.	SWM	SWM	P	2
SCI Systems, Inc.	SCI	SCI	ACPX	1
SciClone Pharmaceuticals, Inc.	SUV	SCLN	AC	1
Scient Corp.	SMQ	SCNT	AP	3
Scientific Games Holdings Corp.	SG	SG	A	2
Scientific-Atlanta, Inc.	SFA	SFA	ACIPX	3
Scios Inc.	UIO	SCIO	AP	2
SciQuest.com	QWQ	SQST	CP	2
Scitex Corp. Ltd.	SXQ	SCIX	AP	1
SCM Microsystems, Inc.	SIU	SCMM	P	3
Scotts Company (The) (Class A)	SMG	SMG	P	1
SDL, Inc.	QSL	SDLI	ACP	3
SeaChange International, Inc.	UEG	SEAC	AC	1
Seacoast Financial Services Corp.	SKQ	SCFS	X	3
SEACOR Smit, Inc.	CKH	CKH	C	3
Seagate Technology, Inc.	SEG	SEG	ACPX	3
Seagram Company, Ltd. (The)	VYG	VO	P	2
Sealed Air Corp. (New)	SEE	SEE	ACX	1
Sears, Roebuck and Company	S	S	ACPX	1
Secure Computing Corp.	UQU	SCUR	AP	1
SED International Holdings	QQE	SECX	C	2
SeeBeyond Technology Corp.	QYS	SBYN	ACP	2
SEI Investments Company	QEI	SEIC	A	3
Seitel, Inc.	SEI	SEI	CX	2
Select Comfort Corp.	AJU	SCSS	C	2
Selectica, Inc.	MUX	SLTC	AP	1
Selective Insurance Group, Inc.	SQZ	SIGI	X	3
SEMA Group plc	QLB	SEMA	ACPX	1
Semiconductor HOLDRS	SMH	SMH	ACP	2
Semotus Solutions, Inc.	DLK	DLK	AP	3
Sempra Energy	SRE	SRE	A	1

Company Name	Option Symbol	Stock Symbol	Exchange(s)	Cycle
Semtech Corp.	QTU	SMTC	ACP	3
Sensormatic Electronics Corp.	SRM	SRM	A	1
Sepracor, Inc.	ERQ	SEPR	ACIPX	1
Sequenom, Inc.	QUK	SQNM	AC	1
SERENA Software, Inc.	NHU	SRNA	ACP	2
Serologicals Corp.	QEO	SERO	A	2
Serono S.A.	SRA	SRA	CP	2
Service Corp. International	SRV	SRV	X	2
Service Experts, Inc.	SVE	SVE	X	2
ServiceMaster Co.	SVM	SVM	X	1
Seven Seas Petroleum Inc.	SEV	SEV	A	3
SFX Entertainment, Inc.	SFX	SFX	ACX	1
Shanghai Petrochemical Company Ltd. ADR	SHI	SHI	C	3
Shared Medical Systems Corp.	SMS	SMS	P	1
Sharper Image Corp.	SAU	SHRP	AP	2
Shaw Group, Inc. (The)	SGR	SGR	AC	1
Shaw Industries, Inc.	SHX	SHX	C	2
Sheidahl Inc.	QSB	SHEL	X	3
Shell Transport & Trading Company, PLC ADR	SC	SC	C	2
Sherwin-Williams Company (The)	SHW	SHW	C	3
Shire Pharmaceuticals, Inc.	UGH	SHPGY	ACIPX	1
Shop At Home	SQR	SATH	ACX	2
Shopko Stores, Inc.	SKO	SKO	X	3
Shuffle Master, Inc.	SQW	SHFL	A	2
Shurgard Storage Center	SHU	SHU	P	1
SICOR Inc.	UEC	SCRI	C	2
Siebel Systems, Inc.	SGQ	SEBL	ACPX	2
Sierra Health Services, Inc.	SIE	SIE	X	3
Sierra Pacific Resources	SRP	SRP	CP	2
Sigma-Aldrich Corp.	IAQ	SIAL	AC	1
SignalSoft Corp.	SUO	SGSF	A	1
Silicon Graphics, Inc.	SGI	SGI	ACP	2
Silicon Image, Inc.	GUD	SIMG	ACP	1
Silicon Laboratories, Inc.	QFJ	SLAB	AC	1
Silicon Storage Technology, Inc.	SSU	SSTI	ACPX	1
Silicon Valley Bancshares	SQU	SIVB	CP	2
Silicon Valley Group, Inc.	VQQ	SVGI	CX	3
Silknet Software	ULI	SILK	AC	1
SilverStream Software, Inc.	QKQ	SSSW	AC	1
Simon DeBartolo Group	SPG	SPG	A	2
Simpson Industries, Inc.	XQX	SMPS	P	2
Sinclair Broadcast Group	JQO	SBGI	A	3
SIPEX Corp.	UQX	SIPX	P	3
Sirius Satellite Radio	QXO	SIRI	ACP	3
Six Flags, Inc.	PKS	PKS	AP	3
Sk Telecom Co., Ltd. ADR	SKM	SKM	C	3

Key to Exchanges: A = AMEX (American Stock Exchange); C = CBOE (Chicago Board Options Exchange); I = International Securities Exchange; P = PCX or PSE (Pacific Stock Exchange); and X = PHLX (Philadelphia Stock Exchange).

Company Name	Option Symbol	Stock Symbol	Exchange(s)	Cycle
Skechers U.S.A., Inc.	SKX	SKX	A	1
Skyline Corp.	SKY	SKY	C	2
SkyWest Inc.	UWQ	SKYW	P	1
SLI Inc.	SLI	SLI	A	3
SMART Modular Technologies, Inc.	UYQ	SMOD	CP	1
SmartForce PLC ADR	QAG	SMTF	AC	2
Smith International, Inc.	SII	SII	ACIPX	1
Smithfield Foods, Inc.	SFD	SFD	X	1
SmithKline Beecham PLC ADR (Class A)	SBH	SBH	ACPX	2
Smurfit Stone Container Corp.	JJQ	SSCC	CP	2
Snap-On, Inc.	SNA	SNA	A	3
Snyder Communications, Inc.	SNC	SNC	AC	3
Sodexho Marriott Services	SDH	SDH	X	1
Softnet Systems	SUC	SOFN	CPX	2
Software HOLDRS Trust	SWH	SWH	A	2
Software.com	UGM	SWCM	ACP	1
Sola International, Inc.	SOL	SOL	C	2
Solectron Corp.	SLR	SLR	ACIPX	1
Solutia Inc.	SOI	SOI	C	1
Somera Communications, Inc.	BQM	SMRA	A	3
Sonat, Inc.	SNT	SNT	A	1
Sonic Automotive, Inc.	SAH	SAH	C	2
Sonic Corp.	YYV	SONC	A	3
Sonic Foundry, Inc.	SQO	SOFO	A	3
SONICblue Incorporated	SQI	SBLU	CPI	1
SonicWall, Inc.	UWL	SNWL	ACP	3
Sonoco Products Company	SON	SON	X	1
Sonus Networks, Inc.	UJS	SONS	ACPX	1
Sony Corp. ADR	SNE	SNE	APX	1
Sorrento Networks Corp.	QFW	FIBR	ACPX	2
SOS Staffing Services, Inc.	SQH	SOSS	P	2
Sotheby's Holdings, Inc. (Class A)	BID	BID	A	1
South Financial Group (The)	QCF	TSFG	P	2
Southdown, Inc.	SDW	SDW	X	3
Southern Company (The)	SO	SO	CI	2
Southern Peru Copper Corp.	PCU	PCU	A	3
Southern Union Company	SUG	SUG	X	3
Southtrust Corp.	SHQ	SOTR	CP	3
Southwest Airlines Co.	LUV	LUV	ACPX	3
Southwest Bancorporation of Texas, Inc.	ZRQ	SWBT	AP	2
Southwest Securities Group, Inc.	SWS	SWS	CP	3
Sovereign Bancorp, Inc.	SQV	SVRN	ACPX	1
SpaceLabs Medical, Inc.	QSQ	SLMD	X	1
Spanish Broadcasting System, Inc.	DFU	SBSA	AC	2
SpectraLink Corp.	SXU	SLNK	A	3
Spectrasite Holdings, Inc.	TUU	SITE	ACX	2
Spectrian Corp.	QCS	SPCT	AC	2
SpeechWorks International Inc.	USP	SPWX	ACP	3
SpeedFam-IPEC, Inc.	FQF	SFAM	CX	1
Speedway Motorsports, Inc.	TRK	TRK	A	3
Spherion Corp.	SFN	SFN	X	2
Spiegel, Incorporated (Class A)	SQE	SPGLA	C	2

Company Name	Option Symbol	Stock Symbol	Exchange(s)	Cycle
Spieker Properties, Inc.	SPK	SPK	P	1
Spinnaker Exploration Company	SKE	SKE	A	3
Splash Technology Holdings, Inc.	QRX	SPLH	AC	1
Splitrock Services, Inc.	KQI	SPLT	A	1
Sportsline USA, Inc.	QSP	SPLN	ACP	1
Springs Industries, Inc. (Class A)	SMI	SMI	P	2
Sprint Corp.	FON	FON	ACPX	2
Sprint Corp. PCS Group	PCS	PCS	ACPX	2
SPX Corp.	SPW	SPW	C	3
Spyglass, Inc.	YQG	SPYG	ACX	1
SS&C Technologies Inc.	QUQ	SSNC	P	1
St. Mary Land & Exploration Company	JQM	MARY	AC	2
St. Joe Company (The)	JOE	JOE	P	3
St. Jude Medical, Inc.	STJ	STJ	AC	1
St. Paul Bancorp, Inc.	HPQ	SPBC	X	1
St. Paul Companies, Inc. (The)	SPC	SPC	C	1
Staff Leasing Inc.	QFF	STFF	C	2
Stage Stores Inc.	SGE	SGE	P	1
Stamps.com	UMT	STMP	ACX	1
Standard Microsystems Corp.	OMQ	SMSC	A	2
Standard Pacific Corp.	SPF	SPF	X	3
Standard Products Company	SPD	SPD	P	2
Stanford Microdevices, Inc.	HTU	SMDI	ACP	1
Stanford Telecommunications	SDQ	STII	X	2
Stanley Works (The)	SWK	SWK	P	1
Staples, Inc.	PLQ	SPLS	ACIPX	3
Star Telecommunications, Inc.	TQQ	STRX	P	2
Starbucks Corp.	SQX	SBUX	ACIPX	1
StarMedia Network	SUF	STRM	ACX	3
STARR Surgical Company	SQT	STAA	C	3
Starwood Hotels & Resorts Worldwide, Inc.	HOT	HOT	CX	2
State Street Corp.	STT	STT	CPX	2
Staten Island Bancorp, Inc.	SIB	SIB	CX	1
Station Casinos, Inc.	STN	STN	AC	1
Steel Dynamics, Inc.	RQL	STLD	P	2
Steelcase Inc. (Class A)	SCS	SCS	AC	1
Stein Mart, Inc.	STQ	SMRT	X	1
Stericycle Inc.	URL	SRCL	AC	2
STERIS Corp.	STE	STE	C	3
Sterling Commerce, Inc.	SE	SE	CX	1
Sterling Software, Inc.	SSW	SSW	CX	3
Steven Madden, Ltd.	SEU	SHOO	P	3
Stewart & Stevenson Services, Inc.	SVQ	SSSS	P	3
Stewart Enterprises, Inc.	EQQ	STEI	P	3
Stillwater Mining Company	SWC	SWC	CP	1
Stilwell Financial, Inc.	SV	SV	ACIPX	3
STMicroelectronics N.V.	STM	STM	CIPX	1

Key to Exchanges: A = AMEX (American Stock Exchange); C = CBOE (Chicago Board Options Exchange); I = International Securities Exchange; P = PCX or PSE (Pacific Stock Exchange); and X = PHLX (Philadelphia Stock Exchange).

Company Name	Option Symbol	Stock Symbol	Exchange(s)	Cycle
Stolt Comex Seaway S.A.	QSO	SCSWF	X	3
Stolt Offshore S.A.	QSO	SOSA	X	3
Stone Energy Corp.	SGY	SGY	P	3
Storage Technology Corp.	STK	STK	CP	3
StorageNetworks, Inc.	OSU	STOR	ACIPX	2
Stratos Lightwave, Inc.	SZQ	STLW	ACPX	3
Stride Rite Corp. (The)	SRR	SRR	P	1
Structural Dynamics Research Corp.	SLQ	SDRC	X	2
Stryker Corp.	SYK	SYK	ACX	3
Sturm Ruger & Co. Inc.	RGR	RGR	C	3
Sugen, Inc.	UGQ	SUGN	P	2
Suiza Foods Corp.	SZA	SZA	X	3
Summit Bancorp	SUB	SUB	CIX	1
Summit Design, Inc.	DQB	SMMT	C	2
Summit Technology, Inc.	BAQ	BEAM	AC	3
Sun International Hotels Ltd.	SIH	SIH	C	2
Sun Microsystems, Inc.	SUQ	SUNW	ACIPX	1
Sunbeam Corp.	SOC	SOC	A	1
Sundstrand Corp.	SNS	SNS	C	3
SunGard Data Systems Inc.	SDS	SDS	CPX	1
Sunglass Hut International, Inc.	RQY	RAYS	C	3
Sunoco, Inc.	SUN	SUN	CX	2
Sunrise Assisted Living, Inc.	QSR	SNRZ	C	1
Sunrise Medical, Inc.	SMD	SMD	P	2
Sunrise Technologies Intl.	RNU	SNRS	ACP	2
Sunterra Corp.	OWN	OWN	C	1
SunTrust Banks, Inc.	STI	STI	CPX	1
Superconductor Technologies, Inc.	OUP	SCON	AC	1
SuperGen, Inc.	UQG	SUPG	ACPX	1
Superior TeleCom, Inc.	SUT	SUT	AP	3
Supertex, Inc.	TXQ	SUPX	X	2
Supervalu, Inc.	SVU	SVU	X	1
Susquehanna Bancshares Inc.	JQW	SUSQ	P	3
Swift Energy Company	SFY	SFY	C	1
Swift Transportation Co., Inc.	SDU	SWFT	CP	1
Sybase, Inc.	SBQ	SYBS	ACPX	3
Sybron Dental Specialities	SYD	SYD	CP	1
Sybron International Corp.	SIW	SYB	ACP	1
Sycamore Networks, Inc.	QSM	SCMR	ACIPX	3
Sykes Enterprises, Inc.	YKQ	SYKE	A	3
Sylvan Learning Systems, Inc.	NQV	SLVN	A	2
Symantec Corp.	SYQ	SYMC	ACPX	1
Symbol Technologies, Inc.	SBL	SBL	ACX	1
Symmetricom, Inc.	SQG	SYMM	P	2
Symyx Technologies, Inc.	OFU	SMMX	P	1
Synaptic Pharmaceutical Corp.	SQS	SNAP	X	3
Syngenta AG	SYT	SYT	ACX	3
Synopsys, Inc.	YPQ	SNPS	APC	3
Synovous Financial Corp.	SNV	SNV	C	2
Synthetech, Inc.	YZQ	NZYM	C	2
Syntroleum Corp.	QSH	SYNM	X	1

Company Name	Option Symbol	Stock Symbol	Exchange(s)	Cycle
Sysco Corp.	SYY	SYY	ACP	2
Systemax, Inc.	SYX	SYX	A	3
Systems & Computer Technology Corp.	YQS	SCTC	A	2
T. Rowe Price Associates	RQW	TROW	C	1
Taiwan Semiconductor Manufacturing Co.	TSM	TSM	ACP	1
Take-Two Interactive Software	TUO	TTWO	ACX	3
Talbots, Inc. (The)	TLB	TLB	P	2
Talk.com, Inc.	QQK	TALK	ACX	1
Tanox, Inc.	TZU	TNOX	ACP	1
Target Corp.	TGT	TGT	ACIX	1
Targeted Genetics Corp.	GNU	TGEN	AC	1
Taro Pharmaceutical Industries Ltd.	QTT	TARO	ACP	1
TBC Corp.	TBQ	TBCC	C	3
TCA Cable TV, Inc.	TTQ	TCAT	C	3
TCF Financial Corp.	TCB	TCB	CP	1
TD Waterhouse Group	TWE	TWE	ACPX	3
Tech Data Corp.	TDQ	TECD	AP	3
Techne Corp.	TGQ	TECH	AX	1
Technitrol, Inc.	TNL	TNL	ACP	1
Technology Solutions Company	QST	TSCC	C	3
Technology SPDR	XLK	XLK	A	3
Tecnomatix Technologies Ltd.	TQY	TCNO	AC	2
TECO Energy, Inc.	TE	TE	X	2
Tecumseh Products Company (Class A)	TUQ	TECUA	A	3
Tekelec	KQ	TKLC	ACP	2
Tektronix Inc.	TEK	TEK	ACP	1
TelCom Semiconductor	TMU	TLCM	ACI	1
Telebras HOLDRS	TBH	TBH	ACIPX	1
Telecom Argentina Stet-France Telecom S.A. ADR	TEO	TEO	ACX	1
Telecom Corp. of New Zealand Limited ADR	NZT	NZT	A	3
Telecom HOLDRS	TTH	TTH	AC	2
Telecom Italia SpA ADS	TI	TI	A	3
TeleCommunications Systems, Inc.	QTY	TSYS	A	1
Telecomunicacoes de Sao Paulo S/A - Telesp	TSP	TSP	AC	1
Telecorp PCS, Inc.	UCA	TLCP	C	2
Teledyne Technologies, Inc.	TDY	TDY	AC	1
Telefonica de Argentina, S.A. ADR	TAR	TAR	ACP	1
Telefonica de Espana, S.A. ADR	TEF	TEF	ACP	3
Telefonica del Peru S.A. ADS	TDP	TDP	C	1
Telefonos de Mexico, S.A. de C.V. ADR	TMX	TMX	ACIPX	2
Teleglobe, Inc.	TGR	TGO	AC	3
TeleNorte Leste Participacoes SA ADS	TNE	TNE	AC	1
Telephone & Data Systems, Inc.	TDS	TDS	AP	2
Telescan, Inc.	TIP	TSCN	ACX	1
Telesp Celular Participacoes SA ADS	TXP	TCP	A	1

Key to Exchanges: A = AMEX (American Stock Exchange); C = CBOE (Chicago Board Options Exchange); I = International Securities Exchange; P = PCX or PSE (Pacific Stock Exchange); and X = PHLX (Philadelphia Stock Exchange).

Company Name	Option Symbol	Stock Symbol	Exchange(s)	Cycle
Telespectrum Worldwide, Inc.	QBA	TLSP	C	3
TeleSudeste Celular Participacoes SA ADS	TSD	TSD	AC	1
TeleTech Holdings, Inc.	QTC	TTEC	CP	1
Teligent, Inc. (Class A)	TNU	TGNT	CPX	2
Tellabs, Inc.	TEQ	TLAB	ACIPX	3
Telular Corp.	QVW	WRLS	A	3
Telxon Corp.	THL	TLXN	C	3
Temple-Inland, Inc.	TIN	TIN	A	2
Templeton Emerging Markets Fund, Inc.	EMF	EMF	A	2
Tenet Healthcare Corp.	THC	THC	ACP	2
Tenneco, Inc.	TEN	TEN	A	2
Teradyne, Inc.	TER	TER	ACIPX	1
Terayon Communication Systems, Inc.	TUN	TERN	ACPX	1
Terex Corp.	TEX	TEX	AX	1
Terra Networks, S.A.	TUR	TRLY	ACP	3
Tesoro Petroleum Corp.	TSO	TSO	X	2
Tetra Tech, Inc.	TQI	TTEK	P	3
TETRA Technologies, Inc.	TTI	TTI	X	3
Teva Pharmaceutical Industries Ltd. ADR	TVQ	TEVA	ACP	3
Texaco, Inc.	TX	TX	ACIPX	1
Texas Biotechnology Corp.	TXB	TXB	A	2
Texas Industries, Inc.	TXI	TXI	P	1
Texas Instruments Incorporated	TXN	TXN	ACPX	1
Textron, Inc.	TXT	TXT	X	3
theglobe.com, Inc.	GLU	TGLO	ACX	2
Theragenics Corp.	TGX	TGX	C	3
Therma-Wave, Inc.	TQB	TWAV	AC	1
Thermedics, Inc.	TMD	TMD	A	2
Thermo Cardiosystems, Inc.	TCA	TCA	A	1
Thermo Electron Corp.	TMO	TMO	CP	3
Thermo Fibertek, Inc.	TFT	TFT	X	3
Thermo Instrument Systems, Inc.	THI	THI	A	3
ThermoTrek Corp.	TKN	TKN	A	1
TheStreet.com	YTQ	TSCM	ACPX	3
THINK New Ideas, Inc.	THU	THNK	A	2
Thomas & Betts Corp.	TNB	TNB	A	3
Thoratec Labs Corp.	TQU	THOR	A	1
THQ Inc.	QHI	THQI	AC	3
Three-Five Systems, Inc.	TFS	TFS	AC	1
TIBCO Software	TIU	TIBX	ACPX	2
Ticketmaster (Class B)	QMF	TMCS	ACPX	1
Ticon Global Restaurants	YUM	YUM	ACIX	1
Tidel Technologies, Inc.	OUA	ATMS	C	1
Tidewater, Inc.	TDW	TDW	CIPX	1
Tier Technologies, Inc.	QTI	TIER	C	1
Tiffany & Co.	TIF	TIF	CIPX	2
Timberland Company (The)	TBL	TBL	AX	2
Timberline Software Corp.	QVT	TMBS	A	1
Time Warner Telecom Inc.	TTU	TWTC	ACPX	3
Times Mirror Company (The)	TMC	TMC	C	3
Timken Company (The)	TKR	TKR	C	3

Company Name	Option Symbol	Stock Symbol	Exchange(s)	Cycle
Titan Corp. (The)	TTN	TTN	ACIPX	1
Titan International, Inc.	TWI	TWI	A	3
Titan Pharmaceuticals, Inc.	TTP	TTP	A	1
Titanium Metals Corp.	TIE	TIE	PX	1
TiVo, Inc.	TUK	TIVO	AC	2
TJ International, Inc.	TJQ	TJCO	X	3
TJX Companies, Inc. (The)	TJX	TJX	AC	1
TLC Laser Center, Inc.	QKR	TLCV	C	2
TMP Worldwide, Inc.	BSQ	TMPW	ACP	3
Toll Brothers, Inc.	TOL	TOL	ACP	3
Tollgrade Communications, Inc.	TQK	TLGD	CP	2
Tom Brown, Inc.	TQF	TMBR	P	3
Tommy Hilfiger Corp.	TOM	TOM	CPX	2
Too, Inc.	TOO	TOO	CX	2
Tootsie Roll Industries, Inc.	TR	TR	CP	1
Topps Company	TOQ	TOPP	CX	3
Torchmark Corp.	TMK	TMK	A	2
Toronto Dominion Bank	TD	TD	A	1
Tosco Corp.	TOS	TOS	ACIPX	1
Total Fina S.A. ADR	TOT	TOT	ACP	2
Total System Services, Inc.	TSS	TSS	X	2
Tower Automotive, Inc.	TWR	TWR	A	2
Tower Semiconductor Ltd.	TWQ	TSEM	PX	1
Toyota Motor Corp. ADR	TM	TM	CP	1
Toys "R" Us, Inc.	TOY	TOY	CIP	3
Trans World Airlines, Inc.	TWA	TWA	AC	1
Trans World Entertainment	TQT	TWMC	A	3
Transaction System Architects, Inc.	TQR	TSAI	X	3
TransCanada PipeLines Ltd.	TRP	TRP	C	3
Transkaryotic	UFT	TKTX	AC	1
Transmeta Corp.	TUE	TMTA	ACPX	1
Transocean Sedco Forex Inc.	RIG	RIG	ACIPX	2
Transportation Technologies, Inc.	JQI	TTII	X	1
TranSwitch Corp.	TZQ	TXCC	ACIPX	2
Travel Service International, Inc.	TVU	TRVL	CX	2
Travelers/Aetna Property Casualty Corp. (Class A)	TAP	TAP	A	3
Travelocity.com	QUT	TVLY	CPX	1
Trex Medical Corp.	TXM	TXM	A	3
Triad Hospitals	TRI	TRI	P	2
Triangle Pharmaceuticals Inc.	VQP	VIRS	PX	3
Triarc Companies, Inc. (Class A)	TRY	TRY	A	1
Tribune Company	TRB	TRB	CP	2
Trico Marine Services, Inc.	MUQ	TMAR	AC	2
Tri-Continental Corp.	TY	TY	X	3
Trigon Healthcare, Inc.	TGH	TGH	ACP	1
Trikon Technologies	QLP	TRKN	PX	3
Trimble Navigation Ltd.	TRQ	TRMB	CP	3

Key to Exchanges: A = AMEX (American Stock Exchange); C = CBOE (Chicago Board Options Exchange); I = International Securities Exchange; P = PCX or PSE (Pacific Stock Exchange); and X = PHLX (Philadelphia Stock Exchange).

Company Name	Option Symbol	Stock Symbol	Exchange(s)	Cycle
Trimeris Inc.	RQM	TRMS	AC	1
Trinity Industries, Inc.	TRN	TRN	A	1
TriPath Imaging, Inc.	TPU	TPTH	X	1
Tripath Technology, Inc.	TQM	TRPH	C	2
Triquint Semiconductor, Inc.	TQN	TQNT	ACPX	2
TriStar Aerospace Co.	TSX	TSX	P	3
Tritel, Inc.	QTK	TTEL	AC	2
Triton Energy Ltd.	OIL	OIL	ACIPX	2
Triton PCS Holdings, Inc.	QUP	TPCS	A	3
Trizec Hahn Corp.	TZH	TZH	C	1
Trustmark Corp.	TKQ	TRMK	X	1
TRW, Inc.	TRW	TRW	A	1
Tubos de Acero de Mexico SA ADR	TAM	TAM	CX	1
Tucker Anthony Sutro	TA	TA	P	3
Tularik, Inc.	TUQ	TLRK	A	2
Tumbleweed Communications Corp.	DQW	TMWD	AC	1
Tupperware Corp.	TUP	TUP	C	1
Turnstone Systems, Inc.	TUA	TSTN	ACPX	1
Tut Systems, Inc.	QSS	TUTS	ACP	2
TV Azteca S.A. de C.V.	TZA	TZA	ACP	2
TV Guide Inc.	UQK	TVGIA	P	3
Tweeter Home Entertainment Group, Inc.	TQZ	TWTR	CP	1
Twinlab Corp.	QBT	TWLB	C	2
TXU Company	TXU	TXU	P	1
Tyco International Limited	TYC	TYC	ACIPX	1
TyCom Ltd.	TCM	TCM	ACP	1
Tyson Foods, Inc. (Class A)	TSN	TSN	ACPX	1
U S WEST, Inc.	USW	USW	ACPX	1
U.S. Bancorp	USB	USB	ACIX	3
U.S. Foodservice	UFS	UFS	C	2
U.S. Interactive, Inc.	UUI	USITQ	A	2
U.S. Plastic Lumber Corp.	QBV	USPL	A	3
UAL Corp.	UAL	UAL	ACP	2
uBid, Inc.	UBD	UBID	ACPX	1
UBS AG	UBS	UBS	AC	3
UCBH Holdings, Inc.	AUW	UCBH	A	3
UGI Corp.	UGI	UGI	C	1
UICI	UCI	UCI	C	2
Ulticom, Inc.	UUL	ULCM	ACP	1
Ultramar Diamond Shamrock Corp.	UDS	UDS	ACPX	3
Ultratech Stepper, Inc.	UQT	UTEK	CP	2
Unibanco Uniao de Bancos Brasileros	UBB	UBB	ACP	1
Unicapital Corp.	UCP	UCP	A	2
Unicom Corp.	UCM	UCM	C	2
Unify Corp.	UFU	UNFY	ACX	2
Unilever N.V.	UN	UN	A	2
Union Carbide Corp.	UK	UK	ACP	1
Union Pacific Corp.	UNP	UNP	CX	2
Union Pacific Resources Group, Inc.	UPR	UPR	CX	1
Union Planters Corp.	UPC	UPC	X	2
UnionBanCal Corp.	UB	UB	P	3

Company Name	Option Symbol	Stock Symbol	Exchange(s)	Cycle
Uniroyal Technology Corp.	URO	UTCI	A	3
Unisource Energy Corp.	UNS	UNS	AP	2
Unisource Worldwide, Inc.	UWW	UWW	C	2
Unisys Corp.	UIS	UIS	ACIPX	1
United Asset Management Corp.	UAM	UAM	P	2
United Auto Group, Inc.	UAG	UAG	A	2
United Dominion Industries Limited	UDI	UDI	X	2
United Dominion Realty Trust	UDR	UDR	A	3
United HealthCare Corp.	UNH	UNH	ACIP	3
United Microelectronics Corp.	UMC	UMC	ACP	3
United Natural Foods, Inc.	JQN	UNFI	C	3
United Pan-Europe Communications (Class A)	UPO	UPCOY	AC	2
United Parcel Service, Inc.	UPS	UPS	ACIPX	1
United Rentals, Inc.	URI	URI	AX	3
United States Cellular Corp.	USM	USM	A	2
United Stationers, Inc.	QTR	USTR	C	3
United Technologies Corp.	UTX	UTX	ACIPX	2
United Therapeutics Corp.	FUH	UTHR	CP	2
Unitedglobalcom, Inc.	QUW	UCOMA	ACPX	2
Unitrode Corp.	UTR	UTR	X	2
Universal Access, Inc.	QXX	UAXS	C	1
Universal Foods Corp.	UFC	UFC	X	3
Universal Health Services, Inc.	UHS	UHS	CP	1
Univision Communications Inc.	UVN	UVN	AC	3
Unocal Corp.	UCL	UCL	CIP	1
Unova Inc.	UNA	UNA	C	3
Unumprovident Corp.	UNM	UNM	ACP	3
Urban Outfitters, Inc.	URQ	URBN	P	3
US Airways Group, Inc.	U	U	ACP	3
US LEC Corp.	QFU	CLEC	A	1
USA Education, Inc.	SLM	SLM	ACP	1
USA Floral Products, Inc.	QRS	ROSI	P	3
USA Networks, Inc.	QTH	USAI	CP	1
USEC, Inc.	USU	USU	AC	1
USFreightways Corp.	UAD	USFC	CP	1
USG Corp.	USG	USG	CP	2
Usinternetworking, Inc.	UUX	USIX	ACX	3
UST Corp.	BTQ	USTB	P	1
UST Inc.	UST	UST	ACP	1
Usweb Corp.	QWB	USWB	ACP	1
USX-Marathon Group	MRO	MRO	ACPX	1
USX-U.S. Steel Group	X	X	AC	1
UTI Energy Corp.	UTI	UTI	AX	1
UtiliCorp United, Inc.	UCU	UCU	A	1
Utilities HOLDRS Trust	UTH	UTH	AC	2
Utilities SPDR	XLU	XLU	A	3
UTStarcom, Inc.	UON	UTSI	AC	2

Key to Exchanges: A = AMEX (American Stock Exchange); C = CBOE (Chicago Board Options
     Exchange); I = International Securities Exchange; P = PCX or PSE (Pacific Stock
     Exchange); and X = PHLX (Philadelphia Stock Exchange).

Company Name	Option Symbol	Stock Symbol	Exchange(s)	Cycle
VA Linux Systems, Inc.	NUU	LNUX	ACP	2
Vail Resorts, Inc.	MTN	MTN	P	3
Valence Technology, Inc.	VHQ	VLNC	ACPX	3
Valero Energy Corp. (New)	VLO	VLO	A	3
Valley National Bancorp	VLY	VLY	X	3
Valspar Corp.	VAL	VAL	P	2
Value America, Inc.	UAS	VUSA	ACX	2
ValueVision Intl. Inc. (Class A)	UVR	VVTV	AC	3
Vans, Inc.	VQG	VANS	A	1
Vantive Corp. (The)	QTZ	VNTV	C	3
Varco International, Inc.	VRC	VRC	AIX	3
Varian Associates, Inc.	VAR	VAR	A	2
Varian Inc.	IUA	VARI	AC	2
Varian Semiconductor Equipment Associates, Inc.	UES	VSEA	ACX	2
Vascular Solutions, Inc.	URB	VASC	A	1
Vastar Resources, Inc.	VRI	VRI	X	3
Vector Group	VGR	VGR	A	2
Veeco Instruments Inc.	QVC	VECO	ACPX	1
Venator Group, Inc.	Z	Z	X	2
Ventana Medical Systems	QMP	VMSI	C	1
Ventiv Health, Inc.	IUI	VTIV	C	3
Ventro Corp.	CKU	VNTR	APX	3
Verio, Inc.	RLQ	VRIO	ACP	2
Verisign Inc.	QVR	VRSN	ACIPX	3
Veritas DGC, Inc.	VTS	VTS	CX	2
VERITAS Software Corp.	VUQ	VRTS	ACIPX	2
Verity, Inc.	YQV	VRTY	ACIP	3
Verizon Communications, Inc.	VZ	VZ	ACIPX	1
Versata, Inc.	DUV	VATA	C	1
Vertel Corp.	TUJ	VRTL	CP	1
Vertex Pharmaceuticals, Inc.	VQR	VRTX	ACPX	1
Verticalnet, Inc.	UER	VERT	ACPX	1
Veterinary Centers of America, Inc.	VQA	VCAI	P	3
Viacom, Inc.	VIA	VIA	CIPX	2
Viacom, Inc. (Class B)	VMB	VIAB	ACPX	3
Viad Corp.	VVI	VVI	A	1
Viant Corp.	VNQ	VIAN	AX	2
ViaSat, Inc.	IQS	VSAT	ACP	2
VIASOFT, Inc.	QVV	VIAS	AC	2
ViaSystems Group, Inc.	VG	VG	AC	2
Viatel, Inc.	VQL	VYTL	ACP	1
Vical Incorporated	VAQ	VICL	P	2
Vicor Corp.	VIQ	VICR	C	1
Viewpoint Corp.	MQZ	VWPT	AC	1
Vignette Corp.	VUO	VIGN	ACPX	3
Vimpel-Communications ADR	VIP	VIP	C	1
Vintage Petroleum, Inc.	VPI	VPI	CX	2
Vion Pharmaceuticals, Inc.	UVP	VION	AC	2
Virata Corp.	UFA	VRTA	ACP	1
Viropharma, Inc.	HPU	VPHM	CX	3
Vishay Intertechnology, Inc.	VSH	VSH	ACPX	1

Company Name	Option Symbol	Stock Symbol	Exchange(s)	Cycle
Visible Genetics, Inc.	UBA	VGIN	AP	1
Visio Corp.	VQJ	VSIO	X	3
Vistana, Inc.	QNM	VSTN	C	2
Visual Data Corp.	UDT	VDAT	CP	2
Visual Networks Inc.	QVN	VNWK	P	1
VISX, Incorporated	EYE	EYE	ACIPX	3
Vitesse Semiconductor Corp.	VQT	VTSS	ACPX	1
Vitria Technology, Inc.	TKU	VITR	ACX	2
Vitro Sociedad Anomina ADR	VTO	VTO	C	2
Vivendi SA	ONV	V	ACPX	3
Vivus, Inc.	VVQ	VVUS	X	3
Vixel Corp.	UTK	VIXL	A	2
Vlasic Food International	VL	VL	C	2
Vodafone Group PLC ADR	VOD	VOD	ACPX	1
Voicestream Wireless Corp.	UVT	VSTR	ACPX	2
Volvo AB ADR	VQY	VOLVY	CX	1
Voyager.net, Inc.	UOY	VOYN	C	2
Vulcan Materials	VMC	VMC	P	2
Vyyo Inc.	QYY	VYYO	A	3
W.R. Berkley Corp.	DQB	BKLY	C	1
Wabash National Corp.	WNC	WNC	C	2
Wachovia Corp.	WB	WB	CPX	1
Wackenhut Corrections Corp.	WHC	WHC	CP	1
Waddell & Reed Financial, Inc.	WDR	WDR	A	3
Walgreen Company	WAG	WAG	ACIP	1
Wall Data, Inc.	WLQ	WALL	C	1
Wallace Computer Services, Inc.	WCS	WCS	X	3
Wal-Mart Stores, Inc.	WMT	WMT	ACPX	3
Walt Disney Internet Group	DIG	DIG	ACX	1
Walter Industries Inc.	WLT	WLT	X	1
Warnaco Group, Inc. (Class A)	WAC	WAC	A	3
Warner-Lambert Company	WLA	WLA	ACP	1
Washington Federal Inc.	WFQ	WFSL	P	2
Washington Gas Light Co	WGL	WGL	P	1
Washington Mutual, Inc.	WM	WM	ACIPX	1
Waste Connections, Inc.	NBU	WCNX	CP	1
Waste Management, Inc.	WMI	WMI	ACIPX	1
WatchGuard Technologies, Inc.	RUH	WGRD	AC	1
Waters Corp.	WAT	WAT	CIX	2
Watsco, Inc.	WSO	WSO	X	2
Watson Pharmaceuticals, Inc.	WPI	WPI	ACX	2
Wave Systems Corp.	AXU	WAVX	ACP	2
WAVO Corp.	WKQ	WAVO	X	2
Weatherford International, Inc.	WFT	WFT	CIP	2
WebEx Communications, Inc.	UWB	WEBX	A	3
WebMD Corp.	HUT	HLTH	ACPX	1
WebMethods,Inc.	OUW	WEBM	ACX	1
Websense, Inc.	DQH	WBSN	C	1

Key to Exchanges: A = AMEX (American Stock Exchange); C = CBOE (Chicago Board Options Exchange); I = International Securities Exchange; P = PCX or PSE (Pacific Stock Exchange); and X = PHLX (Philadelphia Stock Exchange).

Company Name	Option Symbol	Stock Symbol	Exchange(s)	Cycle
WebTrends Corp.	UWE	WEBT	A	1
Webvan Group	UVZ	WBVN	ACX	1
Wellman, Inc.	WLM	WLM	C	3
WellPoint Health Networks, Inc. (Class A)	WLP	WLP	ACP	1
Wells Fargo & Company	WFC	WFC	ACPX	1
Wendy's International, Inc.	WEN	WEN	CP	3
West Marine, Inc.	XWQ	WMAR	A	1
West Teleservices Corp.	IYQ	WTSC	A	3
Westamerica Bankcorporation	QWI	WABC	P	1
Westell Technologies, Inc.	QLW	WSTL	CP	2
Western Digital Corp.	WDC	WDC	ACP	1
Western Gas Resources Inc.	WGR	WGR	PX	1
Western Multiplex Corp.	UPX	WMUX	AC	1
Western Resources, Inc.	WR	WR	A	2
Western Wireless Corp. (Class A)	WRQ	WWCA	PX	2
WestPoint Stevens, Inc.	WXS	WXS	P	3
Westvaco Corp.	W	W	P	1
Westwood One, Inc.	WON	WON	X	1
Wet Seal, Inc. (The) (Class A)	UUQ	WTSLA	C	1
Weyerhaeuser Company	WY	WY	CP	1
Whirlpool Corp.	WHR	WHR	CP	3
Whole Foods Market, Inc.	FMQ	WFMI	AC	2
WHX Corp.	WHX	WHX	C	1
Wild Oats Markets, Inc.	QOQ	OATS	AC	1
Willamette Industries, Inc.	WLL	WLL	AC	1
Williams Communications Group, Inc.	WCG	WCG	ACPX	2
Williams Companies, Inc. (The)	WMB	WMB	ACP	2
Williams-Sonoma, Inc.	WSM	WSM	ACP	2
Wilmington Trust Corp.	WL	WL	P	2
Wind River Systems, Inc.	QWV	WIND	ACP	2
Windmere-Durable Holdings, Inc.	WND	WND	P	3
Wink Communications, Inc.	UII	WINK	AP	1
Winn-Dixie Stores, Inc.	WIN	WIN	C	1
Winnebago Industries, Inc.	WGO	WGO	AC	1
Winstar Communications, Inc.	WQS	WCII	ACP	1
Wireless Facilities, Inc.	QUU	WFII	AP	2
Wireless HOLDRS Trust	WMH	WMH	A	1
Wisconsin Central Transportation Corp.	WQC	WCLX	C	1
Wit Soundview Group, Inc.	IUC	WITC	ACX	1
Witco Corp.	WIT	WIT	C	1
WJ Communications, Inc.	WJQ	WJCI	ACPX	2
WMS Industries, Inc.	WMS	WMS	X	2
Wolverine Tube, Inc.	WLV	WLV	A	3
Wolverine World Wide	WWW	WWW	X	3
Workflow Management, Inc.	WUK	WORK	ACPX	2
World Access, Inc.	WXQ	WAXS	ACX	1
World Wrestling Fed Entmnt.	WWF	WWF	AX	3
WorldCom, Inc.	LDQ	WCOM	ACIPX	3
WorldGate Communications, Inc.	WAQ	WGAT	ACPX	3
Worldwide Xceed Group, Inc.	TQV	XCED	CP	2
Worthington Industries, Inc.	WOR	WOR	X	3
Wrigley (Wm.) Jr. Company	WWY	WWY	A	3

Company Name	Option Symbol	Stock Symbol	Exchange(s)	Cycle
Wyman-Gordon Company	WYG	WYG	CX	3
Xcelera.com	XLA	XLA	ACIP	2
Xeikon N.V.	QIY	XEIK	APX	2
Xerox Corp.	XRX	XRX	ACPX	1
Xicor, Inc.	CIU	XICO	CX	3
Xilinix, Inc.	XLQ	XLNX	ACIPX	3
Xircom, Inc.	XQR	XIRC	CP	3
XL Capital LTD.	XL	XL	X	1
XM Satellite Radio Holdings, Inc.	QSY	XMSR	C	1
XO Communications, Inc.	QNF	XOXO	ACIX	1
XOMA Ltd.	MBU	XOMA	AC	3
Xomed Surgical Products, Inc.	XQK	XOMD	A	3
Xpedior Corp.	UPP	XPDR	CX	3
X-Rite, Incorporated	RQX	XRIT	A	2
Xtra Corp.	XTR	XTR	P	3
Xybernaut Corp.	XUY	XYBR	ACP	2
Yahoo! Inc.	YHQ	YHOO	ACIPX	1
Yankee Candle Company, Inc. (The)	YCC	YCC	AP	1
Yellow Corp.	EEQ	YELL	A	1
York International Corp.	YRK	YRK	C	2
Youbet.com, Inc.	BUB	UBET	ACX	1
Young & Rubicam Inc.	YNR	YNR	AP	1
Youthstream Media Networks	NTU	NETS	ACP	2
YPF Sociedad Anonima ADR	YPF	YPF	A	1
Zale Corp.	ZLC	ZLC	C	2
Zamba Corp.	UYZ	ZMBA	AC	1
Zany Brainy, Inc.	UZB	ZANY	CX	2
Zapata Corp.	ZAP	ZAP	C	2
Zebra Technologies, Inc.	ZBQ	ZBRA	CP	2
Ziff-Davis Inc.	ZD	ZD	AC	1
Ziff-Davis, Inc.-ZDNet	ZDZ	ZDZ	AC	1
Zions Bancorporation	ZNQ	ZION	CX	1
Zix Corp.	HQU	ZIXI	AC	3
Zoltek Companies, Inc.	QOT	ZOLT	C	1
Zomax Incorporated	ZMQ	ZOMX	AP	1
Zonagen, Inc.	NQZ	ZONA	AC	2
Zoran Corp.	ZUO	ZRAN	ACX	3
Z-Tel Technologies	UZT	ZTEL	A	2
Zygo Corp.	UZY	ZIGO	A	1

Key to Exchanges: A = AMEX (American Stock Exchange); C = CBOE (Chicago Board Options Exchange); I = International Securities Exchange; P = PCX or PSE (Pacific Stock Exchange); and X = PHLX (Philadelphia Stock Exchange).

GLOSSARY

Annualized Yield   The actual or potential profit of a transaction divided by the number of days of the investment times 365.

Asset Allocation   An investment theory that suggests investors should diversify their investment holdings into different classes of investments—that is, stocks, bonds, cash, and real estate—in order to reduce the overall risk of a portfolio.

Assign   To require an option seller to perform his or her obligation under an option contract. A put seller would be required to buy stock at a particular price. A call seller would be required to sell stock at a particular price.

Ask   The asking price for a certain security. Buyers usually pay the ask price for a security.

At-the-Money Option   An option with a strike price either at or near the underlying security's current price.

Bear Market   A market that consistently moves down over an extended period of time.

Bid   The price bid by an investor for a particular security. Sellers usually receive the Bid price when they sell a security.

Broker   A registered representative, licensed by the state and the federal governments, who executes security transactions on behalf of investors.

Brokerage Firm   A company that supervises the activities of brokers.

Bull Market   A market that consistently moves up over an extended period of time.

Call Option   An option that gives the holder the right, but not the obligation, to purchase a particular security at a particular price until a specified time in the future.

The Chicago Board Options Exchange (CBOE)   The first exchange to trade equity options.

Clearinghouse   A separate division or corporation of a futures exchange that settles trading accounts, clears trades, regulates delivery, reports trading data, and collects and maintains margin monies. Clearinghouses act as third parties to all futures and options contracts.

Closing Price   The last price at which a security traded during the trading day.

Commission   The fee paid to a broker for executing a security transaction.

Contract Month   The month in which an options contract will expire.

Covered Calls   The practice of selling call options on stocks currently held by the investor. In this way, if the option is exercised, the investor can deliver the stock he or she already owns.

Diversification   The process of spreading out capital over a number of different securities in order to limit the risk that one security will lose a substantial percentage of its original worth, thereby seriously diminishing the total value of an investor's portfolio.

Dow Jones Industrials   A list of 30 stocks designed to represent the overall domestic economy.

Earnings-Per-Share (EPS) Growth Rate   The average earnings-per-share growth rate estimated by analysts covering the stock.

Ex-dividend Date   The date on which the holder of a stock will no longer be eligible to receive the company's current dividend.

Exercise   The action taken by an option holder who wants to buy or sell a security at the prescribed price in the option contract.

Expiration Date   The date on which the option contract will expire.

Fifty-Two-Week High   The highest price at which a security traded over the preceding 52 weeks.

Fifty-Two-Week Low   The lowest price at which a security traded over the preceding 52 weeks.

Fill or Kill   A type of security order that requires that the entire order be filled at a particular price within a few minutes or the order will be cancelled.

First In First Out (FIFO)   One method a brokerage firm can use to determine which option sellers will be assigned options that are being exercised.

Frequency   One of the two components of risk referring to the probability of how often an investor may lose money in a particular investment transaction.

Hedging   The process of taking two positions at the same time with the expectation that if one position loses money, the other will profit to a similar extent.

Index Options   Options traded on an entire market segment such as the S&P 500, the Dow Jones Industrials, or the Nasdaq indexes.

In-the-Money Option   A call option with a strike price that is below the underlying security's current price, or a put option with a strike price that is above the underlying security's current price.

Intrinsic Value (Option)   The amount that an option is currently in the money.

Intrinsic Value (Stock) A method of evaluating the present value of a stock popularized by Warren Buffett. Different investors use various approaches to calculate intrinsic value, however, the primary theory is to discount the future earnings of a company to arrive at the stock's present value.

Leverage The control or investment in a larger amount of securities than an investor maintains in capital.

Limit Order A securities order that is placed to be filled only at a particular execution price.

Margin Call A demand by an investor's brokerage firm to deposit additional capital or to sell currently held securities to cover a shortfall in the account due to market movement that has reduced the value of the investor's account.

Margin Requirements Capital requirements established by brokerage firms, in compliance with federal regulations, detailing the amount of capital required to transact and maintain security positions.

Market Order A securities order that will be executed immediately at the best possible price.

Open Interest The number of call or put option contracts currently sold on a particular underlying security with the same strike price and expiration date.

Option The right to buy or sell a security at a particular price until a specified time in the future.

Option Buyer An investor who buys the right, but not the obligation, to buy or sell a security at a particular price until a specified time in the future.

Option Seller An investor who is obligated, in return for a premium, to purchase or sell a security at a particular price until a specified time in the future.

Premium The consideration paid for an option.

Price-Earnings (P/E) Ratio The current price of a stock divided by its annual after-tax earnings.

Price-Earnings-Growth (PEG) Ratio A measurement of how fast the company is growing in relationship to its present earnings. It is calculated by dividing the company's current "price-to-earnings ratio" by its "estimated growth rate."

Put Option An option that gives the holder the right, but not the obligation, to sell a particular security at a particular price until a specified time in the future.

QQQs   A tracking stock for the Nasdaq-100 index (the 100 largest stocks traded on the Nasdaq Stock Market). The value of each QQQ share equals approximately 1/40 of the value of the Nasdaq-100 index.

Random Selection   A method that can be used by a brokerage firm to determine which option sellers will be assigned options currently being exercised.

Resistance   The price above which many investors are likely to sell a given stock.

Standard & Poor's (S&P) 500   A list of the 500 largest, public U.S. companies.

Severity   One of the two components of risk referring to how much an investor may lose in a particular transaction.

Stop Order   An order to buy or sell a security when it reaches a particular price. A stop order can be entered as either a *limit* or *market order*.

Strike Price   The price at which a call option holder can purchase the underlying security, or the price at which a put option holder can sell the underlying security.

Support Level   The price below which many investors are likely to consider a given stock a good buy.

Time Value   One of the two components of an option premium. For out-of-the-money options, the time value is the entire premium an option buyer is willing to pay for the rights granted under the option contract. For in-the-money options, the time value is the difference between the full premium and the option's intrinsic value.

Treasury Bills   Short-term debt instruments issued by the federal government. These instruments are highly marginable and can be used as collateral for short put positions.

Volatility   A measurement of the change in price experienced by a particular security over a period of time.

Volume   The amount of a particular security transacted during a trading day.

Yield   The actual or anticipated return of a particular investment.

RECOMMENDED READING

James B. Bittman. *Options for the Stock Investor: How Any Investor Can Use Options to Enhance and Protect Their Return,* 4th ed. New York: McGraw-Hill, 1995.

Nicholas R. Bokron. *How to Use Put and Call Options: A Guide to Understanding Options As Traded on the Chicago Board Options Exchange, the American Stock Exchange, and the Over-the-Counter Market.* Boston: J. Magee, 1975.

Lawrence G. McMillan. *Options As a Strategic Investment.* New York Institute of Finance. Paramus, New Jersey: Prentice Hall Press, 1992.

The following books have absolutely nothing to do with investment strategies or options or the stock market, but if you haven't read them, you should. All of them have had a huge impact on my life and they might have a similar effect on you.

Ayn Rand. *Atlas Shrugged.* Seattle, Washington: Signet Press, 1996.

Ayn Rand. *The Fountainhead.* New York: Plume, 2002.

Harry Brown. *Why Government Doesn't Work: How Reducing Government Will Bring Us Safer Cities, Better Schools.* Great Falls, Montana: Liam Works, 1995.

INDEX

ABOUT THE AUTHOR

Jeffrey M. Cohen is a nationally recognized expert in tax and financial planning. He has appeared in several national television programs including *The Investor's Intelligence Report* on the Financial News Network and *Everybody's Money Matters* on the Lifetime cable channel and CNBC.

He has lectured at colleges and universities and is a continuing education instructor for accountants, lawyers, and financial advisors. He is a featured speaker at domestic and offshore financial symposiums. He has been the president and CEO of a life insurance company and currently works as a consultant for large financial management organizations.

Cohen is the author of *Don't Trade Without a Net* and *Personal Success in an Hour or Less*.